Advanced Color Graphics and Animation for the IBM® PC

Don Inman and Kurt Inman

Hayden Book Company

A DIVISION OF HAYDEN PUBLISHING COMPANY, INC.
HASBROUCK HEIGHTS, NEW JERSEY

Acquisitions Editor: RON POWERS
Production Editor: LORI WILLIAMS
Cover Designer: RITTA AND ASSOCIATES
Text Designer: LORRAINE MULLANEY
Illustrator: JOHN McAUSLAND
Compositor: ELIZABETH TYPESETTING COMPANY
Manufacturer: THE MAPLE-VAIL BOOK MANUFACTURING GROUP

EQUIPMENT NEEDED

- IBM PC with at least 128K of memory
- Color/Graphics Adapter
- Disk drive (one or two)
- Color monitor
- Printer

Library of Congress Catalog-in-Publication Data

Inman, Don.
    Advanced color graphics and animation for the IBM PC.

    Includes index.
    1. IBM Personal Computer–Programming. 2. Color computer graphics. I. Inman, Kurt.
II. Title. QA76.8.I2594I56   1986   006.6'765   86-4734
ISBN 0-8104-6390-3

Printed in the United States of America

1	2	3	4	5	6	7	8	9	
86	87	88	89	90	91	92	93	94	YEAR

This book focuses on those graphics commands that are essential for learning fundamental graphics techniques. We assume that you have a reasonable knowledge of Advanced BASIC but are a relative beginner in the use of graphics. If your BASIC is rusty, keep the IBM BASICA reference manual by your side to look up unfamiliar terms. The meanings of BASIC statements and terms used are also included in the glossary at the end of the book. A leisurely trip through the glossary will give you some idea of the material covered here.

Since this is a book about graphics, emphasis will be on software. The hardware configuration of the IBM PC may vary over a tremendously wide range. As a minimum hardware option to the basic IBM PC, we assume that you are using a Color/Graphics Adapter and a color video display. This book was developed using the following configuration: an IBM PC with 256K of memory, a Color/Graphics Adapter, two disk drives, an RGB color monitor, and a printer.

The software assumed is PC DOS and Advanced BASIC (BASICA). PC DOS, Version 2.10, and BASICA, Version 2.10, were used to develop the book, although Version 1.10 of BASICA is discussed at essential points.

The book uses a self-teaching approach. Each graphics command is discussed at the point of its first use. Several examples are given, and one or more demonstration programs are provided to show the use of the command with other BASIC statements. Demonstration programs are written in a modular style with many REMark statements to provide ease of understanding. Clarity is not sacrificed to conserve memory space. Meaningful variable names are used so that their function may be more easily understood.

Illustrations are provided to clarify the text. Screen dumps to a printer are included to show key portions of demonstration runs of all listings.

The book is organized so that statements are encountered in the order needed for efficient learning and use. Each chapter introduces a selected number of graphics statements, functions, and terms. A list of these selections is given at the beginning of each chapter. After discussion and demonstration in the chapter, the items are summarized at the end of each chapter.

Chapter 1 presents only those commands that are necessary for setting up the video display for the text mode. Simple graphics that can be used to enhance text are discussed in Chapter 2 along with animation of crude block graphics.

Chapter 3 covers introductory topics in the medium-resolution mode. Screen resolution and available colors are discussed and demonstrated with programs that set individual points for drawing. The chapter concludes with a discussion and demonstration of the LINE statement and its options.

Methods of drawing circles, arcs, and polygons are presented in Chapter 4. Parameters of the CIRCLE statement are introduced individually. The PAINT statement is used to demonstrate coloring the interior of figures. Sine and cosine functions are used in demonstrating the production of regular polygons.

Chapter 5 is devoted to the graphics definition language (GDL). GDL uses the DRAW statement, which consists of the language commands contained in a string expression. During execution of a DRAW statement, BASICA interprets and carries out the single-letter commands of the string.

Simple animation begins in Chapter 6 and continues in Chapter 7. The concept of linear animation is introduced in Chapter 6. This is accomplished by repeating the following sequence of operations: draw, erase, then move to a new position. A discussion of coordinate systems is included, along with the concept of rotary animation. Chapter 7 introduces more sophisticated animation through GET and PUT statements. Several types of animation are discussed and demonstrated.

Business and scientific applications are presented in Chapter 8 through the construction of line, bar, and pie graphs. The high-resolution graphics mode is introduced and used in this chapter.

Memory that is devoted to the graphics screen is investigated in Chapter 9. Methods of directly turning screen pixels on and off using POKE statements are shown.

Chapter 10 introduces sound and provides demonstrations of methods that integrate sound with animation.

CONTENTS

1

THE VIDEO DISPLAY—TEXT MODE

Graphics Statements, Functions,
and Terms Introduced

WIDTH
KEY
SCREEN O
CLS
COLOR
STRING$

The video display is the link between the computer and the user. It provides a video feedback for the programs and data that you enter and the results that are achieved. Therefore, it is important that you have a detailed understanding of the capabilities of this important link.

The objective of this chapter is to describe how to set up the display screen so that you can use it effectively in the future. The material covered includes the selection of display modes, line width, soft key display, and clearing the screen. The use of foreground, background, and border colors in the text mode is also discussed.

BASIC statements and terms that we assume you are familiar with are the following: FOR-NEXT loops with STEP, GOTO, LEN, LOCATE, PRINT, REM, RIGHT$, and STR$.

BASIC statements that are explained, either as new or as review material, are the following: CLS, COLOR, KEY, SCREEN, STRING$, and WIDTH.

This chapter describes the characteristics of the video display when using a color monitor and the Color/Graphics Adapter with the IBM Personal Computer. These characteristics change whenever you move from one of the three available operating modes to another, as shown in Table 1–1.

MODE	HORIZONTAL RESOLUTION	VERTICAL RESOLUTION	NUMBER OF PIXELS	COLORS AVAILABLE
Text	40	25	1,000	16 foreground
	or 80	25	2,000	8 background
				16 border
Medium-Resolution Graphics	320	200	64,000	3 foreground
				16 background
High-Resolution Graphics	640	200	128,000	black and white only

THE TEXT MODE

When you first turn the computer on and access BASICA, the display is automatically set to the text mode with a black background and border, a white foreground, and a width that produces 80 text characters per line. We are assuming that you are familiar with the text mode of BASICA. However, some of the following text mode material can also be used to produce graphics. Therefore, we will review graphics-related functions and statements of the text mode.

The display we see on start-up is shown in Fig. 1–1.

The line of text at the bottom of the screen shows the keywords for the functions that are initially assigned to the ten function keys (called soft keys) at the left of the keyboard. These keys can be used as shortcuts when entering specific commands. To list a program currently in memory, you can just press the first function key (F1) rather than typing the word LIST. Other soft keys serve other functions, such as RUN, LOAD, SAVE, etc.

When you are in the text mode, the number of characters per row can be switched between 40 and 80 by the WIDTH command. The usual format for this command is

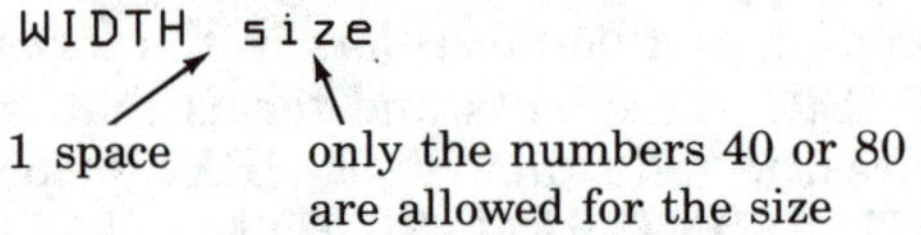

Although the WIDTH command is normally used in the text mode, it can also be used in both graphics modes. If a WIDTH 80 command is given when the screen is in the medium-resolution graphics mode, it forces the computer into high-resolution graphics. If a WIDTH 40 command is given when the screen is in the high-resolution mode, it forces the computer into medium-resolution graphics.

```
The IBM Personal Computer Basic
Version A2.10 Copyright IBM Corp. 1981, 1982, 1983
60891 Bytes free

Ok
_




1LIST   2RUN←   3LOAD"   4SAVE"   5CONT←  6."LPT1 7TRON←  8TROFF← 9KEY    0SCREEN
```

FIG. 1–1. Video display at start-up

> Whenever the screen width is changed, the screen is cleared, and the
> border and background screen colors are set to black. See your
> BASIC manual for other formats for the WIDTH command.

Figure 1–2 shows what we saw on our screen when we typed
WIDTH 40 and pressed the return key ↵ .

Notice that only five of the soft key values are shown in the 40-
character width mode. The other keys are still defined as before but are
not displayed.

To return to the 80-character width mode, a WIDTH 80 command
is entered. The values of all ten soft keys are shown in the 80-character
mode. If you find that the line of soft key values is distracting, you can
turn off the line by typing the command

```
KEY OFF
```

When we entered the KEY OFF command, we saw

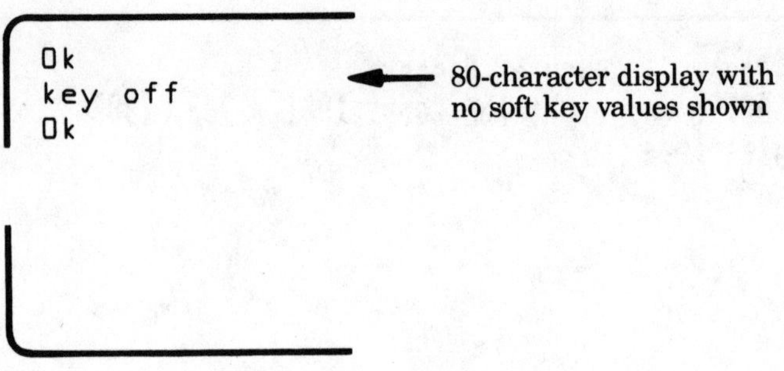

If you cannot remember the key for a function that you wish to use, the bottom line of soft key functions can be displayed again by entering

KEY ON

You may have noticed that a maximum of six characters was shown when the soft key values were displayed. A complete list of soft key values can be obtained by typing the command

KEY LIST

FIG. 1–2. WIDTH 40 display

We will follow the format convention of the IBM PC manuals throughout this book. Keep in mind that the square brackets are used to denote that the material enclosed is optional.

After entering the KEY LIST command, our display showed

```
Ok
key off
Ok
key list
F1 LIST
F2 RUN←
F3 LOAD"
F4 SAVE"
F5 CONT←
F6  ,"LPT1:"←
F7 TRON←
F8 TROFF←
F9 KEY
F10 SCREEN 0,0,0←
Ok
█
```

FIG. 1–3. List of soft key functions

The operating mode is selected by the SCREEN command. The format of this command in the text mode is

```
SCREEN 0 [,[burst][,[apage][, vpage]]]
```

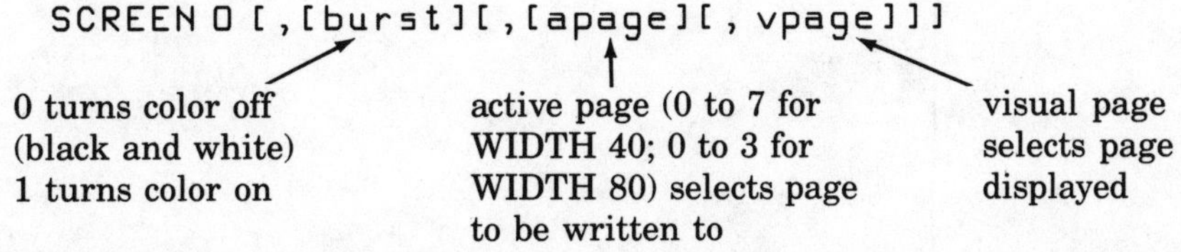

0 turns color off
(black and white)
1 turns color on

active page (0 to 7 for
WIDTH 40; 0 to 3 for
WIDTH 80) selects page
to be written to

visual page
selects page
displayed

> See Chapter 2 for a more detailed description of the apage and vpage parameters. See Chapter 3 for the format for SCREEN for medium-resolution graphics and Chapter 8 for high-resolution. Notice the values used for color burst in the text mode (0 for off, 1 for on). The values are reversed for medium-resolution (1 for off, 0 for on). Since black and white are the only colors used in high-resolution graphics, burst has little effect in that mode.

The three possible screen modes are accessed by the following commands:

```
SCREEN 0      for the text mode
SCREEN 1      for medium-resolution graphics
SCREEN 2      for high-resolution graphics
```

If you do not wish to display any graphics, the text mode is usually selected. The text mode provides a more varied assortment of colors and a wider variety of color uses. Medium-resolution graphics would be selected when colorful graphics are to be displayed. High-resolution graphics would be selected when you need graphics but color is of little importance. High-resolution provides twice the horizontal pixel density as medium-resolution. However, the high-resolution graphics mode is limited to two colors versus four colors for medium-resolution graphics.

Let's pause at this point to demonstrate the text mode with the WIDTH and SCREEN commands. If your computer is not already in the text mode with a column width of 40, enter the following commands:

```
SCREEN 0
KEY OFF
WIDTH 40
```

Next, enter the following command:

```
PRINT "This line will contain forty characters."
```

Our screen showed

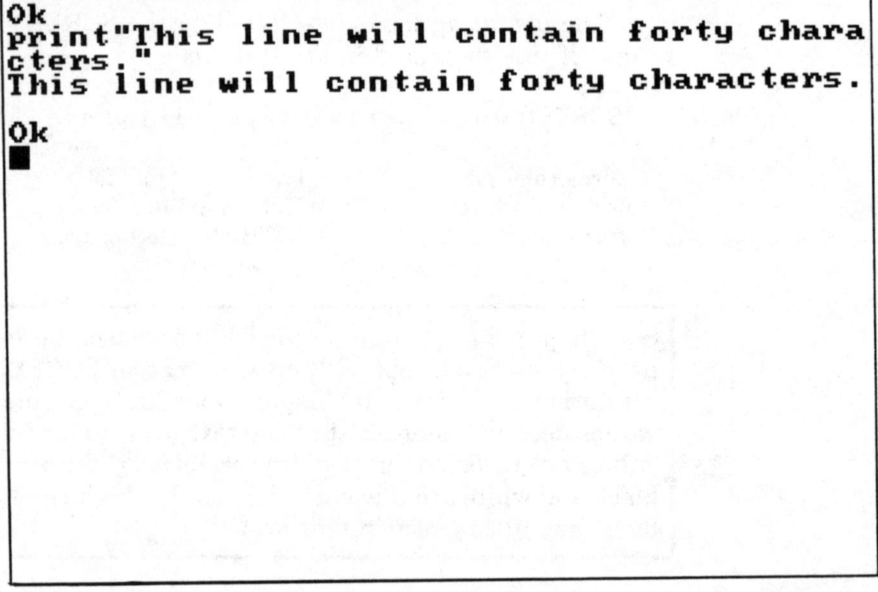

FIG. 1—4. 40-character line

The text displayed by the PRINT statement exactly filled one line of the screen. Change the length of the displayed line by entering

WIDTH 80

Notice that the screen was cleared when the width changed. This happens whenever the width is changed from 40 to 80 or from 80 to 40. Type in the PRINT statement again. This is how our screen looked this time.

```
Ok
print"This line will contain forty characters."
This line will contain forty characters.
Ok
```

FIG. 1–5. 80-character line

Notice that the letters appear closer together and are harder to read than on a 40-character line.

CLEARING THE SCREEN

The screen is cleared whenever you change the character width of the screen by a WIDTH command. The CLS command is also used to clear the screen to the foreground, background, and border colors currently in use. The format for this command is

CLS

The following program module is used to set up the screen in our first demonstration program (Listing 1–1):

```
100 REM * set screen *
110 SCREEN 0,1          ← text mode, color on
120 WIDTH 40            ← width to 40 characters
130 KEY OFF             ← turn off soft keys
140 CLS                 ← clear the screen
```

COLOR

The program will place sixteen color swatches on the screen. Each swatch will be a different color (one of sixteen foreground colors). The value of the color used will be printed near the center of each swatch. The words *color codes* will be printed near the bottom of the screen.

The COLOR command allows the selection of foreground, background, and border colors (see Table 1–2) when the text mode is being used. The format in the text mode is

```
COLOR [foreground][,[background][,border]]
```

codes 0–15 for solid;   codes 0–7   codes 0–15
16–31 for blinking

As mentioned earlier, the video display for the text mode is originally white on black (COLOR 7,0,0). The foreground is white, and both the background and border are black. In the first demonstration program, the COLOR statement changes only the foreground colors. The swatches are drawn by four colored stripes in the following way:

```
210 FORE = 0                          ← set initial foreground color
220 FOR ROW = 1 TO 16 STEP 5
230  FOR COLUMN = 1 TO 31 STEP 10
240   COLOR FORE,0                     ← foreground color changes
250   FOR STRIPE = 0 TO 3              ← 4 stripes of color
260    LOCATE ROW+STRIPE,COLUMN
270    PRINT STRING$(4,219)
280   NEXT STRIPE
290   FORE = FORE+1                    ← increase color code
300  NEXT COLUMN
310 NEXT ROW
```

Notice the indentation of the FOR-NEXT loops. This is a feature of good programming style. The indentation allows you to visualize the order of execution of this section. The inner loop is executed first (FOR STRIPE. .). Then the computer works its way outward (FOR COLUMN. . and then FOR ROW. .).

TABLE 1–2

COLOR CODES FOR TEXT MODE

CODE	COLOR	USE
0	black	foreground, border, background
1	blue	foreground, border, background
2	green	foreground, border, background
3	cyan	foreground, border, background
4	red	foreground, border, background
5	magenta	foreground, border, background
6	brown	foreground, border, background
7	white	foreground, border, background
8	gray	foreground, border
9	light blue	foreground, border
10	light green	foreground, border
11	light cyan	foreground, border
12	light red	foreground, border
13	light magenta	foreground, border
14	yellow	foreground, border
15	bright white	foreground, border
16	* black	foreground
17	* blue	foreground
18	* green	foreground
19	* cyan	foreground
20	* red	foreground
21	* magenta	foreground
22	* brown	foreground
23	* white	foreground
24	* gray	foreground
25	* light blue	foreground
26	* light green	foreground
27	* light cyan	foreground
28	* light red	foreground
29	* light magenta	foreground
30	* yellow	foreground
31	* bright white	foreground

* signifies blinking color

Variables used in this section of the program include

FORE, the foreground color varies from 0 through 15

ROW, the screen row (values of 1, 6, 11, and 16)

COLUMN, the screen column (values of 1, 11, 21, and 31)

STRIPE, an offset added to ROW varies from 0 through 3

The STEP options in the FOR ROW and FOR COLUMN loops allow the placement of the color swatches at reasonable positions on the screen.

The STRING$ function is used in this program for the first time. It returns a string of a specified number of characters. It has the format

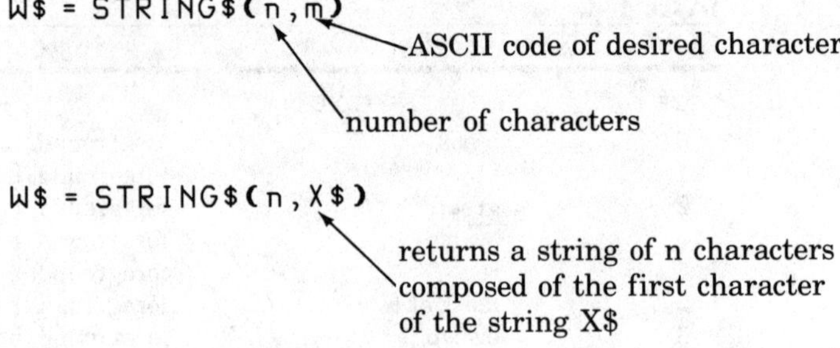

Line 270 of our program prints a string of four characters whose ASCII code is 219. This forms a strip of color four character widths long.

The section of statements in lines 400–480 prints the corresponding code inside each color swatch. Line 450 is of particular importance. Ordinarily, a positive number is printed with a leading blank space and a trailing blank space. We would like to suppress the blanks so that each of the numbers 0 through 15 fits inside the appropriate color swatch, which is only four characters wide.

The numeric variable NUMBER is converted to string form by STR$(NUMBER). The STR$ function returns a string representation of the value of NUMBER. It strips off the trailing blank but leaves a leading blank.

The string representation is stripped of the leading blank by RIGHT$(STR$(NUMBER),LEN(STR$(NUMBER))−1). The LEN function returns the length of the string form of NUMBER. One is subtracted from the length. The RIGHT$ function then returns the right portion of the string form of NUMBER minus one character, the leading blank.

EXAMPLE

When NUMBER = 12, PRINT NUMBER would print

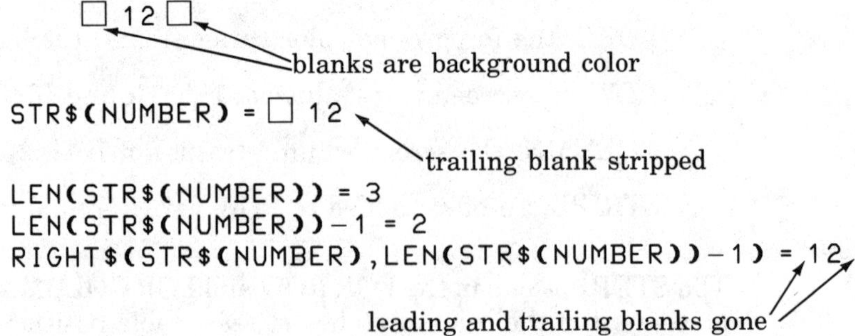

Therefore, each color code printed is no greater than two characters and will fit inside the swatch.

Enter the complete program of Listing 1–1 (REM lines may be omitted). Then run the program. The results can be used to adjust the controls of your video monitor until you are satisfied with the shades of color.

LISTING 1–1. Changing Foreground Colors

```
100 REM * set screen *
110 SCREEN 0,1
120 WIDTH 40
130 KEY OFF
140 CLS
199 '
200 REM * place color swatches *
210 FORE = 0
220 FOR ROW = 1 TO 16 STEP 5
230   FOR COLUMN = 1 TO 31 STEP 10
240     COLOR FORE,0
250     FOR STRIPE = 0 TO 3
260       LOCATE ROW+STRIPE,COLUMN
270       PRINT STRING$(4,219)
280     NEXT STRIPE
290     FORE = FORE+1
300   NEXT COLUMN
310 NEXT ROW
399 '
400 REM * print color codes *
410 NUMBER = 0
420 FOR ROW = 2 TO 17 STEP 5
430   FOR COLUMN = 2 TO 32 STEP 10
440     LOCATE ROW,COLUMN
450     PRINT RIGHT$(STR$(NUMBER),LEN(STR$(NUMBER))-1);
460     NUMBER = NUMBER+1
470   NEXT COLUMN
480 NEXT ROW
499 '
500 REM * draw title *
510 LOCATE 22,12
520 PRINT "color codes"
530 GOTO 530
```

If you wish to see the blinking effect of the color codes 16 through 31, change the listing as follows. Then run the program again.

```
change      210 FORE = 16
change      410 NUMBER = 16
add         415 COLOR 7
```

To stop the blinking press CTRL BREAK. Then clear the screen with CLS.

The COLOR statement controls the background and border colors as well as the foreground color in the next demonstration program. Referring back to Table 1–1, you will see that all 16 colors are available for the border but only 8 colors can be used for the background.

The COLOR statement does not change the foreground or background colors that are already on the screen. It affects only those characters printed on the screen after the COLOR statement is executed. However, the border color changes immediately when a COLOR statement that specifies a new color is executed.

The program of Listing 1–2 displays the same foreground swatches as the Changing Foreground Colors program. However, each background color is displayed in turn with the appropriate color code printed in text at the bottom of the screen. After all 16 background colors have been displayed, the 8 border colors are displayed in turn with the appropriate border color code printed in text. The color code text is printed using white as foreground and blue as background. Note again that the foreground and background colors already on the screen do not change. Only the border color and the text that is printed following the COLOR 7,1, BORDER statement (line 720) change.

After all 8 border colors have been displayed, the screen is cleared (lines 810, 820) to black border, black background, and white foreground. The message "Done. Press CTRL BREAK to stop." is displayed. The program loops at line 840 until you follow those directions.

Notice that the screen colors for the foreground, background, and border were reset to their original colors at the end of the program. All the programs in the book assume that the screen has been set to this white on black condition before the programs are run.

LISTING 1–2. Background and Border Colors

```
100 REM * set screen *
110 SCREEN 0,1
120 WIDTH 40
130 KEY OFF
140 BORDER = 9
150 FOR BACK = 0 TO 7
160   FORE = 0
170   COLOR FORE,BACK,BORDER
180   CLS
199   '
200   REM * place color swatches *
210   FOR ROW = 1 TO 16 STEP 5
220     FOR COLUMN = 1 TO 31 STEP 10
230       COLOR FORE,BACK,BORDER
240       FOR STRIPE = 0 TO 3
250         LOCATE ROW+STRIPE,COLUMN
260         PRINT STRING$(4,219)
270       NEXT STRIPE
280       FORE = FORE+1
290     NEXT COLUMN
300   NEXT ROW
399   '
400   REM * print color codes *
410   NUMBER = 0
```

```
420   FOR ROW = 2 TO 17 STEP 5
430     FOR COLUMN = 2 TO 32 STEP 10
440       LOCATE ROW,COLUMN
450       PRINT RIGHT$(STR$(NUMBER),LEN(STR$(NUMBER))-1);
460       NUMBER = NUMBER+1
470     NEXT COLUMN
480   NEXT ROW
499   '
500   REM * draw title *
510   LOCATE 22,12
520   PRINT "color codes"
530   LOCATE 24,10
540   PRINT "background =";STR$(BACK);
599   '
600   REM * time delay and end outside loop *
610   FOR REPEAT = 1 TO 2000
620   NEXT REPEAT
630 NEXT BACK
699 '
700 REM * change border *
710 FOR BORDER = 0 TO 15
720   COLOR 7,1,BORDER
730   LOCATE 24,10
740   PRINT"  border = ";BORDER;
750   FOR TIME = 1 TO 1000: NEXT TIME
760 NEXT BORDER
799 '
800 REM * restore screen *
810 COLOR 7,0,0
820 CLS
830 PRINT"Done.   Press CTRL BREAK to stop."
840 GOTO 840
```

SUMMARY

In this chapter we discussed the control of the video display in the text
mode. You learned the following.

- Text can be displayed in two sizes.
    - 40 characters per row with 25 rows
    - 80 characters per row with 25 rows
- The original text screen displays white characters on a black
  screen.
- The WIDTH command controls the number of characters per
  line.
    - WIDTH 40 provides 40 characters/line
    - WIDTH 80 provides 80 characters/line
- The KEY command controls the display of soft key (function
  key) values.
    - KEY ON turns on the display of values
    - KEY OFF turns off the display of values
    - KEY LIST provides a list of complete functions for each soft
      key

- The SCREEN command controls the operation mode to be used.
  SCREEN 0 text mode
  SCREEN 1 medium-resolution graphics mode
  SCREEN 2 high-resolution graphics mode
- The CLS command clears the screen.
- The COLOR command controls the color of the display.

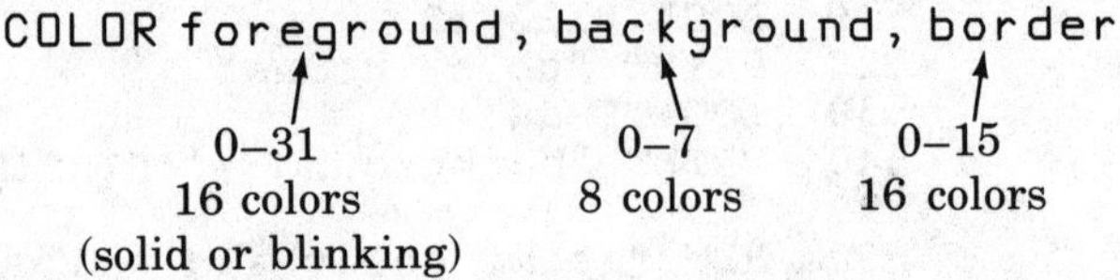

- The STRING$ function returns a string of text characters.

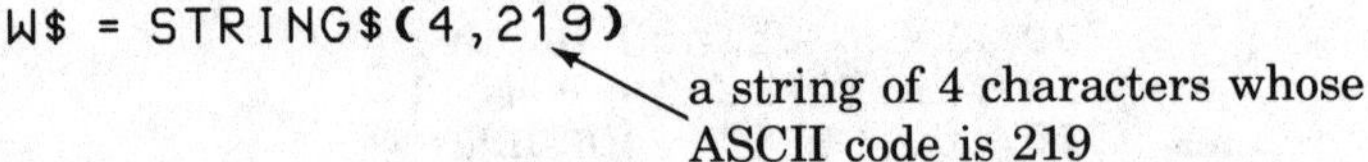

Tables were given for the screen resolution of the operating modes and for the color code values used for the display. Two demonstration programs were given to show how the foreground, background, and border colors can be controlled.

<h1 style="text-align:center">2</h1>

TEXT-MODE GRAPHICS

Graphics Statements, Functions,
and Terms Introduced

PRINT
CHR\$(n)
SPACE\$(n)
apage
vpage
concatenation

The objective of this chapter is to demonstrate the unique capabilities of graphics in the text mode. The material covered includes the use of character-size blocks of color for text messages and for simple shapes used for animation. Also included is the use of active and visual page options for the SCREEN statement.

BASIC statements and terms that we assume you are familiar with include all those in the previous chapter, plus DATA and READ, GOSUB and RETURN, IF-THEN, and INKEY\$.

BASIC statements and terms that are explained in this chapter are apage, vpage, CHR\$, concatenation, PRINT, and SPACE\$.

The keyboard of your computer contains the letters of the alphabet, numbers, punctuation marks, and many special characters. Some of these characters are graphics shapes. They can be displayed on the screen by pressing the appropriate key. They can also be displayed from a program in another way. A standard ASCII code, in the range of 1–128, is assigned to each one of these shapes (see Appendix A). Therefore, each shape can be displayed by a PRINT statement such as

```
PRINT CHR$(n)
```

The CHR\$(n) part of the statement produces the character associated with the specified code number n. The PRINT part of the statement displays the character on the screen.

```
PRINT CHR$(65)
```
ASCII code for uppercase A

```
PRINT CHR$(97)
```
ASCII code for lowercase a

The program shown in Listing 2–1 displays 15 uppercase and 15 lowercase letters. Each pair of letters is displayed in a different color, as seen in Fig. 2–1, by means of the COLOR statement

```
250 COLOR FOREGROUND,0,0
```

LISTING 2–1. Colored Letters

```
100 REM * set screen *
110 SCREEN 0,1
120 KEY OFF
130 WIDTH 40
140 CLS
199 '
200 REM * print letters *
210 FOR CHARACTER = 65 TO 79 STEP 5
220   FOR COLUMN = 0 TO 4
230     LETTER = CHARACTER+COLUMN
240     FOREGROUND = LETTER-64            colors 1 through 15
250     COLOR FOREGROUND,0,0
260     PRINT CHR$(LETTER)CHR$(LETTER+32)"    ";
270   NEXT COLUMN                                4 spaces
280   PRINT:PRINT
290 NEXT CHARACTER
300 PRINT:PRINT
```

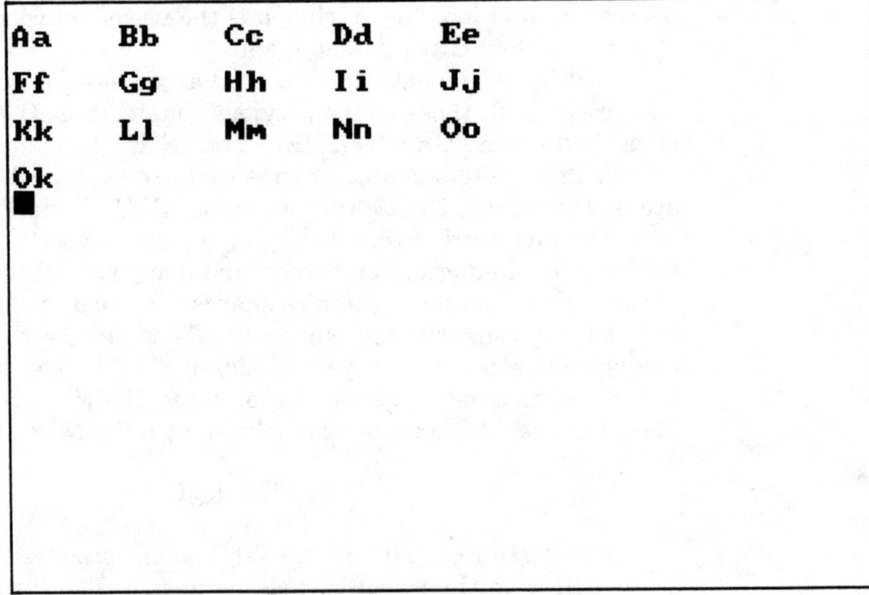

FIG. 2–1. Display of colored characters

ASCII codes in the range of 128–255 of the IBM PC character set contain other useful shapes. Included are lines, corners, intersections, and blocks. Some of these shapes can be joined together to form larger shapes that can be used in diagrams and charts. You can even combine some of them into simple figures that can be used in animation.

Rather than try to explain each individual shape, we'll provide two demonstration programs that display each shape along with the character code that produces it. The first of the two programs uses 80 characters/line and prints the codes and shapes with black on white. The arrangement of the codes and shapes is shown in Fig. 2–2.

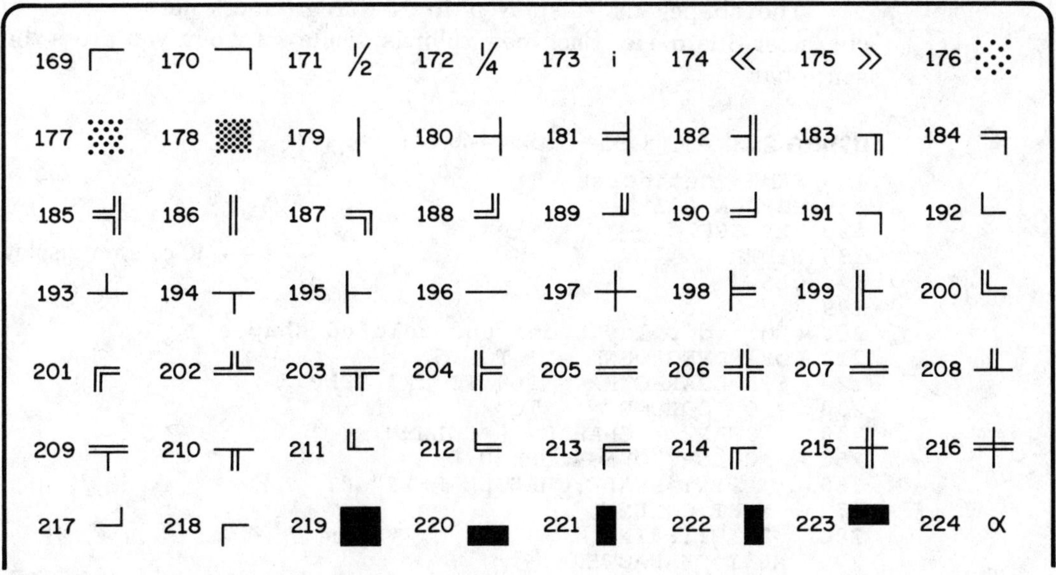

FIG. 2–2. Character codes—80 columns

Listing 2–2 produces the display of Fig. 2–2. Notice its similarity to Listing 2–1.

LISTING 2–2. ASCII Code Display—80 Columns

```
100 REM * set screen *
110 SCREEN 0,1
120 KEY OFF
130 WIDTH 80                          ←——— 80-column display
140 CLS
199 '
200 REM * display codes and shapes *
210 FOR CHARACTER = 169 TO 223 STEP 8
220   FOR COLUMN = 0 TO 7
230     SHAPE = CHARACTER+COLUMN
240     PRINT SHAPE;CHR$(SHAPE);SPACE$(3);   ← shape, followed
250   NEXT COLUMN                                by 3 spaces
260   PRINT:PRINT:PRINT
270 NEXT CHARACTER
```

The SPACE$ function is used for the first time in this program. It provides a short way to insert spaces in text or text graphics. Its format is

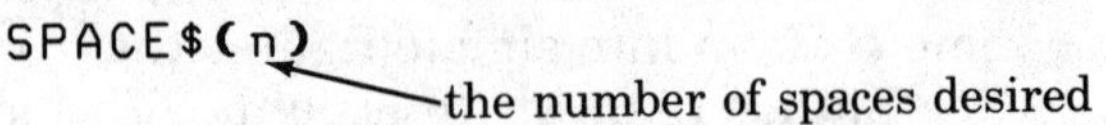

The shapes in the previous program may be a little bit small for you to visualize what might be produced by joining them. Therefore, the next program uses a 40-character/line WIDTH to enlarge the shapes.

The shapes are displayed in 15 foreground colors in the 40 character/line mode. Each new color is displayed when you press the space bar.

LISTING 2–3. ASCII Code Display—40 Columns

```
100 REM * set screen *
110 SCREEN 0,1
120 KEY OFF
130 WIDTH 40                              ←——————— 40-column display
140 CLS
199 '
200 REM * display codes and colored shapes *
210 FOR FOREGROUND = 1 TO 15
220   FOR CHARACTER = 169 TO 223 STEP 5
230     FOR COLUMN = 0 TO 4
240       SHAPE = CHARACTER+COLUMN
250       COLOR FOREGROUND,0,0
260       PRINT SHAPE;CHR$(SHAPE);" ";
270     NEXT COLUMN                          ↑
280     PRINT:PRINT              1 space
290   NEXT CHARACTER
300   IF INKEY$<>CHR$(32) THEN 300 ←——— wait for press of space bar
310   IF FOREGROUND<>15 THEN CLS
320 NEXT FOREGROUND
```

USING CHARACTER CODES

The program Color Windows (see Listing 2–4) uses some of the upper character codes to "paint" color swatches of various sizes on the screen. Messages are printed on the color swatches, and borders are drawn around some of them. This has the effect of placing colored text in various colored "windows" on an overall black background.

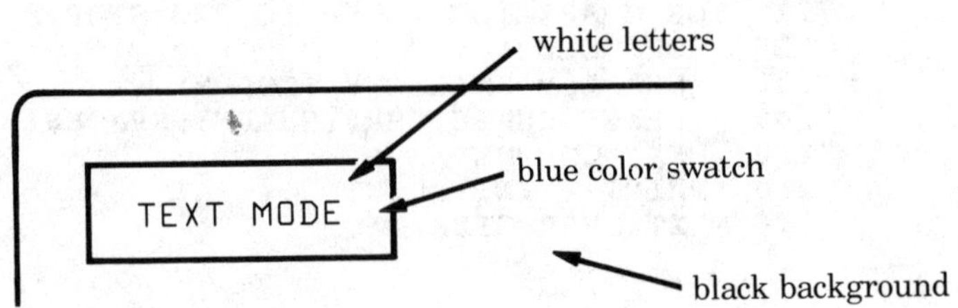

The program opens with the usual preparation of the screen.

```
100 REM * set screen *
110 SCREEN 0,1
120 KEY OFF
130 WIDTH 80
140 CLS
```

A blue rectangular swatch, 3 rows high by 21 columns wide, is then displayed using character code 176.

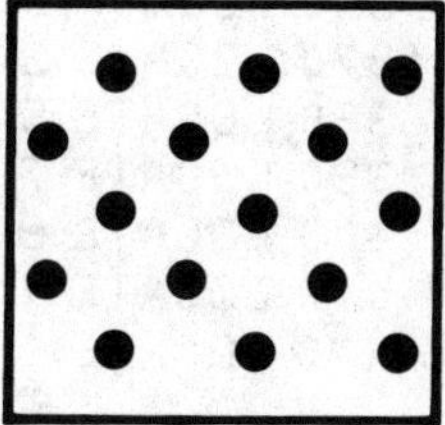

character code 176

The color is selected in line 210. Each row of blue characters is printed by line 240 PRINT STRING$(21,176). The row is selected by lines 220, 230, and 250. The message "TEXT MODE" is printed in white near the center of the rectangle by lines 260 through 280.

```
200 REM * blue swatch - code 176 *
210 COLOR 1,0,0
220 FOR ROW = 1 TO 3
230   LOCATE ROW,1
240   PRINT STRING$(21,176);
250 NEXT ROW
260 LOCATE 2,6
270 COLOR 7,0,0
280 PRINT "TEXT MODE";
```

A yellow swatch is displayed at the top-center of the screen using character code 177.

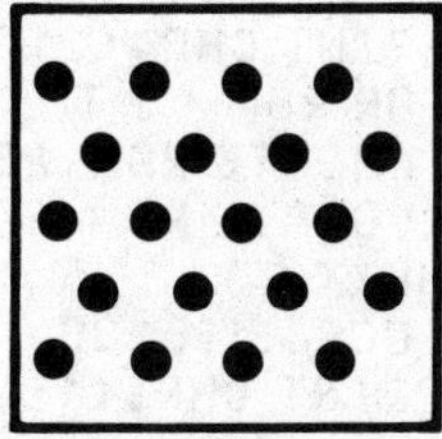

character code 177

The color is selected in line 310. Lines 320 through 350 print the strings of yellow blocks that form the rectangle. The message "YELLOW SWATCH USED FOR THIS MESSAGE" is printed in light magenta diagonally across the yellow rectangle by lines 360 through 420.

```
300 REM * yellow swatch & message *
310 COLOR 14,0,0
320 FOR ROW = 1 TO 15
330   LOCATE ROW,25
340   PRINT STRING$(36,177);
350 NEXT ROW
360 COLOR 13,0,0
370 LOCATE 3,34: PRINT "YELLOW";
380 LOCATE 5,36 : PRINT "SWATCH";
390 LOCATE 7,38: PRINT "USED";
400 LOCATE 9,40: PRINT "FOR";
410 LOCATE 11,42: PRINT "THIS";
420 LOCATE 13,44: PRINT "MESSAGE";
```

A white border is then drawn around the yellow rectangle. Character codes 179, 191, 192, 196, 217, and 218 are used to form the border.

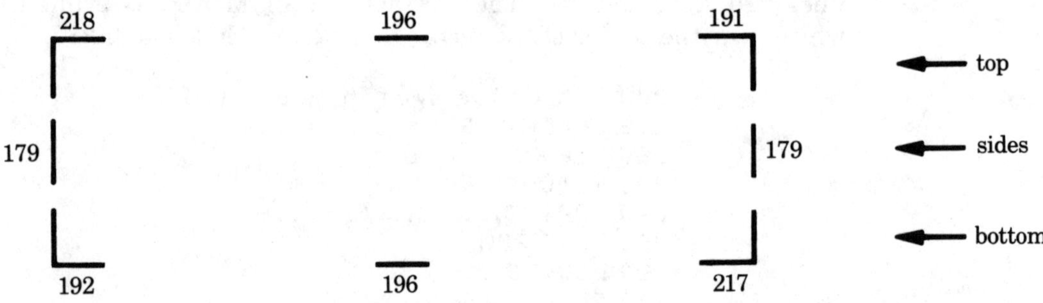

Lines 510 through 530 form the top border. Lines 540 through 570 form the sides, and lines 580 and 590 form the bottom.

```
500 REM * white border around yellow swatch *
510 LOCATE 1,25
520 COLOR 15,0,0
530 PRINT CHR$(218)STRING$(34,196)CHR$(191);
540 FOR ROW = 2 TO 15
550   LOCATE ROW,25: PRINT CHR$(179);
560   LOCATE ROW,60: PRINT CHR$(179);
570 NEXT ROW
580 LOCATE 16,25
590 PRINT CHR$(192)STRING$(34,196)CHR$(217);
```

A magenta swatch with the light cyan message "CHARACTER CODE = 176" is placed at the bottom-right of the screen by lines 610 through 670. Character code 176 is used again for the rectangle.

```
600 REM * magenta swatch & message *
610 COLOR 5,0,0
620 FOR ROW = 18 TO 22
630   LOCATE ROW,25: PRINT STRING$(54,176);
640 NEXT ROW
650 COLOR 11,0,0
660 LOCATE 20,40
670 PRINT "CHARACTER CODE = 176";
```

A wide blue border is placed around the magenta rectangle, using character code 219, by lines 710 through 770.

```
700 REM * blue border around magenta swatch *
710 COLOR 1,0,0
720 LOCATE 18,25: PRINT STRING$(54,219);
730 LOCATE 22,25: PRINT STRING$(54,219);
740 FOR ROW = 19 TO 21
750   LOCATE ROW,25: PRINT STRING$(2,219);
760   LOCATE ROW,77: PRINT STRING$(2,219);
770 NEXT ROW
```

The program ends by restoring the screen to a white foreground with black background and border at lines 810 and 820.

```
800 REM * restore colors *
810 COLOR 7,0,0
820 LOCATE 23,1
```

The complete program is given in Listing 2–4. The result is shown in Fig. 2–3.

LISTING 2–4. Colored Windows

```
100 REM * set screen *
110 SCREEN 0,1
120 KEY OFF
130 WIDTH 80
140 CLS
199 '
200 REM * blue swatch - code 176 *
210 COLOR 1,0,0
220 FOR ROW = 1 TO 3
230   LOCATE ROW,1
240   PRINT STRING$(21,176);
250 NEXT ROW
260 LOCATE 2,6
270 COLOR 7,0,0
280 PRINT "TEXT MODE";
```

```
299 '
300 REM * yellow swatch & message *
310 COLOR 14,0,0
320 FOR ROW = 1 TO 15
330   LOCATE ROW,25
340   PRINT STRING$(36,177);
350 NEXT ROW
360 COLOR 13,0,0
370 LOCATE 3,34: PRINT " YELLOW ";
380 LOCATE 5,36: PRINT " SWATCH ";
390 LOCATE 7,38: PRINT " USED ";
400 LOCATE 9,40: PRINT " FOR ";
410 LOCATE 11,42: PRINT " THIS ";
420 LOCATE 13,44: PRINT " MESSAGE ";
499 '
500 REM * white border around yellow swatch *
510 LOCATE 1,25
520 COLOR 15,0,0
530 PRINT CHR$(218)STRING$(34,196)CHR$(191);
540 FOR ROW = 2 TO 15
550   LOCATE ROW,25: PRINT CHR$(179);
560   LOCATE ROW,60: PRINT CHR$(179);
570 NEXT ROW
580 LOCATE 16,25
590 PRINT CHR$(192)STRING$(34,196)CHR$(217);
599 '
600 REM * magenta swatch & message *
610 COLOR 5,0,0
620 FOR ROW = 18 TO 22
630   LOCATE ROW,25: PRINT STRING$(54,176);
640 NEXT ROW
650 COLOR 11,0,0
660 LOCATE 20,40
670 PRINT " CHARACTER CODE = 176 ";
699 '
700 REM * blue border around magenta swatch *
710 COLOR 1,0,0
720 LOCATE 18,25: PRINT STRING$(54,219);
730 LOCATE 22,25: PRINT STRING$(54,219);
740 FOR ROW = 19 TO 21
750   LOCATE ROW,25: PRINT STRING$(2,219);
760   LOCATE ROW,77: PRINT STRING$(2,219);
770 NEXT ROW
779 '
800 REM * restore colors *
810 COLOR 7,0,0
820 LOCATE 23,1
```

← 1 space before and after each word

SIMPLE ANIMATION

Some of the character codes can be joined to form simple figures that can be used to produce animation. An object can move in a vertical direction if you change the row at which it is displayed. Horizontal motion can be achieved by changing the column at which an object is displayed.

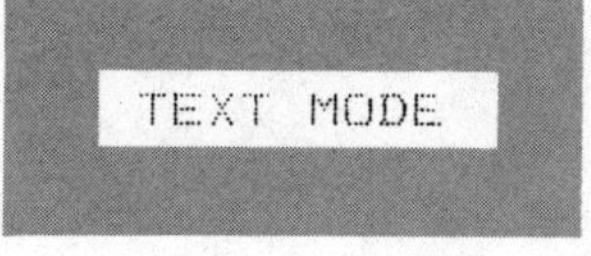

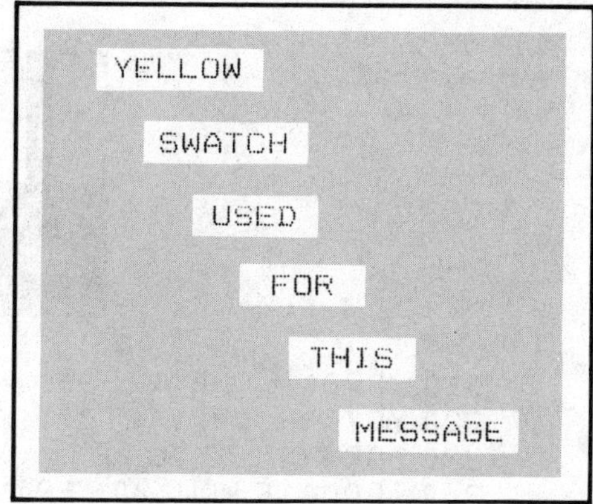

FIG. 2–3. Colored windows—text mode

The program of Listing 2–5 produces vertical motion by using character codes 32, 179, 219, and 220.

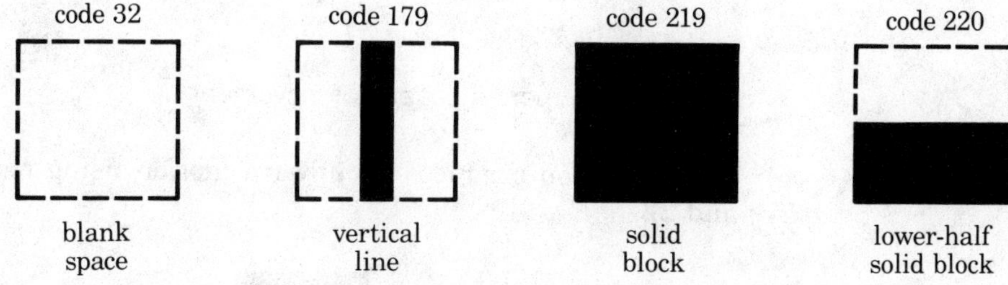

Character code 220 is used three times to provide a visual support for the moving object.

```
210 LOCATE 1,19
220 PRINT STRING$(3,220)
```

Character codes 179 and 219 are used to provide the vertical motion by moving them down one row at a time.

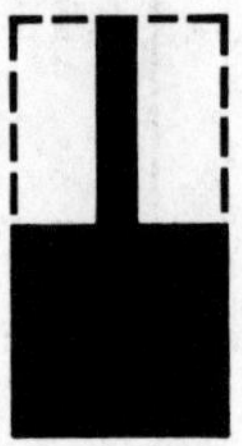

```
310 CORD$ = CHR$(179)
320 YOYO$ = CHR$(219)
330 FOR ROW = 2 TO 22
340   LOCATE ROW,20: PRINT CORD$
350   LOCATE ROW+1,20: PRINT YOYO$
360   FOR DELAY = 1 TO 20: NEXT DELAY  ←——— speed factor
370 NEXT ROW
```

This loop produces a series of displays with the "string" supporting the object growing longer each time through the loop.

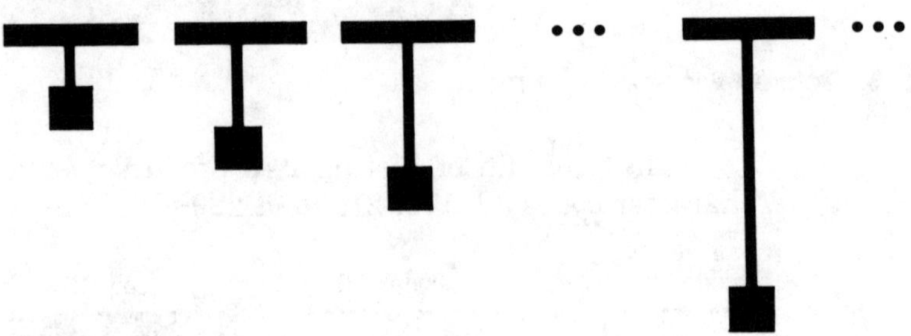

FIG. 2—4. Sequence of vertical movement

Another loop produces an upward motion using character codes 219 and 32.

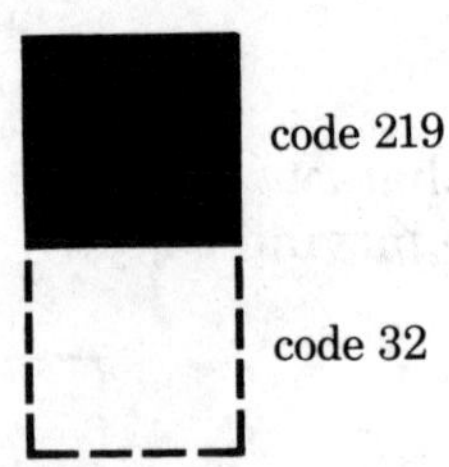


```
410 BLANK$ = CHR$(32)
420 FOR ROW = 22 TO 2 STEP -1
430   LOCATE ROW+1,20: PRINT BLANK$;
```

```
440  LOCATE ROW,20: PRINT YOYO$;
450  FOR DELAY = 1 TO 20: NEXT DELAY
460 NEXT ROW
```

This loop erases the current object and prints the object one row higher than it was. This gives the effect of a string that gets shorter.

The up and down action is repeated over and over, creating a display similar to that of a yoyo.

LISTING 2–5. Yoyo Action

```
100 REM * set screen *
110 SCREEN 0,1
120 KEY OFF
130 WIDTH 40
140 CLS
199 '
200 REM * draw support *
210 LOCATE 1,19
220 PRINT STRING$(3,220)
299 '
300 REM * downward animation *
310 CORD$ = CHR$(179)
320 YOYO$ = CHR$(219)
330 FOR ROW = 2 TO 22
340   LOCATE ROW,20: PRINT CORD$;
350   LOCATE ROW+1,20: PRINT YOYO$;
360   FOR DELAY = 1 TO 20: NEXT DELAY
370 NEXT ROW
399 '
400 REM * upward animation *
410 BLANK$ = CHR$(32)
420 FOR ROW = 22 TO 2 STEP -1
430   LOCATE ROW+1,20: PRINT BLANK$;
440   LOCATE ROW,20: PRINT YOYO$;
450   FOR DELAY = 1 TO 20: NEXT DELAY
460 NEXT ROW
499 '
500 REM * repeat the animation *
510 GOTO 330
```

Page flipping is a second method that can be used to animate objects. There are eight separate "pages" of memory that can be used to produce displays in the 40-character text mode. Each page will produce a separate screen display. The pages being used are controlled by the SCREEN command. The active page is the page on which you can currently "draw," or print. The visible page is the one that is currently being displayed. The active and visible pages are normally the same so that you can see what is being produced. The format for SCREEN is

```
SCREEN [mode][,[burst][,[apage][,[vpage]]]
```

        active page   visible page

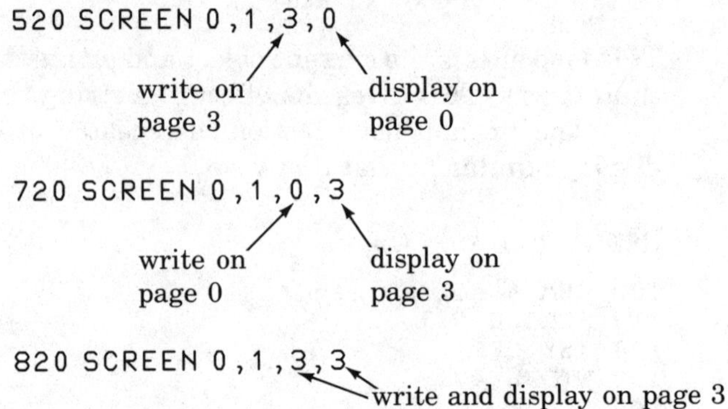

The program of Listing 2–6 uses page flipping to display the movement of four pistons in a cutaway engine, as shown in Fig. 2–5.

FIG. 2–5. Animated engine

The engine parts are created by character codes. Character code 220 is used for the shaft to which the pistons are attached. This shaft shape is assigned to a string variable A\$. A\$ is developed in lines 210 through 240 by concatenation. Concatenation (also catenation) is simply tying together several parts into one piece.

In line 210, A\$ starts out as two blanks □□. The FOR-NEXT loop (lines 220–240) catenates CHR\$(220) to A\$ for each pass through the loop. A\$ ends up as

Lines 210 through 240 could be replaced by

```
210 A$ = STR$(2,32) + STR$(12,220)
```

Catenation was used in this section to be consistent with the method of forming B$, which is a more complex structure.

Shapes were assigned in this manner to A$, B$, and C$ so that the engine could be drawn more quickly and more easily placed on multiple pages in lines 500–640 of the program.

The top portion of the engine block is formed by six rows of character code 219 separated by spaces. The bottom of the engine is one solid row of character code 219. Light blue is used for the engine's color.

The pistons are formed in various positions by character codes 179 and 219.

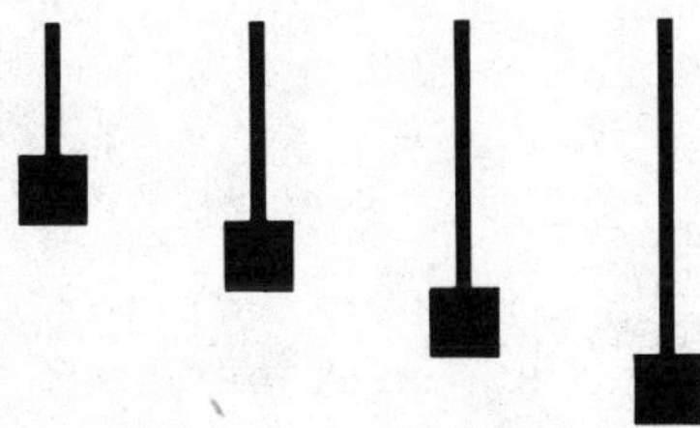

The four pistons are drawn in six unique positions. Each arrangement is placed on a different screen page. The pages are then flipped to display the "moving" pistons.

```
700 REM * flip pages *
710 FOR PAGE = 0 TO 5
720   SCREEN 0,1,PAGE,PAGE
730   FOR DELAY = 1 TO 80: NEXT DELAY
740 NEXT PAGE
750 GOTO 710
```

LISTING 2–6. Engine Action

```
100 REM * set screen *
110 SCREEN 0,1
120 KEY OFF
130 WIDTH 40
140 CLS
199 '
200 REM * define A$ *
210 A$ = CHR$(32)+CHR$(32)
220 FOR NUMBER = 1 TO 12
```

```basic
230   A$ = A$+CHR$(220)
240 NEXT NUMBER
299 '
300 REM * define B$ *
310 B$ = ""
320 FOR NUMBER = 1 TO 5
330   B$ = B$+CHR$(32)+CHR$(219)+CHR$(219)
340 NEXT NUMBER
399 '
400 REM * define C$ *
410 C$ = CHR$(32)
420 FOR NUMBER = 1 TO 14
430   C$ = C$+CHR$(219)
440 NEXT NUMBER
499 '
500 REM * draw engine on 6 pages *
510 FOR AP = 0 TO 5
520   SCREEN 0,1,AP,0
530   COLOR 9
540   LOCATE 7,13
550   PRINT A$;
560   FOR ROW = 9 TO 14
570     LOCATE ROW,13
580     PRINT B$;
590   NEXT ROW
600   LOCATE 15,13
610   PRINT C$;
620   COLOR 7
630   GOSUB 1010
640 NEXT AP
699 '
700 REM * flip pages *
710 FOR PAGE = 0 TO 5
720   SCREEN 0,1,PAGE,PAGE
730   FOR DELAY = 1 TO 80: NEXT DELAY
740 NEXT PAGE
750 GOTO 710
799 '
1000 REM * subroutine for piston data *
1010 FOR PISTON = 1 TO 4
1020   READ COLUMN,NUMBER
1030   GOSUB 1110
1040 NEXT PISTON
1050 RETURN
1099 '
1100 REM * subroutine to draw pistons *
1110 FOR ROW = 8 TO NUMBER
1120   LOCATE ROW,COLUMN
1130   PRINT CHR$(179);
1140 NEXT ROW
1150 LOCATE ROW,COLUMN
1160 PRINT CHR$(219);
1170 IF NUMBER <> 12 THEN 1180
1175 LOCATE ROW+1,COLUMN: COLOR 12,0,0: PRINT CHR$(177);: COLOR 7,0,0
1180 RETURN
1199 '
```

```
1200 REM * data for pistons *
1210 DATA 16,9,19,10,22,11,25,12
1220 DATA 16,10,19,11,22,12,25,11
1230 DATA 16,11,19,12,22,11,25,10
1240 DATA 16,12,19,11,22,10,25,9
1250 DATA 16,11,19,10,22,9,25,10
1260 DATA 16,10,19,9,22,10,25,11
```

SUMMARY

In this chapter you learned to create and animate simple graphics using character codes in the text mode. The information needed to do this follows.

- Keyboard characters can be displayed in any of 16 colors by using the COLOR statement and an appropriate character code (an integer, n).

```
PRINT CHR$(n)
```

- High-numbered character codes can be used to produce a variety of shapes. See Fig. 2–2 and Listings 2–2 and 2–3.
- Special character codes can be used to produce colorful windows of text, as seen in Fig. 2–3.
- Simple animation can be created in the text mode by moving shapes, created by character codes, to different screen positions.
- Simple animation can also be created in the text mode by flipping pages by means of the SCREEN command.

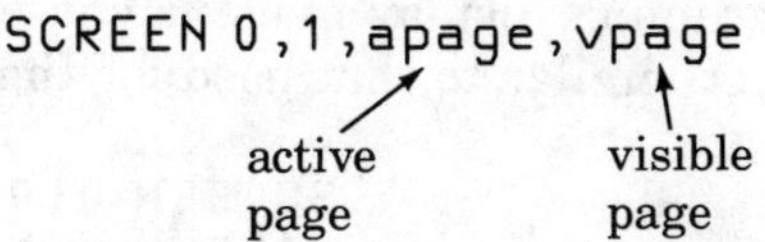

- Spaces can be inserted in text or graphics by the SPACE$ statement.

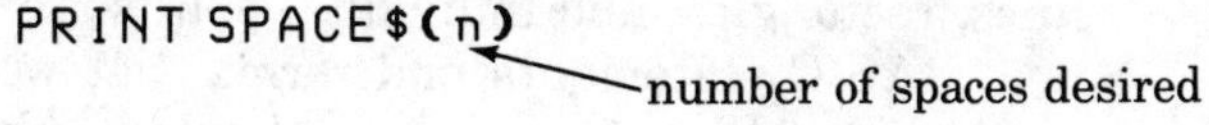

3
LINES AND RECTANGLES

The first two chapters have shown how crude graphics can be created in the text mode. We now enter the true graphics modes of the IBM PC. The graphics display mode is chosen by the SCREEN command in a manner similar to that used for the text mode, which is

```
SCREEN 0,0      color off
SCREEN 0,1      color on
```

Your objective in this chapter is to learn to set up the screen for the medium-resolution graphics mode and to draw objects composed of lines, rectangles, and individual points.

BASIC statements and terms that we assume you are familiar with are all those in previous chapters, plus COS, END, INT, RAN-DOMIZE, RND, and SIN.

BASIC statements and terms that are explained in this chapter are COLOR and SCREEN for medium-resolution, LINE, PSET, PRE-SET, and LINE style.

The command SCREEN 1 selects a medium-resolution graphics display. The screen is divided horizontally into 320 dots and vertically into 200 dots in this mode. This provides a total of 64,000 individually controlled dots. Each dot on the screen can be set to one of four different colors. Only 40 characters per line of text are allowed in this mode. Text may be in color or black and white only depending on whether the color burst value is a 1 or a 0.

SCREEN 1 , 0 ←————turns on colors
SCREEN 1 , 1 ←————turns off colors

Notice that the values for controlling the color burst are the reverse of those used in the text mode (SCREEN 0). Enter and run the following BASIC program to see the effect of the color-burst parameter.

LISTING 3–1. Color Burst

```
100 REM * set screen for color *
110 SCREEN 1,0: CLS
120 KEY OFF
199 '
200 REM * print in color *
210 FOR BACKGROUND = 0 TO 15
220   SCREEN 1,0: CLS
230   COLOR BACKGROUND
240   PRINT "SCREEN 1,0": PRINT
250   PRINT "turns color on": GOSUB 1010
260   CLS: SCREEN 1,1
270   PRINT "SCREEN 1,1": PRINT
280   PRINT "turns color off": GOSUB 1010
290 NEXT BACKGROUND
299 '
300 REM * end program *
310 END
399 '
1000 REM * time delay subroutine *
1010 FOR DELAY = 1 TO 1000: NEXT DELAY
1020 RETURN
```

When the Color Burst program is run, the screen alternately displays a message on 1 of the 16 available colored backgrounds (SCREEN 1,0—color on) and a message with white letters on a black background (SCREEN 1,1—color off). Figure 3–1 shows the display. The 16 background colors are those of Table 3–1.

```
SCREEN 1,0
turns color on
```

FIG. 3–1(a). Color on

```
SCREEN 1,1
turns color off
```

FIG. 3–1(b). Color off

TABLE 3—1
BACKGROUND COLOR CODES

NUMBER CODE	COLOR
0	black
1	blue
2	green
3	cyan
4	red
5	magenta
6	brown
7	white
8	gray
9	light blue
10	light green
11	light cyan
12	light red
13	light magenta
14	yellow
15	bright white

MEDIUM-RESOLUTION GRAPHICS MODE

The screen allows 64,000 individual points in the medium-resolution graphics mode. There are 320 horizontal points (columns) and 200 vertical points (rows).

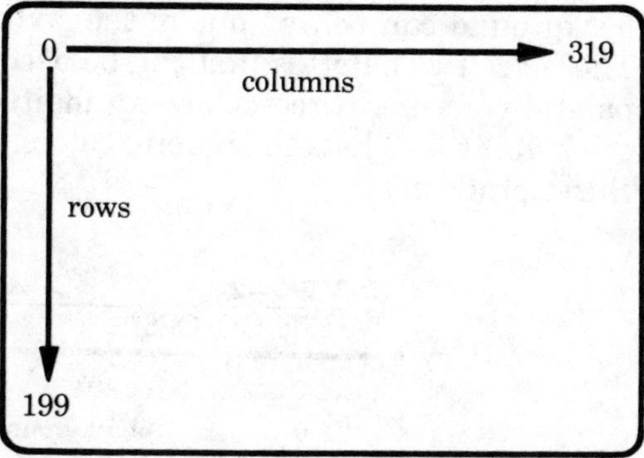

Each point in the display is designated by two numbers, one for column and one for row. The rows are numbered from top to bottom. Thus, the point at the extreme upper-left corner is designated 0,0 whereas the point at the extreme lower-right corner is called 319,199. Notice that the column is given first, then a comma, then the row. This is the reverse order from the LOCATE command used in the text mode. A point is located at the intersection of the specified row and column.

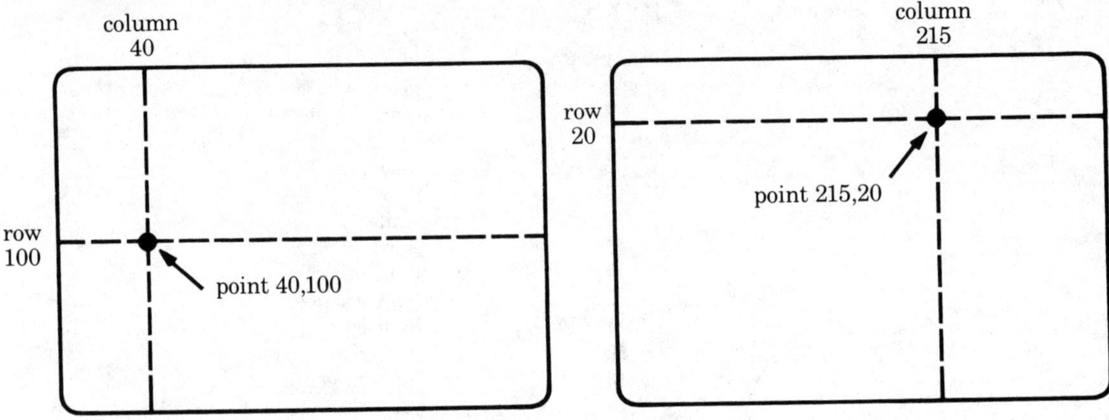

COLORS FOR MEDIUM-RESOLUTION

The COLOR command has a different format in this mode from the one it had in the text mode. For medium-resolution graphics, it is

```
COLOR [background][,palette]
```

As demonstrated in the Color Burst program of Listing 3–1, the background can be any one of the sixteen colors shown in Table 3–1. There are two palettes that can be used for the foreground color. Each palette contains three colors in addition to the selected background color. Table 3–2 lists the palette colors. Palette 1 was used in the Color Burst program.

TABLE 3–2

PALETTE COLORS

COLOR CODE	PALETTE 0	PALETTE 1
0	background	background
1	green	cyan
2	red	magenta
3	brown	white

LINE STATEMENT

The LINE statement provides a shortcut for drawing straight lines and rectangles. This statement needs only the location of the end points to draw a line or the location of the opposite corners to draw a rectangle. The format for LINE is

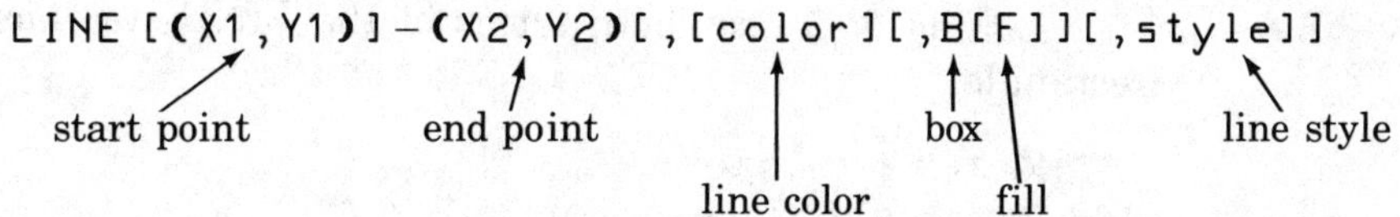

Note: Line style is not available on Advanced BASIC versions that are earlier than version 2.

The starting-point parameter of the LINE statement is optional. If it is not specified, the last point referenced is used as the starting point for the new line.

EXAMPLE

When two end points are given, the line is drawn from the start point to the end point.

```
LINE (100,50)-(210,50)
```

start point   end point

When only one point is given, the line is drawn from the last point that has been referenced to the end point that is specified.

```
LINE-(210,150)
```

end point

When the two examples are combined, two connecting lines are drawn.

```
210 LINE(100,50)-(210,50)
220 LINE-(210,150)
```

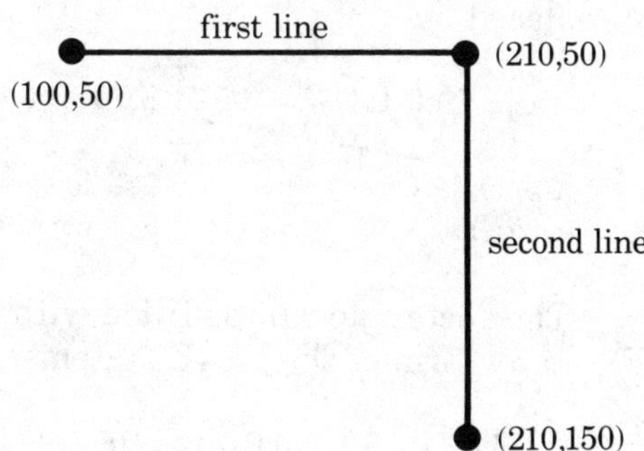

Listing 3–2 uses both forms of the LINE statement to draw a rectangle.

LISTING 3–2. Rectangle

```
100 REM * set screen for color *
110 SCREEN 1,0: COLOR 5,1: KEY OFF
120 CLS
199 '
200 REM * solid-line rectangle *
210 LINE(100,50)-(210,50)          'top line
220 LINE-(210,150)                 'side
230 LINE-(100,150)                 'bottom
240 LINE-(100,50)                  'side
```

The color of the lines to be drawn can be defined in the LINE statement. The color parameter follows the end point and is separated from it by a comma.

LINE(100,50)-(210,50),3 ← color code

LINE-(210,150),2 ← color code

If the color code is not specified, the computer will use the default code (number 3). So that all lines of the rectangle in the previous program will be the same color, the color code is specified in each line.

```
210 LINE(100,50)-(210,50),1
220 LINE-(210,150),1
230 LINE-(100,150),1
240 LINE-(100,50),1
```

The BOX option (B) of the LINE statement allows a more convenient method for drawing rectangles whose sides are all the same color. If the LINE statement is to be used to draw a rectangle, the location of two opposite corners of the rectangle are used in place of the start and end points of a line. Lines 210 through 240 of Listing 3–2 can be replaced by

210 LINE (100,50)-(210,150),1,B

upper-left corner   lower-right corner   color is cyan   draw a box

The rectangle can be filled with color by adding the FILL option (F) to any form of the LINE statement.

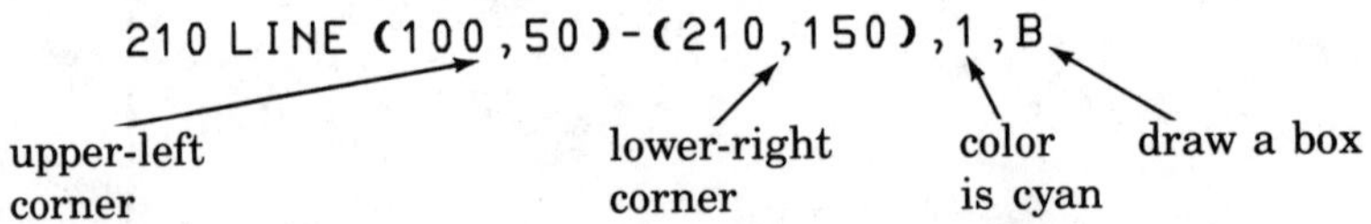

310 LINE-(300,180),,BF

color not specified   fill the box with default color (white in palette 1 or brown in palette 0)

If no color is specified, the current color is used. However, the position of the color option must be maintained by the two consecutive commas following the end point of the LINE statement. Figure 3–2 shows a large empty rectangle and two smaller rectangles filled with color.

FIG. 3–2. Boxes

LISTING 3–3. Box and Fill

```
100 REM * set screen *
110 SCREEN 1,0: KEY OFF
120 COLOR 5,1: CLS
199 '
200 REM * draw box *
210 LINE(100,50)-(210,150),1,B          ←————open box
299 '
300 REM * add filled box *
310 LINE-(300,180),,BF                   ←————filled box
```

LINE 210 SETS THE SCENE

The order of the start and end points in line 210 of Listing 3–3 is very important. The shortened form of the LINE statement uses the end point of line 210 as its start point. After running the Box and Fill program, change the order of the points in line 210 to

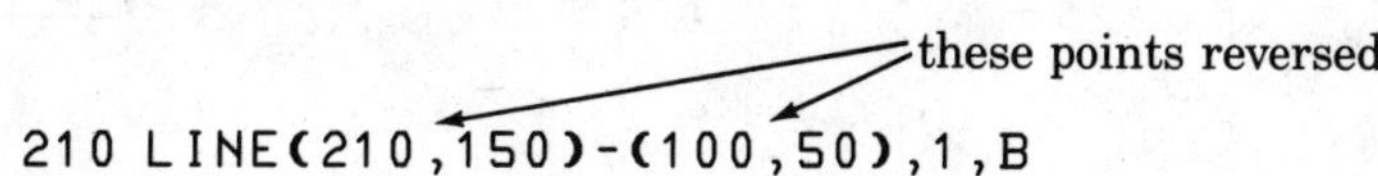

Run the program with this change, and you will see only one large filled rectangle. In this case, line 310 uses the last referenced point (which is now 100,50) as its starting point. Thus, the filled rectangle is drawn from 100,50 to 300,180. This covers the first rectangle, as shown in Fig. 3–3.

FIG. 3–3. Covered box

This shows that you must be careful in using filled rectangles, for they may hide something that you want to be visible.

The STEP option may also be used in the LINE statement. Listing 3–4 produces a series of rectangles using the last referenced point as one corner. The first referenced point is turned on by PSET in line 210. PSET is more fully discussed later in this chapter. Thirty units are added to X, and twenty units are added to Y to calculate the corner opposite the last referenced point.

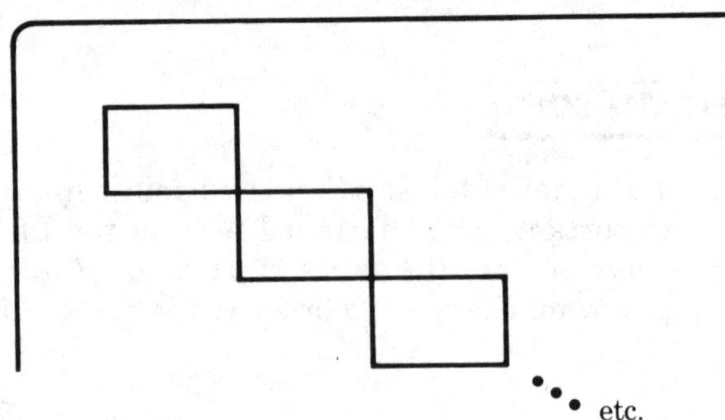

LISTING 3–4. Boxes by STEP

```
100 REM * set screen *
110 SCREEN 1,0: KEY OFF
120 COLOR 12,1: CLS            ←——— light red background,
199 '                                palette 1
200 REM * draw 10 boxes *
210 PSET(10,40),2             ←——— set 1 point
220 FOR NUMBER = 1 TO 10
230   LINE-STEP(30,20),,BF    ←——— draw boxes 30 by 20
240 NEXT NUMBER
```

As can be seen in Fig. 3–4, only eight rectangles are visible. The last two rectangles drawn do not fit on the screen. When the coordinates of a point are beyond the limits of the screen, the last possible coordinate value is used. Therefore, you see a white line at the bottom-right of the screen.

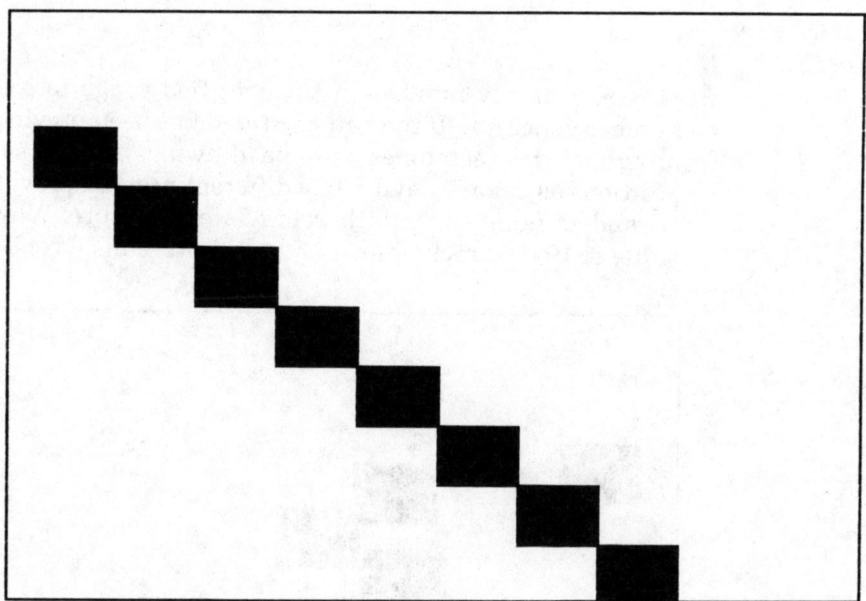

FIG. 3–4. Series of boxes

To fit all rectangles on the screen, change line 210 to

```
210 PSET(10,10),1
```

Another form of the STEP option is used in Listing 3–5. This time, the starting point of each rectangle is randomly chosen. A step of 30,20 is then used to locate the opposite corner. The color of the rectangle is also randomly chosen.

```
100 REM * set screen *
110 SCREEN 1,0: KEY OFF
120 COLOR 6,1: CLS
130 RANDOMIZE
140 CLS
199 '
200 REM * draw boxes *
210 FOR NUMBER = 1 TO 10
220   KOLOR = INT(RND*3)+1
230   X = INT(RND*280)+1
240   Y = INT(RND*180)+1
250   LINE(X,Y)-STEP(30,20),KOLOR,BF
260 NEXT NUMBER
```

When the program is run, the screen first shows

```
Random number seed (-32768 to 32767) ?
```

Key in any number in the specified range to seed the random-number generator. If the value entered has been previously used in the program, the rectangles will be drawn with the same colors and positions as before. Keying in a different number provides a new series of random numbers and, therefore, a new picture. When we entered a value of 10, the rectangles of Fig. 3–5 were displayed.

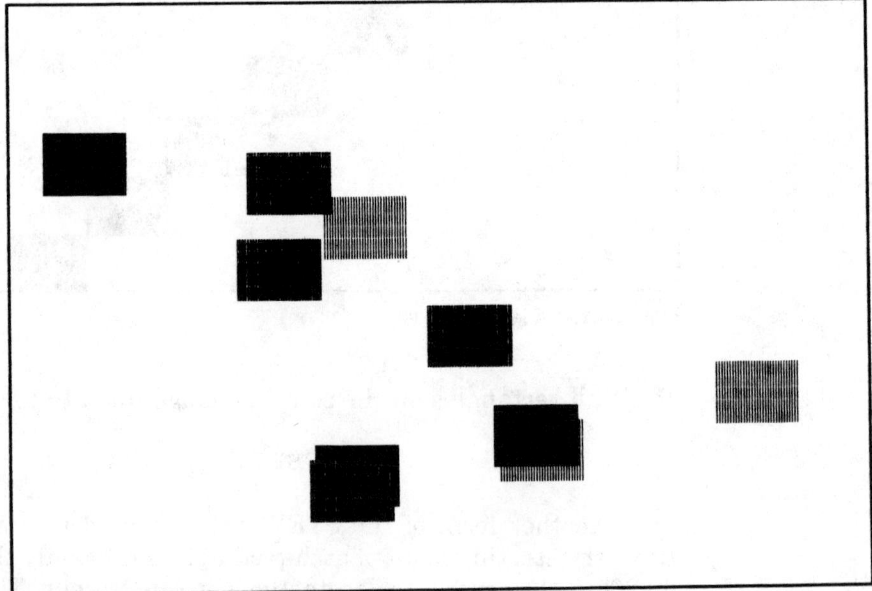

FIG. 3–5. Random rectangles

The final option of the LINE statement is STYLE. This option can be used to draw lines composed of dots and dashes as well as solid lines. It uses 16-bit binary numbers to form a pattern as the line is drawn. A binary value of one (1) specifies that a point on the line is to be drawn. A binary value of zero (0) specifies that a point is not to be drawn.

EXAMPLE

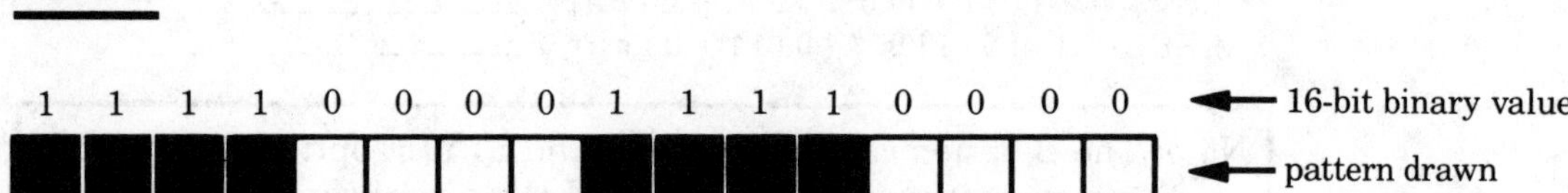

Because 16-bit binary numbers are very long, the hexadecimal equivalents of groups of 4 binary digits (bits) are usually used in programs. Table 3–3 shows the hexadecimal equivalents of 4-bit binary groups. Four hexadecimal digits can represent 16 binary digits. For convenience, decimal equivalents are also shown in the table.

TABLE 3–3

BINARY/HEXADECIMAL/DECIMAL EQUIVALENT VALUES

BINARY	HEXADECIMAL	DECIMAL
0000	0	0
0001	1	1
0010	2	2
0011	3	3
0100	4	4
0101	5	5
0110	6	6
0111	7	7
1000	8	8
1001	9	9
1010	A	10
1011	B	11
1100	C	12
1101	D	13
1110	E	14
1111	F	15

EXAMPLES

STYLE VALUE	BINARY VALUE	PATTERN PRODUCED
CCCC	1100110011001100	
9A9A	1001101010011010	
5757	0101011101010111	

Hexadecimal values are preceded by the symbols &H to let the computer know that the value is a hexadecimal value rather than a decimal value that would normally be used. Here are some examples of LINE statements using the STYLE option with hexadecimal values.

```
LINE(10,10)-(130,10),,,&HEE88
LINE-(130),,,&H5577
LINE(20,20)-(100,90),3,B,&HEEEE

&HEE88 = 1110111010001000 binary ____ ____ _  _
&H5577 = 0101010101110111 binary _ _ _ _ ____ ____
&HEEEE = 1110111011101110 binary ____ ____ ___ ____
```

> Note: The B option can be used with the STYLE option, but the BF option cannot be used with STYLE, as it causes a syntax error.

The pattern produced by the STYLE option is repeated over and over as the line is drawn. Listing 3–6 produces a screen that is similar to that of Fig. 3–6. Dotted and dashed rectangles are drawn within a solid-line rectangle.

LISTING 3–6. Rectangles by Style
```
100 REM * set screen *
110 SCREEN 1,0: KEY OFF
120 COLOR 5,1: CLS
199 '
200 REM * solid rectangle *
210 LINE(100,50)-(210,150),,B,&HFFFF
```

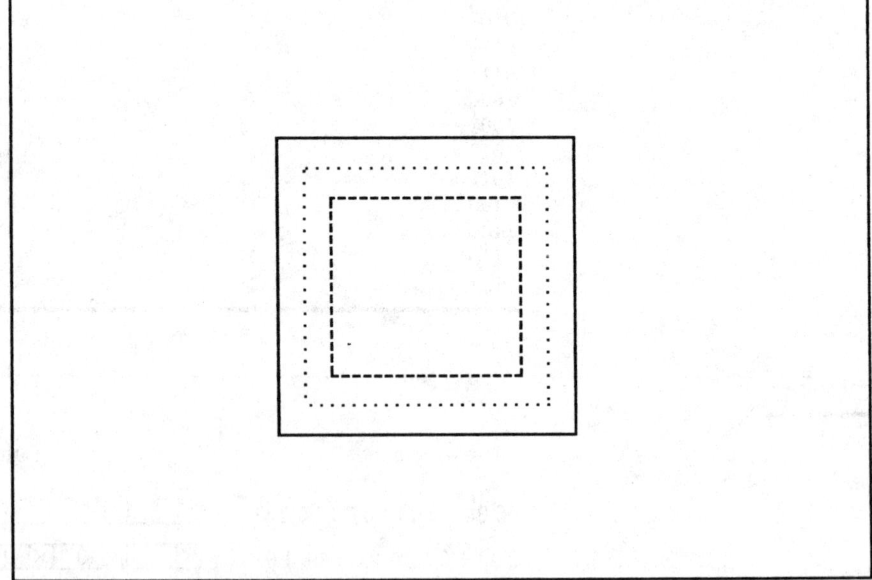

FIG. 3–6. Rectangles using style

```
299 '
300 REM * dotted rectangle *
310 LINE(110,60)-(200,140),,B,&H8888
399 '
400 REM * dashed rectangle *
410 LINE(120,70)-(190,130),,B,&HEEEE
```

PSET COMMAND

The numerical color codes are used as parameters in commands that "set," or turn on, points of color. Individual points are colored by the PSET command:

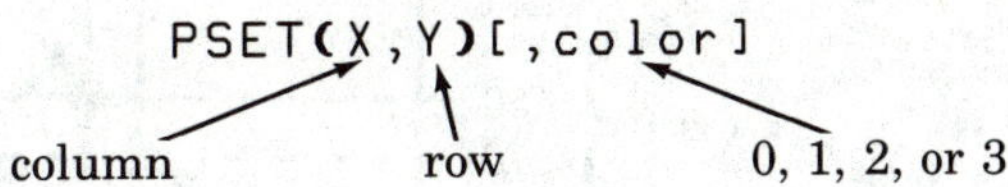

EXAMPLES

PSET(100,150)
PSET(300,50)

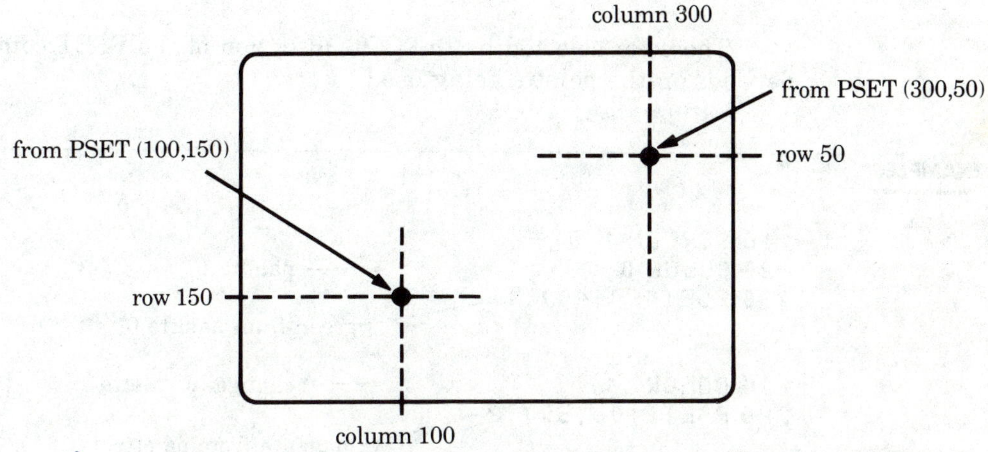

The X,Y values can be the absolute column and row numbers for the screen positions, as previously indicated, or they can be expressed in the following relative form:

PSET STEP(x-offset,y-offset)[,color]

The offset values of the relative form give the horizontal and vertical change from the last point referenced.

```
210 PSET(100,150)       ← turns on point 100,150
220 PSET STEP(-10,20)   ← turns on the point 90,170
                                (100−10,150+20)
```

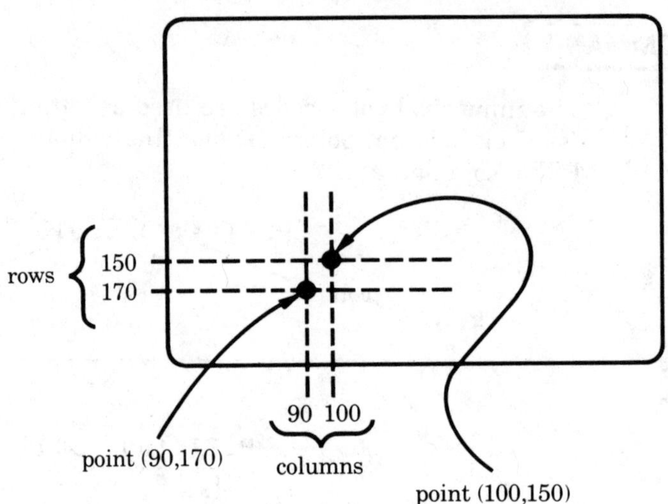

The color selected by the COLOR option of the PSET command depends on the palette being used.


```
110 SCREEN 1,0
120 COLOR 0,0           ←——— palette 0
130 PSET(90,40),1 ←
      .                    green from palette 0
      .
210 COLOR ,1            ←——— change to palette 1
220 PSET(100,50),2 ←
                         magenta from palette 1
```

If no color is selected for PSET, the foreground color (number 3) is used. If the color value is less than 0, an "Illegal function call" error is given. If the color value is greater than 3, Version 2.0 uses the foreground color.

Since PSET draws individual points, it can be used to draw curved lines much like those found in mathematical expressions such as

```
Y = SIN(ANGLE)

Y = COS(ANGLE)

Y = .002*X^2-180
```

PSET is used in Listing 3–7 to draw these three mathematical expressions with parameters adjusted so that the results will fit on the screen as shown in Fig. 3–7. The curves are each drawn in a different color.

LISTING 3–7. Curves of Mathematical Expressions

```
100 REM * set screen *
110 SCREEN 1,0: KEY OFF: CLS
199 '
200 REM * draw curve *
210 PI = 3.14159
220 FOR ANGLE = 0 TO 2*PI STEP .05
230   X = ANGLE*40+40
240   YSIN = -(SIN(ANGLE)*80-90)
250   YCOS = -(COS(ANGLE)*80-90)
260   YSQR = -(.002*X^2-180)
270   PSET(X,YSIN),1          'green
280   PSET(X,YCOS),2          'red
290   PSET(X,YSQR),3          'brown
300 NEXT ANGLE
```

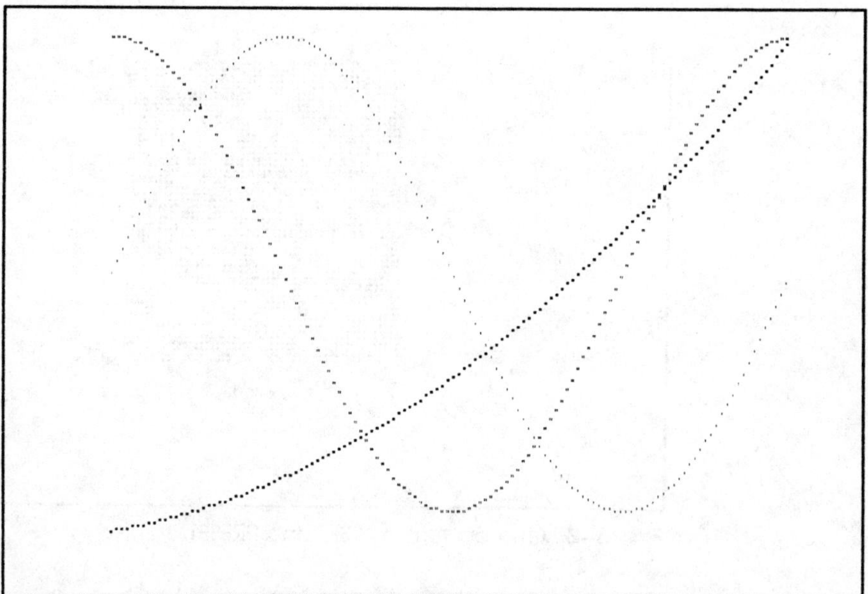

FIG. 3–7. Curved lines by PSET

PRESET STATEMENT

Individual points are set, or turned on, by PSET. Points can also be turned off by using PSET with the COLOR option set to the background color. However, points are more conveniently reset to the background color by the PRESET statement.

```
PRESET(X,Y)[,color]
```

reset this point   optional

If no color is selected for PRESET, the background color is automatically selected. This can be used to erase points that have been previously PSET (or PRESET with a selected color). If a color value is included with PRESET, it acts exactly like PSET turning on the specified point to that color.

The next program, in Listing 3–8, selects palette 0 of the medium-resolution graphics mode. It then sets a grid of green points on a red background. We use PSET to make a grid of 51 rows of dots, with 51 dots in each row. After all points have been set, the program instructs the computer to pause for a few seconds.

Then PRESET is used to erase every fifth point in every fifth row leaving the pattern shown in Fig. 3–8 on the display. The original number of points (51) was chosen as 1 more than an even multiple of 5 points so that the final pattern would be symmetrical.

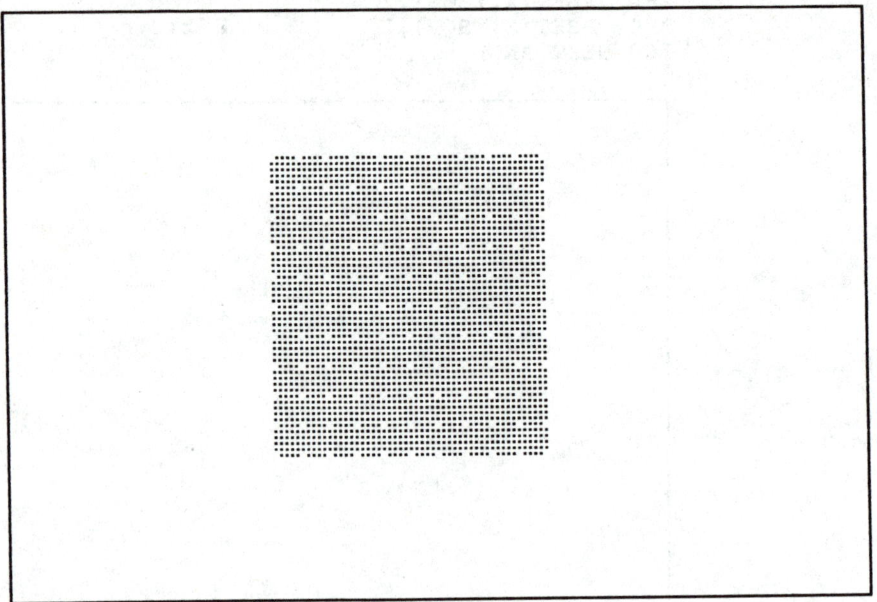

FIG. 3–8. Grid pattern by PSET and PRESET

LISTING 3–8. Setting a Grid of Points

```
100 REM * set screen *
110 SCREEN 1,0: CLS
120 KEY OFF
199 '
200 REM * set all points *
210 COLOR 4,0                    ◄─── red background, palette 0
220 FOR X = 100 TO 200 STEP 2
230   FOR Y = 50 TO 150 STEP 2
240     PSET(X,Y),1              ◄─── green points
250   NEXT Y
```

```
260 NEXT X
299 '
300 REM * wait a bit *
310 FOR DELAY = 1 TO 500: NEXT DELAY
399 '
400 REM * erase some points *
410 FOR X = 200 TO 100 STEP -10
420   FOR Y = 150 TO 50 STEP -10
430     PRESET(X,Y)
440   NEXT Y
450 NEXT X
```

The same display can be made using the relative form for PSET by changing the following lines:

```
230   Y = 50: PSET(X,Y),1
240    FOR NUMBER = 1 TO 50
250      PSET STEP(0,2),1
260    NEXT NUMBER
270 NEXT X
        .
        .
420   Y = 150: PRESET(X,Y)
430    FOR NUMBER = 1 TO 10
440      PRESET STEP(0,-10)
450    NEXT NUMBER
460 NEXT X
```

increase Y by 2

decrease Y by 10

DRAWING LINES AT ODD ANGLES

Trigonometric functions can be used to draw a series of points to form lines in various directions. Consider the following line of dots turned a given angle from the solid line.

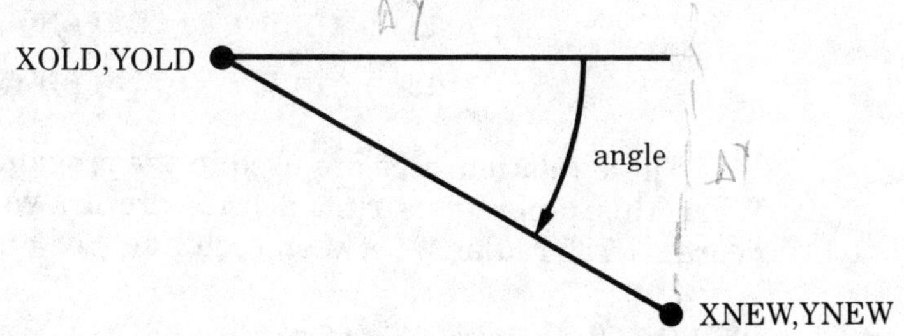

The end point of the dotted line is found by adding a given amount to the X-coordinate and a given amount to the Y-coordinate of the starting point of the line.

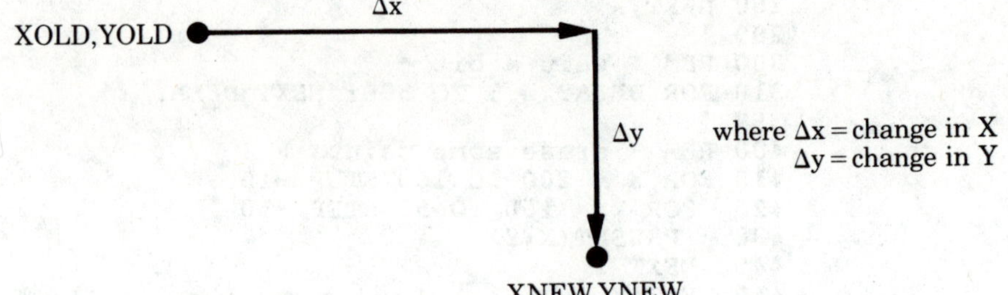

If you look at the triangle formed by a line drawn between the two points and the lines formed by Δx and Δy, you can take advantage of sine and cosine functions to calculate the X-coordinate and Y-coordinate of the new point.

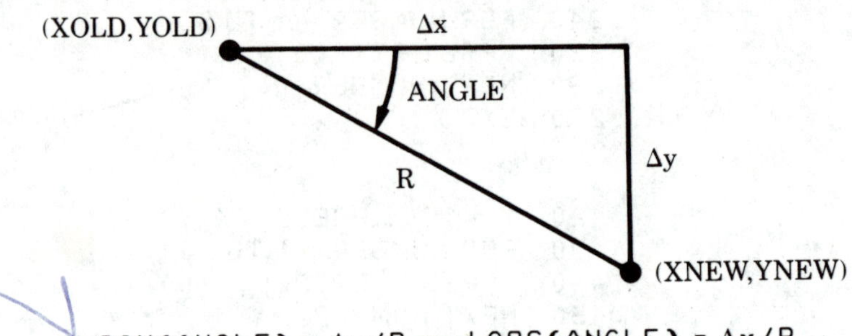

$$\text{SIN(ANGLE)} = \Delta y/R \text{ and } \text{COS(ANGLE)} = \Delta x/R$$

Therefore,

$$\Delta x = R * \text{COS(ANGLE)}$$

$$\Delta y = R * \text{SIN(ANGLE)}$$

The coordinates of the end points can then be found by

$$\text{XNEW} = \text{XOLD} + R*\text{COS(ANGLE)}$$

$$\text{YNEW} = \text{YOLD} + R*\text{SIN(ANGLE)}$$

These relationships are used in the progam Lines at Odd Angles. When this program is run, 8 lines are drawn with an angle of 45 degrees (.785 radians) between each line. See Fig. 3–9.

LISTING 3–9. Lines at Odd Angles

```
100 REM * set screen *
110 SCREEN 1,0: KEY OFF
120 CLS
130 COLOR 5,1                          ←——— magenta
199 '
200 REM * draw lines *
210 FOR ANGLE = 0 TO 6.28 STEP .785
```

```
220    XOLD = 100: YOLD = 100
230    XNEW = XOLD + 80*COS(ANGLE)
240    YNEW = YOLD + 80*SIN(ANGLE)
250    LINE(XOLD,YOLD)-(XNEW,YNEW)
260  NEXT ANGLE
```

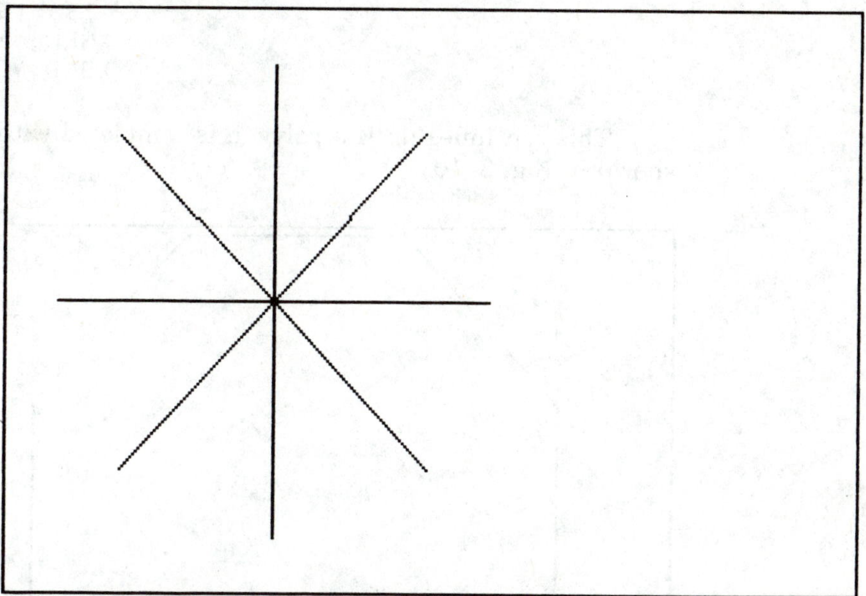

FIG. 3–9. Lines using sines and cosines

An interesting display is created in Fig. 3–10 by making the following changes to Listing 3–9.

```
210 XOLD = 100: YOLD = 3
```
X and Y starting values outside the loop

```
220 FOR ANGLE = 0 TO 6.28 STEP .785
```

The initial values for X and Y are moved outside the ANGLE loop. The Y value is changed from 100 to 3. In addition, a line is added that converts the end point of each line to the starting point of the next line.

```
255 XOLD = XNEW: YOLD = YNEW
```


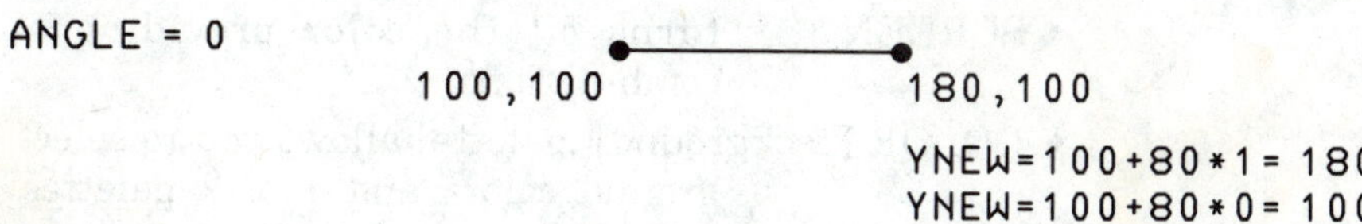


```
YNEW=100+80*1= 180
YNEW=100+80*0= 100
```

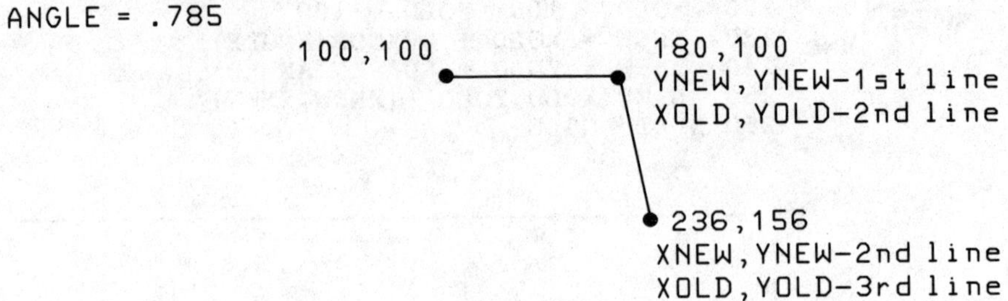

This continues until a polygon is completed with eight sides, as shown in Fig. 3–10.

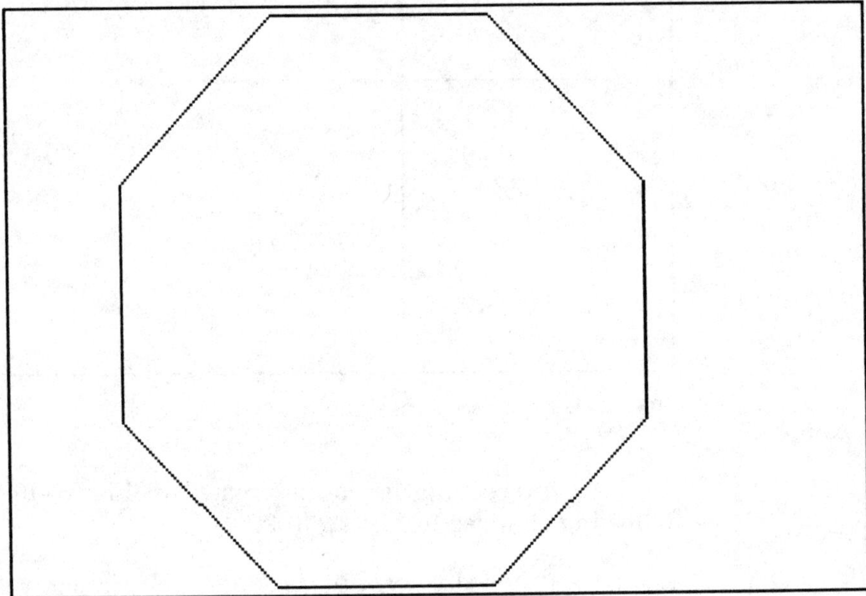

FIG. 3–10. Octagon

SUMMARY

In this chapter you learned how to set up the screen for medium-resolution graphics. Medium-resolution graphics provides 64,000 individual points, 320 columns by 200 rows. You learned how to use the following statements:

- SCREEN 1,0   selects medium-resolution with 1 to 2 four-color palettes.
- SCREEN 1,1   turns off the color providing only black/white combinations.
- COLOR [background][,palette] allows you to select 1 of 16 background colors and 1 of 2 palettes from which the

foreground color is selected. Background colors were given in Table 3–1 and palette colors in Table 3–2.

- LINE [(X1,Y1)] – (X2,Y2)[,color][,B[F]][,style] allows you to draw lines, rectangles, rectangles filled with color, and lines of many styles.

- PSET (X,Y)[,color] allows you to turn on a point defined by X,Y coordinates to 1 of the four colors of a specified palette.

- PRESET (X,Y)[,color] allows you to erase a point specified by the X,Y coordinates.

Programs demonstrated how to draw solid, dashed, and dotted lines. Trigonometric functions were used to demonstrate lines drawn at any specified angle. Parallel lines were used to draw rectangles with PSET. Programs were given to demonstrate the many options of the LINE statement.

4

CIRCLES AND POLYGONS

Graphics Statements, Functions,
and Terms Introduced

CIRCLE
aspect
sine
cosine
PAINT

The objective of this chapter is to teach you how to use the CIRCLE statement to draw an ellipse, a circle, or a part of either an ellipse or a circle. The PAINT statement is introduced to show you how to color the interior of a closed area.

BASIC statements and terms that we assume you are familiar with are all those used in previous chapters, plus IF-THEN-ELSE, INPUT, and LEFT$.

BASIC statements and terms that are explained are CIRCLE with its radius, color, and aspect ratio; sine and cosine functions; and PAINT.

The IBM PC can draw curves as well as straight lines. In fact, BASICA contains a powerful command that can draw an arc, a circle, or even an ellipse.

CIRCLES, ARCS, AND ELLIPSES

The CIRCLE statement contains several parameters to control placement on the screen, size, color, the start and end points of an arc, and an aspect ratio, which "squeezes" the shape into an ellipse. The format of this statement is

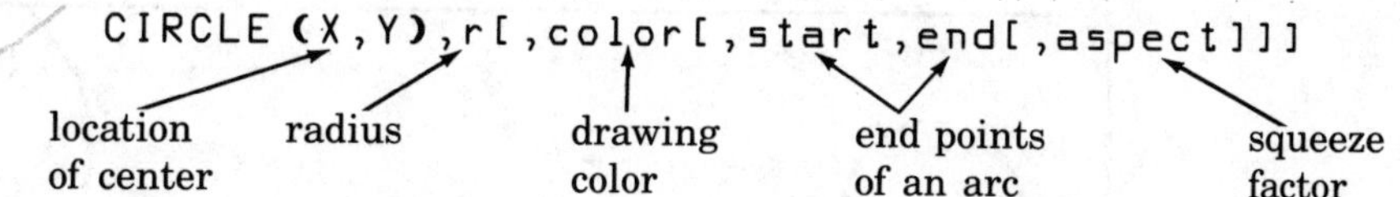

Let's consider the simplest form of a circle first.

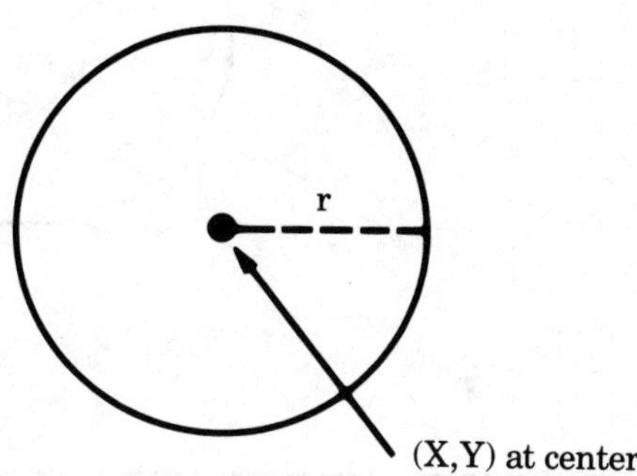

The X,Y coordinates determine where the center of the circle is located on the screen. The limits in the medium-resolution graphics mode are 0 through 319 for X and 0 through 199 for Y. The size of the circle is determined by the radius, r. If the circle is to lie completely within the limits of the screen, care must be taken in the selection of both coordinates and radius.

EXAMPLES

`CIRCLE(160,100),50` ←——— center of circle near center of screen; radius 50

`CIRCLE(40,40),20` ←——— center at upper-left of screen; radius 20

`CIRCLE(280,30),50` ←——— center at upper-right of screen; radius will cause part of the circle to go off the screen (invisible)

Listing 4–1 draws the three circles given in the examples. Note that the third figure is not a complete circle; parts of it lie off the screen because some of the X,Y coordinates exceed the screen's limits. These gaps can be seen in Fig. 4–1.

Medium-resolution is used in Listing 4–1. The background color is white and palette 0 is used. The circles are drawn in brown (color 3, the default color for palette 0). A time delay is placed between each execution of the CIRCLE statement so that you can readily see which

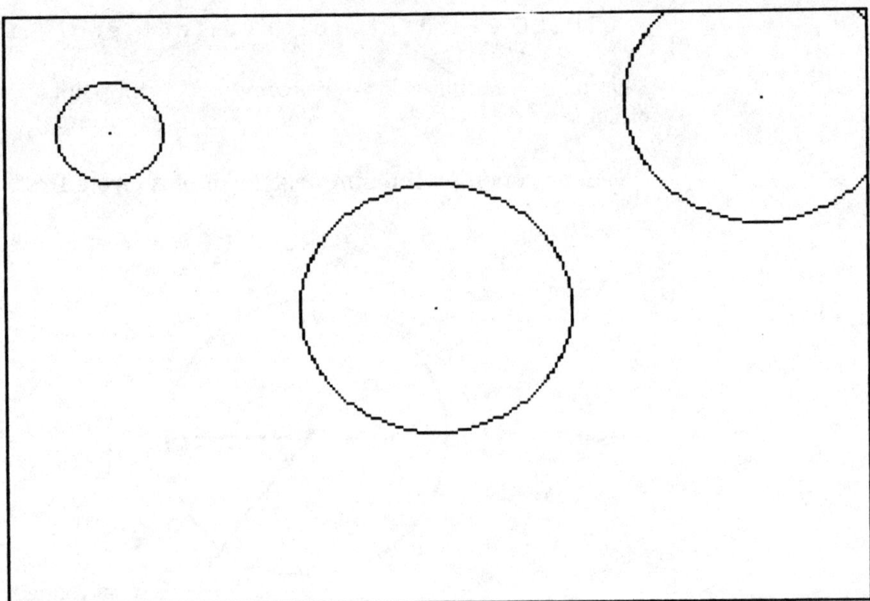

FIG. 4–1. Circle examples

LISTING 4–1. Circles

```
100 REM * set scren *
110 SCREEN 1,0: KEY OFF
120 COLOR 7,0: CLS
199 '
200 REM * draw circles *
210 PSET(160,100)
220 CIRCLE(160,100),50
230 FOR DELAY = 1 TO 500: NEXT DELAY
240 PSET(40,40)
250 CIRCLE(40,40),20
260 FOR DELAY = 1 TO 500: NEXT DELAY
270 PSET(280,30)
280 CIRCLE(280,30),50
```

CIRCLE statement causes the off-screen figure. The center of each circle is PSET for emphasis.

The color with which circles are drawn can be changed from the default color by including the COLOR option.


```
220 CIRCLE(160,100),50,1
250 CIRCLE(40,40),20,2
```

Use these two examples in place of lines 220 and 250 in Listing 4–1. The first circle will be drawn in green and the second in red.

The START and END options specify where an arc (a part of a circle) will begin and end. Start and end are specified as angles measured in radians. Angles are measured in standard mathematical order; zero is at the right (three o'clock) position and angles increase counterclockwise. There are $2 \times$ pi radians in a circle. Arcs are drawn from the start angle to the end angle.

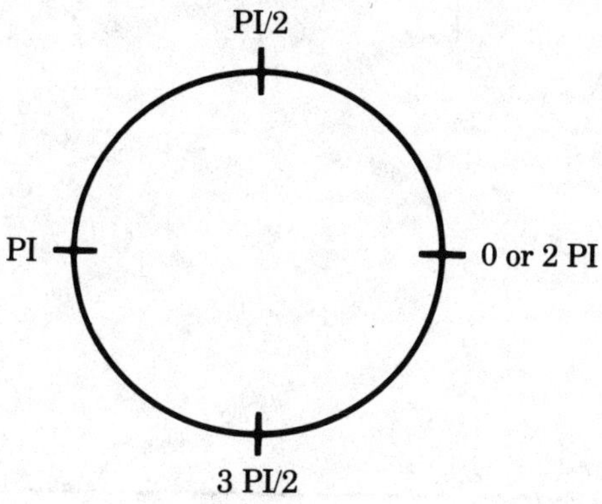

EXAMPLES

```
130 PI = 3.141593
210 CIRCLE(160,100),50,1,0,PI
310 CIRCLE(150,50),40,2,PI,0
410 CIRCLE(240,140),30,3,PI/2,PI
```

If the start or end angle is specified as negative (-0 not allowed), that point is connected to the center of the circle by a straight line.

EXAMPLES

```
PI = 3.141593
CIRCLE(100,50),40,2,-PI*3/2,-PI*2
CIRCLE(240,140),30,3,-PI*3/2,PI*2
```

Listing 4–2 uses the START and END options to draw three arcs as shown in Fig. 4–2.

The first arc is drawn in green at the center of the screen and uses zero for the start and a positive value for the end. The second arc is drawn in red at the upper-left. It has negative values for both start and

FIG. 4–2. Arcs

end. Therefore, lines are drawn from both ends of the arc to the center of the circle. The third arc is drawn in brown at the lower-right. The start value is negative, and the end value is positive. Therefore, a line is drawn from the start to the center of the circle but not from the end of the arc.

LISTING 4–2. Arcs and Circle Sections

```
100 REM * set screen and PI value *
110 SCREEN 1,0: KEY OFF
120 COLOR 0,0: CLS
130 PI = 3.141593
199 '
200 REM * circle, no negatives *
210 CIRCLE(160,100),50,1,0,3*PI/4
299 '
300 REM * circle, 2 negatives *
310 CIRCLE(40,50),40,2,-PI*3/2,-PI*2
399 '
400 REM * circle, 1 negative *
410 CIRCLE(240,140),30,3,-PI*3/2,PI*2
```

The ASPECT option changes the circle into an ellipse. It may be considered as the ratio of the Y-axis to the X-axis. Thus, an aspect value greater than one squeezes the circle along the X-axis (Y greater than X). Y becomes the radius, r. If the aspect value is less than one, the circle is squeezed along the Y-axis (X greater than Y). X becomes the radius, r.

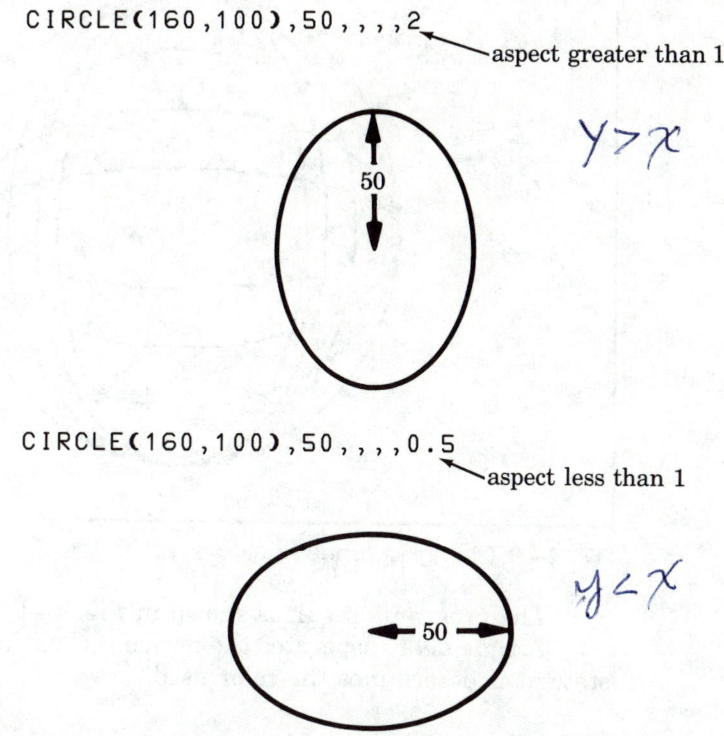

Various values are used in Listing 4–3 for the aspect. When aspect is greater than or equal to one, green is used to draw the ellipse. When the aspect ratio is less than one, red is used. The choice of color is made in line 220 by an IF-THEN-ELSE statement:

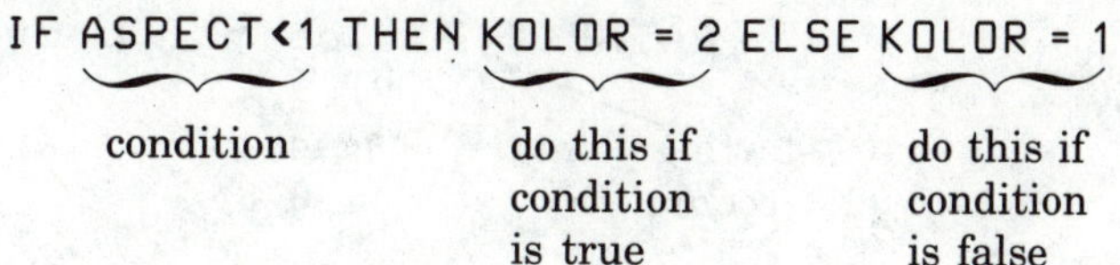

LISTING 4–3. Circle to Ellipse

```
100 REM * set screen and PI *
110 SCREEN 1,0: KEY OFF
120 COLOR 0,0: CLS
130 PI=3.141593
199 '
200 REM * draw ellipses *
210 FOR ASPECT = .25 TO 1.75 STEP .25
220  IF ASPECT<1 THEN KOLOR = 2 ELSE KOLOR = 1
230  CIRCLE(160,100),80,KOLOR,,,ASPECT
240  FOR DELAY = 1 TO 500: NEXT DELAY
250 NEXT ASPECT
```

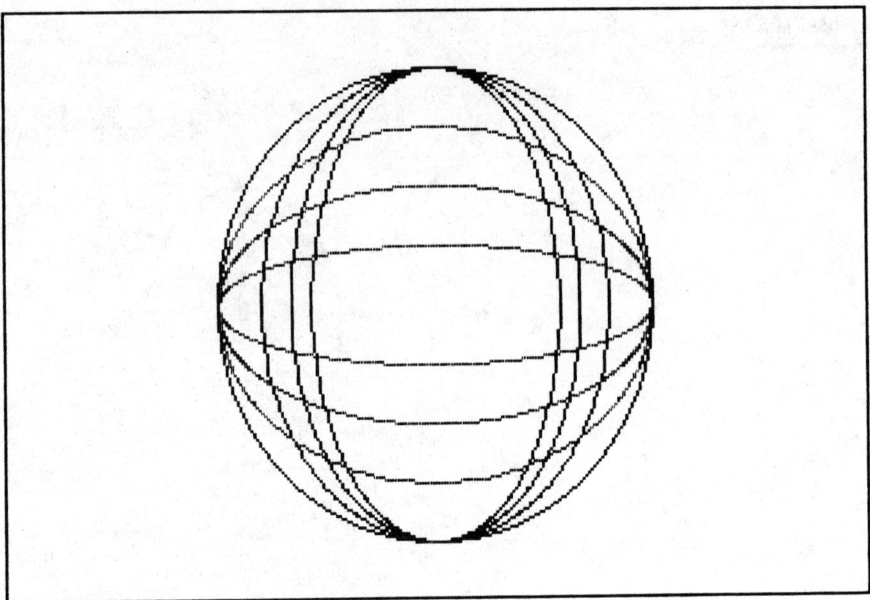

FIG. 4–3. Changing aspect

The program's result is shown in Fig. 4–3.

A time delay separates the drawing of each ellipse. An IF-THEN statement determines the color used.

INTERIOR PAINTING

The interior of a closed figure can be colored by a PAINT statement that provides the point at which the painting is to begin, the paint color, and the boundary color that encloses the area to be painted.

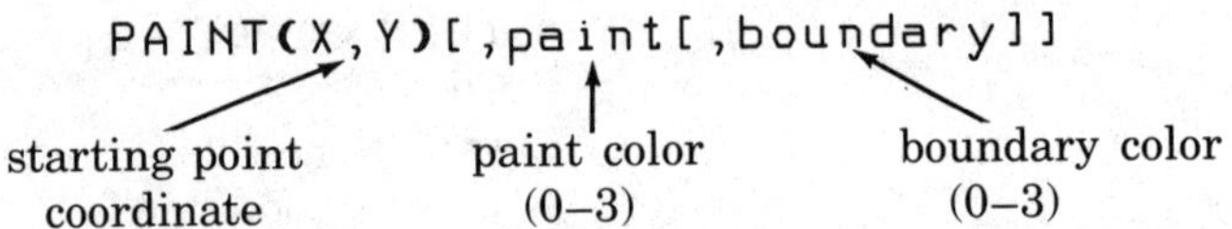

```
PAINT(X,Y)[,paint[,boundary]]
```

starting point   paint color   boundary color
coordinate   (0–3)   (0–3)

The paint and boundary color values are chosen from the palette currently in use. The starting point must be inside the figure to be painted.

EXAMPLE

```
120 COLOR 0,0
210 CIRCLE(160,100),80,1  ←—— produces a green circle on a
                               black background
220 PAINT(170,100),3,1    ←—— paints the inside brown up to a
                               green boundary
```

Suppose that you wish to create two sectors of a circle as shown in Fig. 4–4. The large sector is to be painted brown, and the small sector is to be painted green.

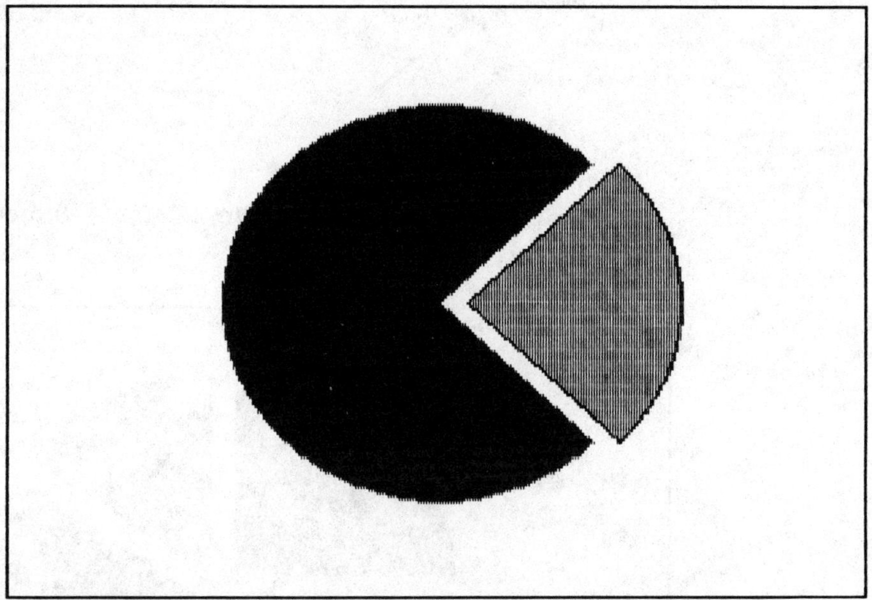

FIG. 4–4. Two colored sections of a circle

Listing 4–4 produces Fig. 4–4 by drawing the large sector with a green boundary. Negative start and end points are used for the arc so that they will be connected to the circle's center. The small sector is drawn in red. The PAINT statement in line 310 paints from the point 155,100 using brown paint from green boundary to green boundary. Line 320 uses point 175,100 to paint green from red boundary to red boundary. Other color combinations within the palette could be used.

LISTING 4–4. Painting Circle Sectors

```
100 REM * set screen and pi *
110 SCREEN 1,0: KEY OFF
120 COLOR 0,0: CLS
130 PI=3.141593
199 '
200 REM * draw sectors *
210 CIRCLE(160,100),80,1,-PI/4,-PI*7/4
220 CIRCLE(170,100),80,2,-PI*7/4,-PI/4
299 '
300 REM * paing sectors *
310 PAINT(155,100),3,1
320 PAINT(175,100),1,2
```

Notice that the starting points of the PAINT statements are inside the boundaries of the appropriate figures.

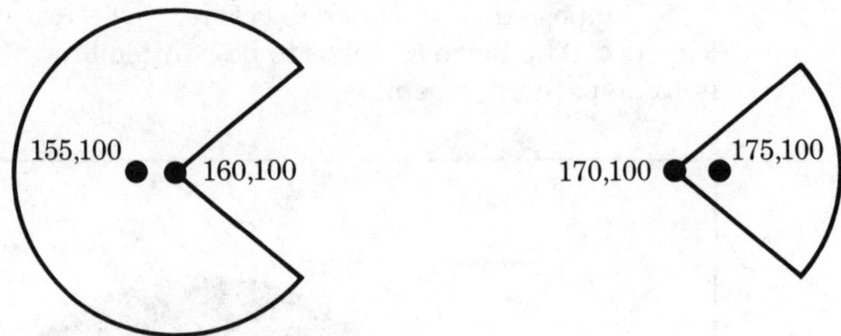

As a final circle demonstration, Listing 4–5 produces the circle graph, or pie chart, of Fig. 4–5.

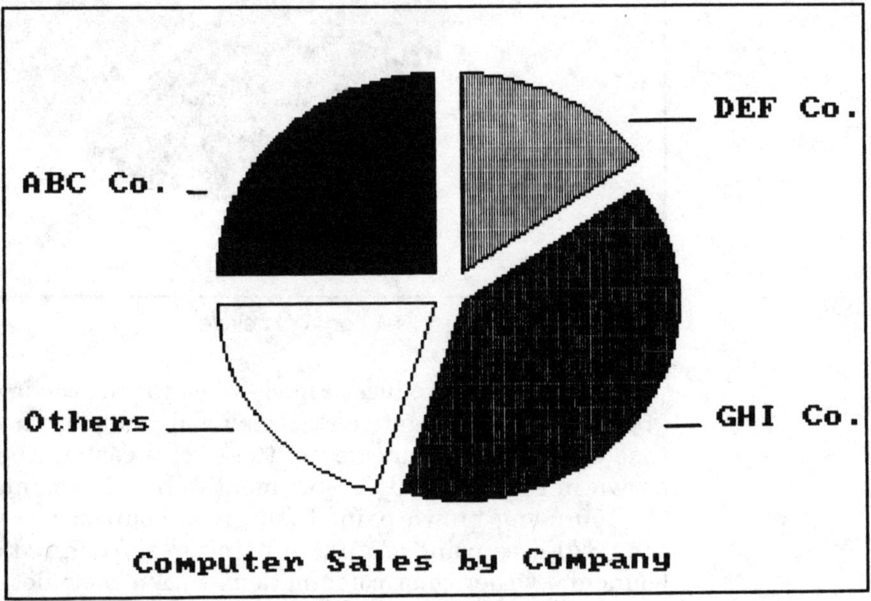

FIG. 4–5. Business pie chart

LISTING 4–5. Computer Sales Pie Chart

```
100 REM * set screen and pi *
110 SCREEN 1,0: KEY OFF
120 COLOR 0,0: CLS
130 PI = 3.141593
199 '
200 REM * draw sectors *
210 CIRCLE(170,90),80,,-PI/5,-PI/2
220 CIRCLE(160,90),80,,-PI/2,-PI
230 CIRCLE(160,100),80,,-PI,-PI*7/5
240 CIRCLE(170,100),80,,-PI*7/5,-PI/5
299 '
300 REM * paint sectors *
310 PAINT(180,80),1,3
320 PAINT(180,100),2,3
330 PAINT(150,80),3,3
```

310 ← green to brown
320 ← red to brown
330 ← brown to brown

```
399 '
400 REM * labels *
410 LOCATE 24,7: PRINT"Computer Sales by Company";
420 LOCATE 8,1: PRINT"ABC Co. __";
430 LOCATE 5,30: PRINT"___ DEF Co.";
440 LOCATE 18,2: PRINT"Others ___";
450 LOCATE 18,31: PRINT"__ GHI Co.";
460 LOCATE 1,1                        ◄——— moves cursor back to top
470 '
```

FROM CIRCLES TO REGULAR POLYGONS

The start and end points of an arc, as discussed previously in this chapter, are specified as angles of a standard circle measured counterclockwise from zero at the right (three o'clock) position.

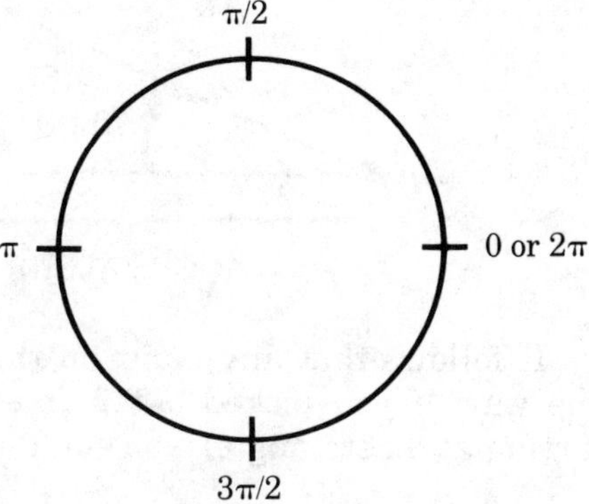

Consider the start and end points (X1,Y1) and (X2,Y2) of an arc.

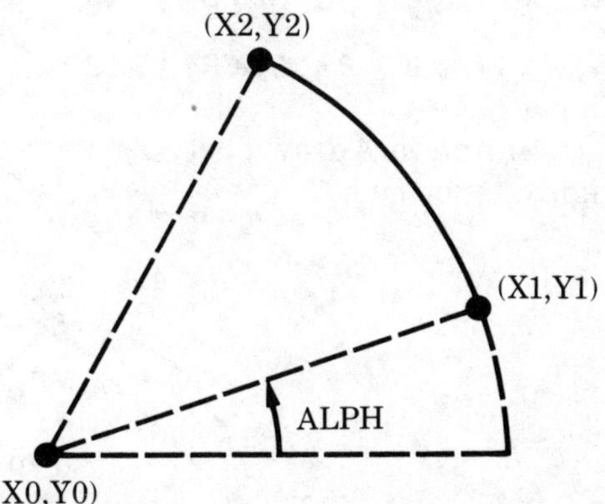

The point (X1,Y1) is at an angle named ALPH. If we look at this point with reference to the zero angle, a right triangle can be formed by dropping a perpendicular line from (X1,Y1).

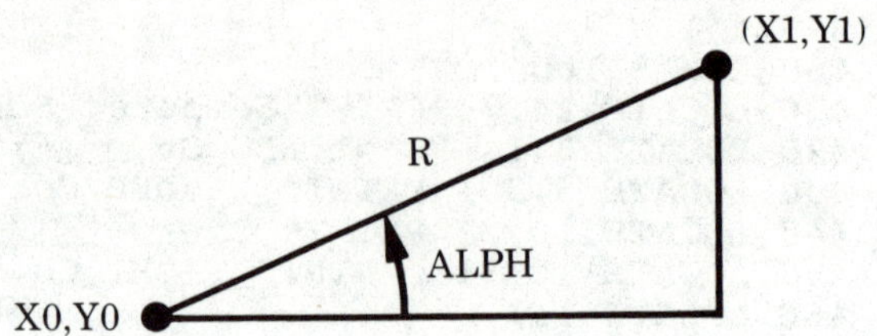

If we know where the center of the circle is, how large the radius is, and the size of ALPH, then the point (X1,Y1) is found to be

$$X1 = X0 + R*COS(ALPH)$$

$$Y1 = Y0 + R*SIN(ALPH)$$

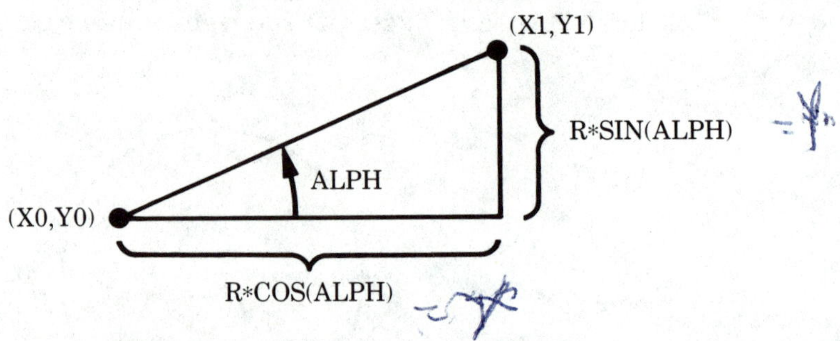

It follows that any point on the circle can be referenced in the same way. If you picked out four equally spaced points on a circle (starting at a zero angle), you could specify the points by

```
X1 = X0 + R*COS(0)          Y1 = Y0 + R*SIN(0)
X2 = X0 + R*COS(PI/2)       Y2 = Y0 + R*SIN(PI/2)
X3 = X0 + R*COS(PI)         Y3 = Y0 + R*SIN(PI)
X4 = X0 + R*COS(PI*3/2)     Y4 = Y0 + R*SIN(PI*3/2)
```

If lines are drawn between successive points, a regular four-sided figure is formed.

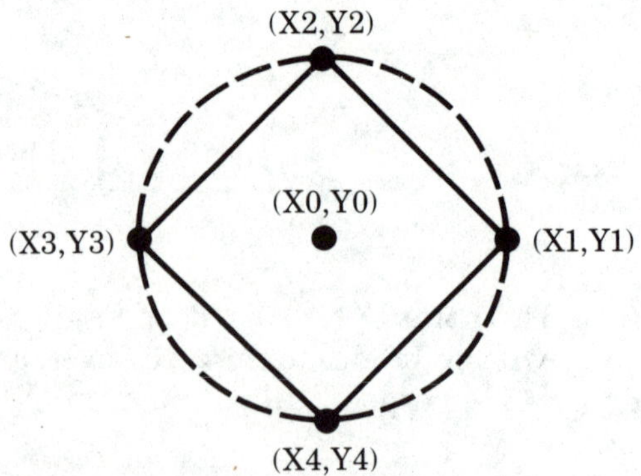

The size of the figure depends on the size of the radius. The location of the figure depends on where the center of the circle is located. A regular polygon with any desired number of sides can be drawn in a similar manner by dividing the number of sides into 2*PI to find the change in angle for each point.

The previous description must be modified when you transfer the mathematical model to the video screen. The standard mathematical notation for positive X-coordinates and Y-coordinates is

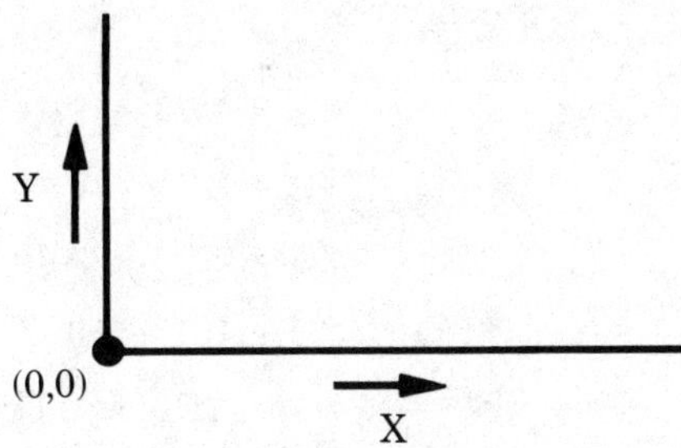

The video screen reverses the direction for positive Y values.

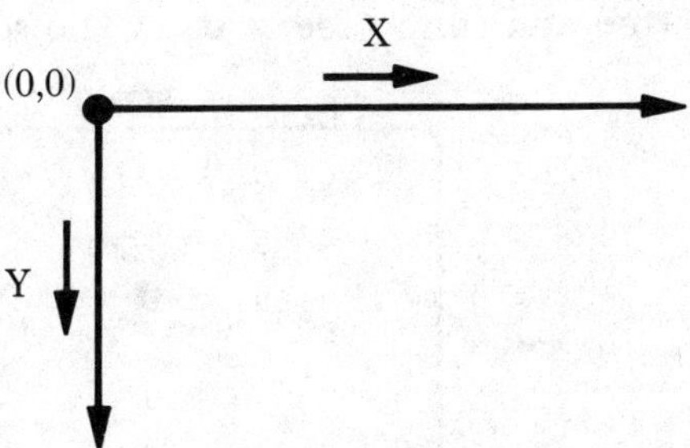

An immediate solution to this difference is to change the sign of R*SIN(ALPH) to

```
Y1 = Y0 - R * SIN(ALPH)
```

Suppose you want to draw a square on the screen. If the first point has been predetermined, the remaining points for a square whose sides are 30 units can be calculated.

```
XNEW = XOLD + R*COS(ALPH)
YNEW = YOLD - R*SIN(ALPH)
X1 = 100
Y1 = 80
R = 30
ALPH = 0, PI/2, PI, PI*3/2
```

The sines and cosines for these angles are

ALPH	SIN	COS
0	0	−1
PI/2	1	0
PI	0	−1
PI*3/2	−1	0

Therefore,

$$X2 = 100 + 30*1 = 130$$

$$Y2 = 80 - 30*0 = 80$$

$$X3 = 130 + 30*0 = 130$$

$$Y3 = 80 - 30*1 = 50$$

$$X4 = 130 + 30*(-1) = 100$$

$$Y4 = 50 - 30*0 = 50$$

The four coordinate pairs that have been calculated can then be plotted and connected to draw the square.

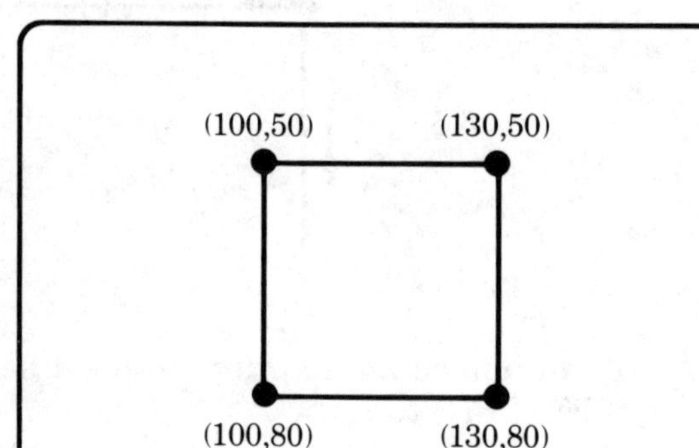

The computer can be used to calculate the points and draw the lines. One method is

```
210 XOLD = 100: YOLD = 80
220 FOR ALPH = 0 TO PI*3/2+.1 STEP PI/2
230 XNEW = XOLD + 30*COS(ALPH)
240 YNEW = YOLD - 30*SIN(ALPH)
250 LINE(XOLD,YOLD)-(XNEW,YNEW)
260 XOLD = XNEW: YOLD = YNEW
270 NEXT ALPH
```

.1 is added to allow for round-off error

make end point the next start point

The program can be modified to draw other regular polygons by changing line 220.

triangle	`220 FOR ALPH = 0 TO PI*4/3+.1 STEP PI*2/3`
pentagon	`220 FOR ALPH = 0 TO PI*8/5+.1 STEP PI*2/5`
hexagon	`220 FOR ALPH = 0 TO PI*5/3+.1 STEP PI/3`

.
.
.

etc.

Listing 4–6 makes use of the computer's ability to accept values of your choice for the polygon's shape and size. It lets you enter the number of sides and their length in lines 130 and 140. INPUT statements can contain a string prompt so that you will know what the computer expects you to enter.

From line 130 the display shows the following:

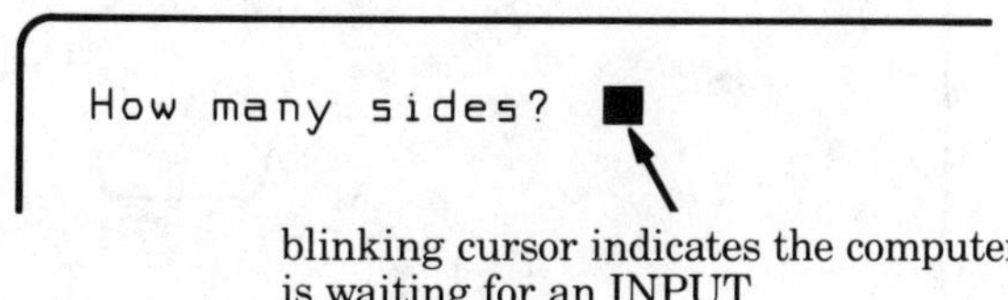

blinking cursor indicates the computer
is waiting for an INPUT

LISTING 4–6. Drawing Regular Polygons

```
100 REM * set text screen and get inputs *
110 SCREEN 0,0: KEY OFF
120 WIDTH 40: CLS
130 LOCATE 1,1: INPUT "How many sides"; NUMBER
140 LOCATE 3,1: INPUT "Length of sides"; SIZE
199 '
200 REM * set graphics screen and PI *
210 SCREEN 1,0
220 COLOR 0,1: CLS
230 PI = 3.141593
299 '
300 REM * draw polygon *
310 XOLD = 140: YOLD = 170
320 INC = PI*2/NUMBER
330 FOR ALPH = 0 TO PI*2-INC+.1 STEP INC
340   XNEW = XOLD+SIZE*COS(ALPH)
350   YNEW = YOLD-SIZE*SIN(ALPH)
360   LINE(XOLD,YOLD)-(XNEW,YNEW),1
370   XOLD = XNEW: YOLD = YNEW
380 NEXT ALPH
```

Some sample runs of Listing 4–6 are shown in Fig. 4–6.

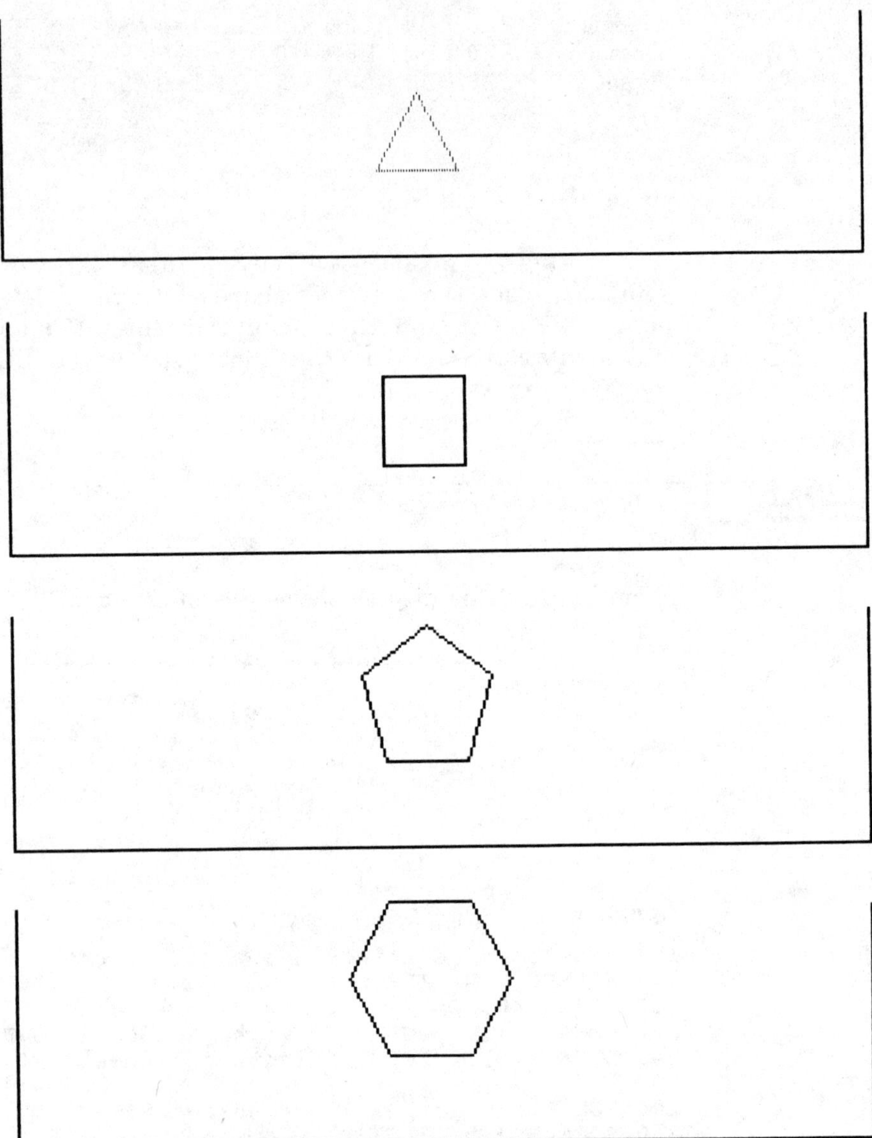

FIG. 4—6. Regular polygons: triangle, rectangle, pentagon, hexagon

The program can be made even more flexible by adding a choice
for the location of the original point (XOLD,YOLD).

```
170 LOCATE 5,1: INPUT "Start at X ="; XOLD
180 LOCATE 7,1: INPUT "Start at Y ="; YOLD
Delete line 310
```

You might also want to provide a choice of the color value or even
PAINT the interior.

Figure 4–7 and Listing 4–7 show how subroutines can be used for drawing and painting the interior of polygons. The program allows you to draw as many polygons as desired. You have the choice of size, color, and paint. You can add to the screen or clear it and start over.

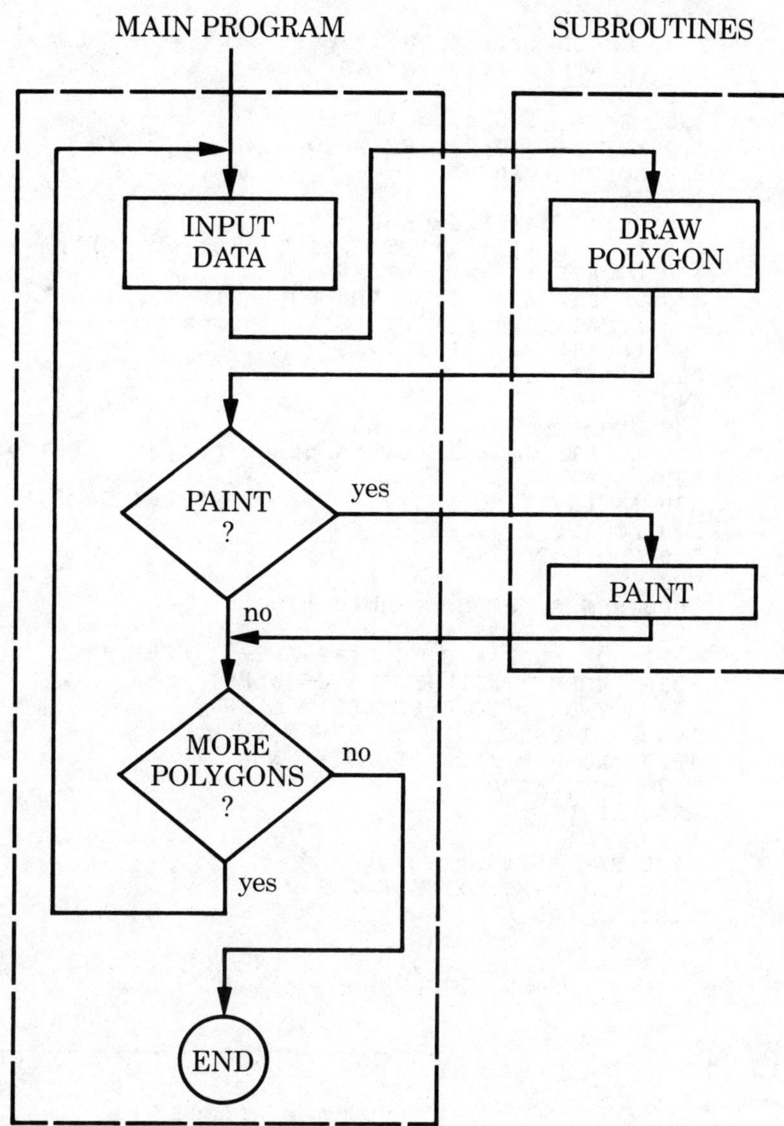

FIG. 4–7. Flowchart for polygons

LISTING 4–7. Polygon Choice

```
100 REM * set screen and variables *
110 SCREEN 1,0: KEY OFF
120 COLOR 0,0: CLS
130 PI = 3.141593
140 A$=SPACE$(35)
199 '
```

```
200 REM * polygon data *
210 LOCATE 1,1: INPUT "How many sides"; NUMBER
220 LOCATE 1,1: PRINT A$
230 LOCATE 1,1: INPUT "Length of sides"; SIZE
240 LOCATE 1,1: PRINT A$
250 LOCATE 1,1: INPUT "Start at X ="; XOLD
260 LOCATE 1,1: PRINT A$
270 LOCATE 1,1: INPUT "Start at Y ="; YOLD
280 LOCATE 1,1: PRINT A$
299 '
300 REM * go draw polygon *
310 XPT = XOLD+2: YPT = YOLD-2
320 GOSUB 1010
399 '
400 REM * paint or not *
410 LOCATE 1,1: INPUT "PAINT (Yes or No)"; P$
420 LOCATE 1,1: PRINT A$
430 IF LEFT$(P$,1) = "N" OR LEFT$(P$,1) = "n" THEN 520
440 LOCATE 1,1: INPUT "Color of paint (0-3)"; KOLOR
450 LOCATE 1,1: PRINT A$
460 GOSUB 1110
499 '
500 REM * more polygons *
510 LOCATE 1,1: INPUT "Another polygon (Yes or NO)"; MORE$
520 LOCATE 1,1: PRINT A$
530 IF LEFT$(MORE$,1) = "N" OR LEFT$(MORE$,1) = "n" THEN END
540 LOCATE 1,1: PRINT A$
550 CLS:GOTO 210
599 '
1000 REM * Polygon Subroutine *
1010 INC = PI*2/NUMBER
1020 FOR ALPH = 0 TO PI*2-INC+.1 STEP INC
1030   XNEW = XOLD+SIZE*COS(ALPH)
1040   YNEW = YOLD-SIZE*SIN(ALPH)
1050   LINE(XOLD,YOLD)-(XNEW,YNEW)
1060   XOLD = XNEW: YOLD = YNEW
1070 NEXT ALPH
1080 RETURN
1099 '
1100 REM * Paint Polygon *
1110 PAINT(XPT,YPT),KOLOR,3
1120 RETURN
```

The program requests, in order:

1   How many sides?

2   Length of sides?

3 | Start at X = ?

4 | Start at Y = ?

Then the subroutine is called to draw the polygon. On returning from the subroutine, the paint request is displayed.

5 | PAINT (Yes or No) ?

If the answer is yes, the program then requests:

6 | Color of paint (0–3) ?

When the color code is entered, the program goes to the paint subroutine to color the polygon. It then returns to request number 7.

If the answer to the paint request is no, the program skips the sixth request and asks:

7 | Another polygon (Yes or No) ?

A No answer stops the program. A Yes answer returns to request number 1. Your response is detected in line 530.

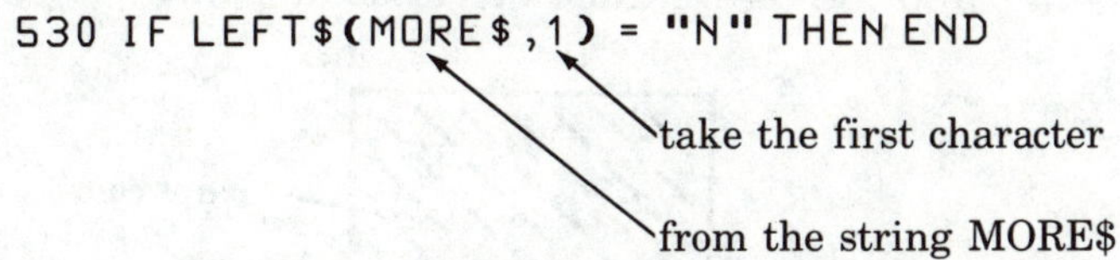

The LEFT\$ function looks at the leftmost character of your response. If it is an *N* (for no), then the program ends. A response not beginning with an *N* allows the computer to go on to line 540.

SUMMARY

This chapter described the use of the CIRCLE statement and the use of trigonometric functions to draw regular polygons. The PAINT statement, which provides a means of coloring the interior of closed figures, was introduced. The uses of these two new graphics statements were demonstrated through several examples and programs.

- CIRCLE (X,Y),R[,color[,start,end[,aspect]]] allows you to place the center of a circle of radius r at the specified X,Y coordinates. The color may be controlled by the COLOR option allowing for one of four colors of the specified palette. Arcs may be drawn, instead of complete circles, by specifying angles for start and end. The circle may be squeezed along the X-axis or the Y-axis to form an ellipse using the aspect ratio.

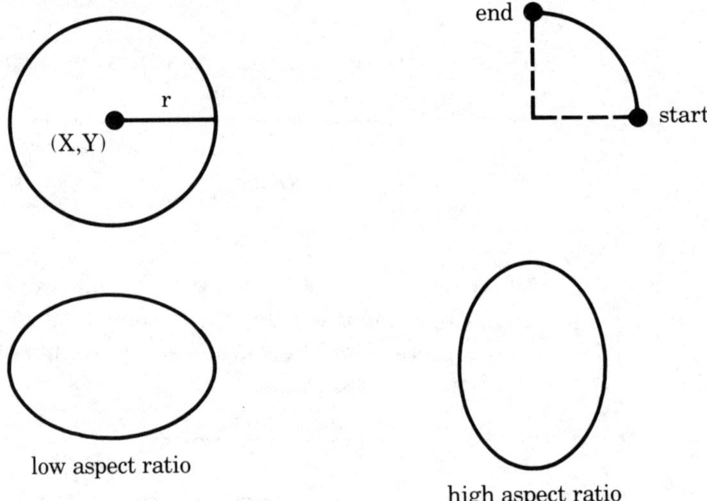

- PAINT (X,Y)[,paint[,boundary]] allows you to color the interior of a closed figure. The painting begins at the specified X,Y point in the specified paint color until the boundary color is reached. The starting point, of course, must be inside the figure, and the figure must be closed or paint will "leak" out.

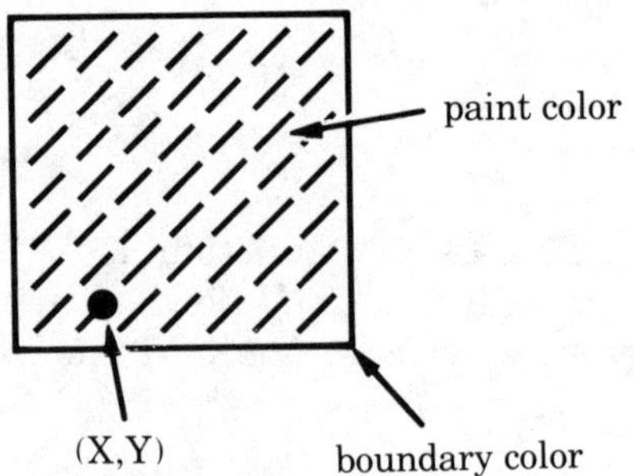

Sine and cosine functions were used to describe a point referenced from the center of an imaginary circle. This technique was used in demonstration programs to draw regular polygons.

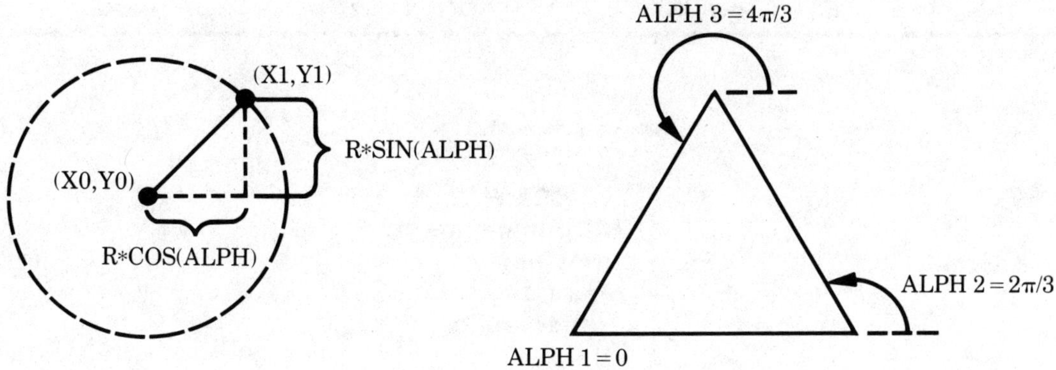

5
GRAPHICS DEFINITION LANGUAGE

Graphics Statements, Functions,
and Terms Introduced

DRAW
GDL commands
string
turn angle
aspect ratio

We have shown you how to draw figures with points, lines, and circles. We have also shown you how to "paint" these figures in different ways. To do these things, it was necessary to use many separate statements (such as LINE, PSET, PRESET, and CIRCLE) to create parts of the overall picture. You have also seen that trigonometric calculations are sometimes necessary if you want to draw a figure using an unusual orientation.

Your objective in this chapter is to learn how to use the wide variety of options provided by the DRAW statement. It is the most versatile of all the graphics statements.

BASIC statements and terms that are explained in this chapter are DRAW, GDL commands, string, turn angle, and aspect ratio.

The DRAW statement interprets a text string as a series of commands in a "graphics definition language." When combined, these commands provide a powerful, yet simple method of creating figures with many advantages over normal BASICA statements. In addition, there are many new operations that you can easily perform on a figure, such as scaling and rotation, which would take many lines of code if performed with the usual BASICA statements.

We will consider the GDL (graphics definition language) commands one at a time, giving an example of each as used in a program. Some of the commands are available only in the newer versions of

BASICA. Unless otherwise stated, the commands described will work in all versions of the language.

We will begin with how to set up and use the DRAW statement, which takes the form

```
DRAW string
```

where "string" is either a series of characters enclosed in quotation marks or the name of a BASICA string variable.

```
DRAW "U90 D90"
```

or

```
A$ = "U90 D90"
DRAW A$;
```

Using a variable allows you to change the figure being drawn simply by changing the variable's contents. As you will see later, GDL commands themselves can have variables as arguments so that it is not even necessary to change the contents of the DRAW string when you want to change drawing parameters.

The DRAW string consists of combinations of the GDL commands (M, B, N, A, C, S, X, P, TA, U, D, L, R, E, F, G, H), special characters (=, +, −, ;, space), numbers, and variable names. The string can contain as many GDL commands and characters as will fit within BASICA's maximum string length.

SPECIAL CHARACTERS

At this point, some generalizations about special characters are in order:

- Spaces are optional and can be used within the command string to make it more readable. The only thing that a space cannot be used for is to separate the digits of a single numeric value or the letters of a single variable name.

- Semicolons are optional for some commands and not for others. The semicolon is used to separate commands from each other in the DRAW string. The commands that *must* be separated by semicolons are indicated in their descriptions. All commands *may* be separated by semicolons for readability if you desire. If a command does not require a semicolon, it is not necessary to use any character at all to separate it from the next command.

- The plus and minus signs are used only with the relative movement commands. They will be described in that section.
- The equal sign is used to assign a variable to a GDL command. Its use will be described later.

RELATIVE DRAWING COMMANDS

The most basic commands of the GDL are used for relative line drawing. There are eight of these: U, D, L, R, E, F, G, and H. Each corresponds to a different direction: up, down, left, right, and four diagonals.

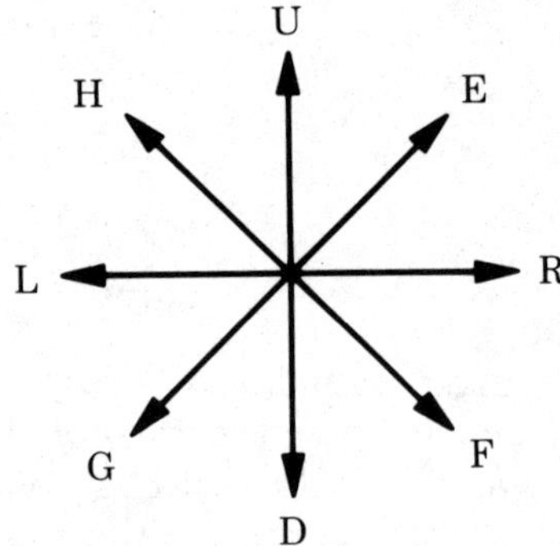

The form the command takes is as follows:

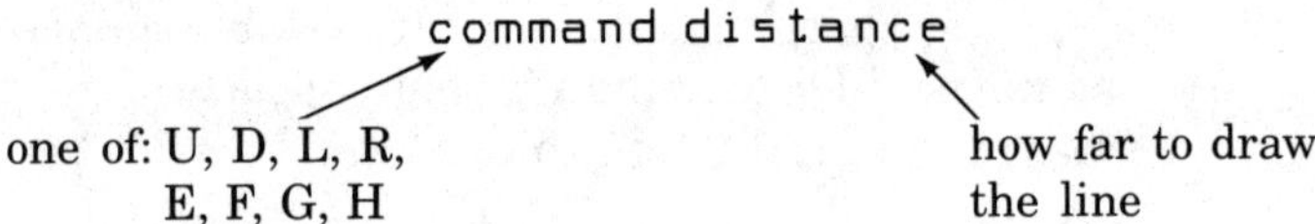

The line is drawn from the last referenced screen position in the current color (set by a previous COLOR statement). The end point of the new line then becomes the "last referenced point." We will find out later how to change the drawing color using another GDL command, C.

The distance parameter can take one of two forms. It can be just a number that specifies how long the line to be drawn should be.

EXAMPLE

U20 ←——— draws a line 20 positions long in the up direction

Alternatively, it can be an equal sign followed by a variable name followed by a semicolon.

$$R = dist ;$$

number of units to move to the right

You *must* use the semicolon to tell the interpreter where the variable name stops and the next GDL command in the string begins.

To show how this feature might be used, consider the following example, which will draw five diamonds on the screen at the current position. The DRAW statement is placed in a loop that updates the distance parameter. This makes it easy to create diamonds of different sizes.


```
300 FOR DIST = 1 TO 10 STEP 2
310 DRAW "E = DIST; F = DIST; G = DIST; H = DIST;"
320 NEXT DIST
```

Note the use of the last semicolon in the DRAW string. Even though there are no more commands in the string, it is still required.

In our example, all the diamonds were drawn on top of each other because we always ended up back at the starting point after each diamond was drawn.

Listing 5–1 illustrates the use of all our relative DRAW commands in both constant and variable forms. PSET is used to set a new "last referenced point" for the DRAW commands so that each figure is located at a different position on the screen. The output of the program is shown in Fig. 5–1.

LISTING 5–1. Variable Figures

```
100 REM * set screen *
110 SCREEN 1,0: KEY OFF
120 COLOR 0,0: CLS
199 '
200 REM * draw figures *
210 PSET(160,100)
220 DRAW "U20 R30 D20 L30"        'draw a box
230 PSET(220,15): SIZE = 5
240 GOSUB 310                      'draw small diamond (size 5)
250 PSET(50,160): SIZE = 20
260 GOSUB 310                      'draw big diamond (size 20)
270 GOTO 270                       'loop
299 '
300 REM * subroutine to draw diamond with sides SIZE long *
310 DRAW "E = SIZE; H = SIZE;"
320 DRAW "G = SIZE; F = SIZE;"
330 RETURN
```

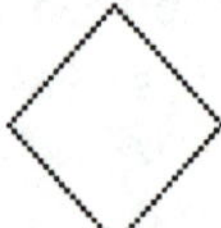

FIG. 5—1. Variable figures

PREFIX COMMANDS

In addition to the relative drawing commands we have already described, there are two useful "prefix" commands, which can be inserted in front of the relative commands to modify their operation. These are B (blank move) and N (nulled move).

The B command changes the "last referenced point" on the screen to a new position. Using this command, it is easy to place many different objects on the screen: simply draw an object, do a blank move to the position where you want to place the next object, draw the object, and so on. The B command can be used with all the relative draw commands (U, D, L, R, E, F, G, H) and with the M movement command, which will be described later. For example, the DRAW string "U10 BL20 D10" will draw up 10 positions, then move 20 positions to the left without drawing anything, then draw down 10 positions. The result on the screen will be 2 horizontal lines.

Notice that only the command to move left was blanked; the B prefix affects only the next command, not the rest of the commands in the string.

The N (nulled move) prefix command executes the next command in the DRAW string and then returns to where it was just before the command with the N prefix was executed. Our example shows how this feature is used to draw several lines, all originating from the same point, to form the letter *T*.

The figure is created with a single DRAW string: "NL20 NR20 ND30". This string tells BASICA to start at the "last referenced point," draw left for 20 positions, return to the previous point, draw right for 20 positions, return to the previous point, draw down 30 positions, and again return to the previous point. Any further DRAW commands would continue from this point. The result of the DRAW string is shown here:

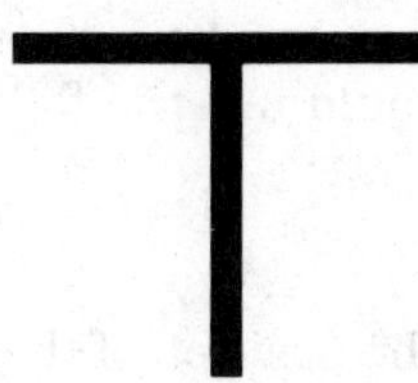

Notice again that the N command applies only to the single command following it in the DRAW string, and not to the entire portion of the string that follows it. Also, it does not matter whether a number or a variable name is used with the prefixed relative DRAW command. We could just as easily have performed the same operation as above by assigning the value 20 to a variable called LONG and executing the DRAW string: "NL=LONG; NR=LONG; ND30".

MOVEMENT COMMAND

The GDL has one basic movement command, M. This command draws a line from the "last referenced point" to a point specified in the M command. The coordinates given for the new point can be either absolute or relative to the previous position. The form of the command is

```
M [{+,-}] x-value, [{+,-}] y-value
```

The brackets indicate that the presence of a sign is optional, and the braces indicate the choices for the sign. If a sign is present immediately after the M, BASICA interprets the X and Y values given to be relative to the "last referenced point." If no sign is present, the coordinates are interpreted as being absolute.

For the following examples, assume that the current point is (160,100). The DRAW string "M 1,1" would draw a line from (160,100) to (1,1). The absence of a sign following the M indicates that the line is to be drawn to absolute position (1,1). The string "M 1,-1" would have the same effect because there is no sign *immediately following* the M. Even though there is a sign attached to the Y value, it is ignored; the instruction is interpreted as a draw to absolute position (1,1). Whenever there *is* a sign immediately following the M, the X value is given that sign and the Y value is assumed to be positive unless there is a negative sign preceding it. "M +1,1" would draw to (161,101), "M +1,-1" would draw to (161,99), "M -1,1" would draw to (159,101), and "M -1,-1" would draw to (159,99).

It is possible to assign the X and Y values to variables as well. The method is the same for all cases where variables are used: replace what would have been a numeric value with an equal sign followed by the variable name followed by a semicolon. The M command looks a little peculiar when this is done, but it works. For example, to do an absolute move to the point whose X-coordinate is in X and whose Y-coordinate is in Y, you would use the following string:

```
M = X ; , = Y ;
```

Note the position of the comma, which is still required to separate the X and Y values. A relative move would also include a sign immediately after the M.

```
M + = X ; , = Y ;
```

It is also possible to place a sign in front of the Y value. Note that any signs introduced into the actual DRAW string take into consideration the sign of the numeric value already stored in the corresponding variable. For example, suppose the current position is (160,100), X contains the value -4, Y contains the value -3, and the string "M + = X; , − = Y;" is executed. The result is a draw to absolute position (156,103), because 160 + (−4) = 156 and 100 − (−3) = 103.

This movement command is similar to the BASICA LINE statement. However, the M command is usually used in conjunction with the B command to do blank moves. Using B and M together is like doing a PSET in the background color. It provides an easy way to get from one point to another on the screen without drawing anything. Earlier we showed how to do this using B with the relative draw commands. The program in Listing 5–2 draws two boxes on the screen, positioning them using blank moves rather than PSETs. The boxes are shown in Fig. 5–2.

LISTING 5–2. Boxes with B and M

```
100 REM * set screen *
110 SCREEN 1,0: KEY OFF
120 COLOR 0,0: CLS
199 '
200 REM * draw boxes *
210 DRAW "BM 10,10"              'set initial position
220 DRAW "R10 D10 L10 U10"       'draw a box
230 DRAW "BM 160,100"            'change position
240 DRAW "R20 D20 L20 U20"       'draw another box
250 GOTO 250                     'loop
```

FIG. 5–2. Boxes with B and M

A FINAL MOVEMENT EXAMPLE

So far we have covered the basic GDL commands that let us move around the screen and draw figures. The program shown in Listing 5–3 is an example of all these commands. The program draws and labels a diagram of the eight possible movement directions. A blank move command is used to position the diagram at the center of the screen, followed by a series of relative draw commands, each preceded by an N (null move) command. These draw lines that extend in all eight directions from the center of the screen. Each direction on the diagram is then labeled using BASICA's LOCATE and PRINT statements. The result of the program is shown in Fig. 5–3.

LISTING 5–3. Movement Diagram

```
100 REM * set screen *
110 SCREEN 1,0: KEY OFF
120 COLOR 0,0: CLS
199 '
200 REM * draw the 8 movement directions *
210 DRAW "BM 160,100"                 'move to center of the screen
220 DRAW "NU30 ND30 NL30 NR30"        'draw up, down, left, and right
230 DRAW "NE30 NF30 NG30 NH30"        'draw the diagonals
240 FOR X = 1 TO 8                    'label each direction
250   READ R,C,A$
260   LOCATE R,C: PRINT A$;
270 NEXT X
280 GOTO 280                          'loop
299 '
300 REM * data for letter location *
310 DATA 8,21,U,18,21,D
320 DATA 13,15,L,13,26,R
330 DATA 8,26,E,18,26,F
340 DATA 18,15,G,8,15,H
```

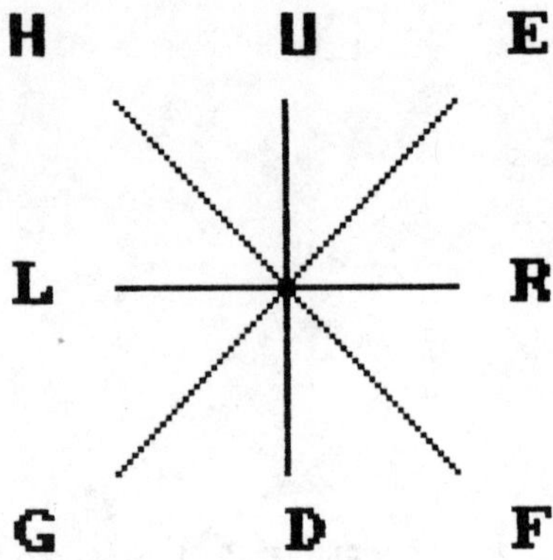

FIG. 5–3. Movement diagram

COLOR (C) COMMAND

The C command allows you to change the drawing color. If you are using the medium-resolution graphics mode, there are four colors available from which to choose: 0 (the background color), 1, 2, and 3 (the foreground color). As with other BASICA drawing statements, the actual colors depend on whether you have selected palette 0 or 1 in the COLOR statement. If you are using the high-resolution graphics mode, the colors may either be 0 (black) or 1 (white). The form of the color command is shown here:

```
C color-number
```

where color-number is either one of the numbers above or an equal sign followed by the name of a numeric variable containing the color number followed by a semicolon.

In our earlier examples, we did not specify a drawing color using the C command. Instead, as with other BASICA drawing statements, the draw color was set automatically to the current foreground color. Let's now make the following changes to our program in Listing 5–3. We will add two color commands to the DRAW statement in line 220.

```
220 DRAW "C1 NU30 ND30 C2 NL30 NR30"
```

We will also add a color command to the DRAW statement in line 230.

```
230 DRAW "C3 NE30 NF30 NG30 NH30"
```

The result will be that the up/down lines of our diagram will be drawn in color 1 (green in our case), the left/right lines will be drawn in color 2 (red), and the diagonal lines will be drawn in color 3 (brown). Notice that it would not be effective to place another color command at the end of the string in line 230, in hopes of changing the color that the text is printed in. When working in a graphics mode, any text displayed using BASICA's PRINT statement is always shown in the palette's foreground color, no matter which drawing color is selected.

PAINT (P) COMMAND

Note: The P command is available only in BASICA Version 2.0 or higher.

The P command allows you to paint the interior of a figure that you have drawn, just like BASICA's PAINT statement. The command takes the form

```
P paint-color , boundary-color
```

As with the M command, each color parameter may be either a number or an equal sign followed by the name of a numeric variable followed by a semicolon. If both colors are specified with variables, the DRAW string might look like this:

```
DRAW "P = PC; , = BC;"
```

The P command fills the figure with the paint color, up to the edges that were drawn with the boundary color. Since the paint command does not allow you to specify a location to start painting from, you must do a blank move beforehand to position the "cursor" for painting. Also, when a paint command is executed, the paint color becomes the drawing color for the next DRAW command. Therefore, if you want to keep the original drawing color, you must use a C (color) command to return to the original drawing color after each P (paint).

The program in Listing 5–4 demonstrates the operation of the paint command. First, lines 210 and 220 draw a box in the foreground color (brown). Then we move to a point within the box in line 230, and paint the box in color 2 (red) in line 240. In line 250, we draw another box on the screen. This box is drawn in red (color 2) since that was the

LISTING 5–4. Painting Boxes

```
100 REM * set screen *
110 SCREEN 1,0: KEY OFF
120 COLOR 0,0: CLS
199 '
200 REM * painting figures *
210 DRAW "BM 160,100"                    'set initial position
220 DRAW "R10 D10 L10 U10"               'draw box in foreground color
230 DRAW "BM 165,105"                    'move inside the box
240 DRAW "P2,3"                          'paint interior in color 2
250 DRAW "BM 200,150 R20 D20 L20 U20"    'draw a box in color 2
260 DRAW "BM 210,160"                    'move inside the box
270 DRAW "P1,2"                          'paint this box in color 1
280 DRAW "C3"                            'change back to color 3
290 DRAW "BM 10,10 R30 D10 L30 U10"      'draw another box
300 GOTO 300                             'loop
```

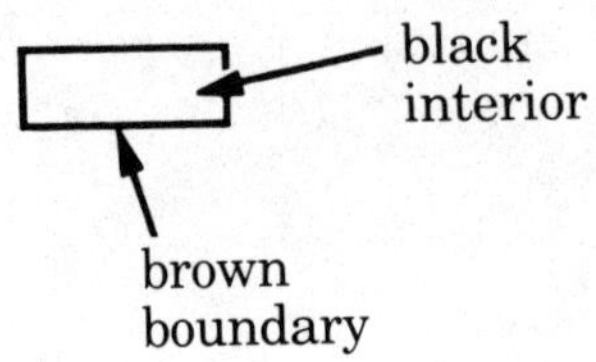

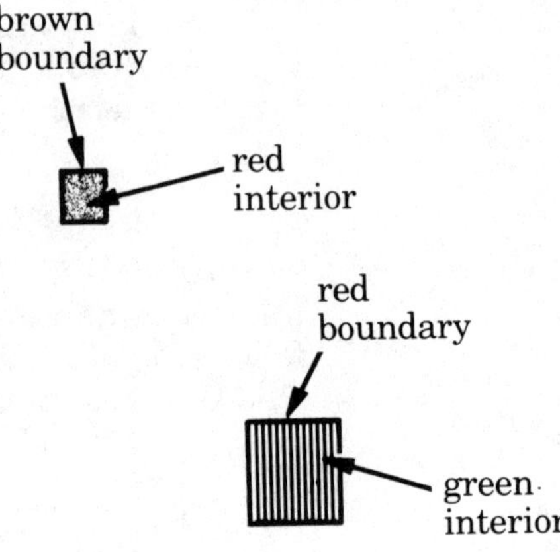

FIG. 5–4. Painting boxes

most recent paint color. Once again, in line 260, we move to a point within the box, and paint the interior green (color 1) in line 270. Now we are going to draw another box, but we want it to be brown (color 3), not the most recent paint color, green. We do this by using the C command in line 280 to change the draw color back to brown. Finally, line 290 draws the box. Figure 5–4 shows the result of running the program.

When using the paint command, it is very important that you set up the position you wish to begin painting from. For example, in the program of Listing 5–4, line 260 positions the cursor within a box known to have a closed, red boundary. The paint command that follows it paints in green from the current cursor position outward until it runs into red boundaries. If we were to change line 260 to read

```
260 DRAW "BM 10,10"
```

we would be positioning the cursor at a point on the screen that is outside the box with the red boundary. The result of running the program would be to draw and paint the first box (brown), draw the second box (red), paint the *entire* screen green, except for the interior of the first box (since it was painted in red) and the exterior and interior of the second box (since the closed exterior is red, the paint is kept outside the box's interior), and then draw the last box in brown as before. This result is shown in Fig. 5–5.

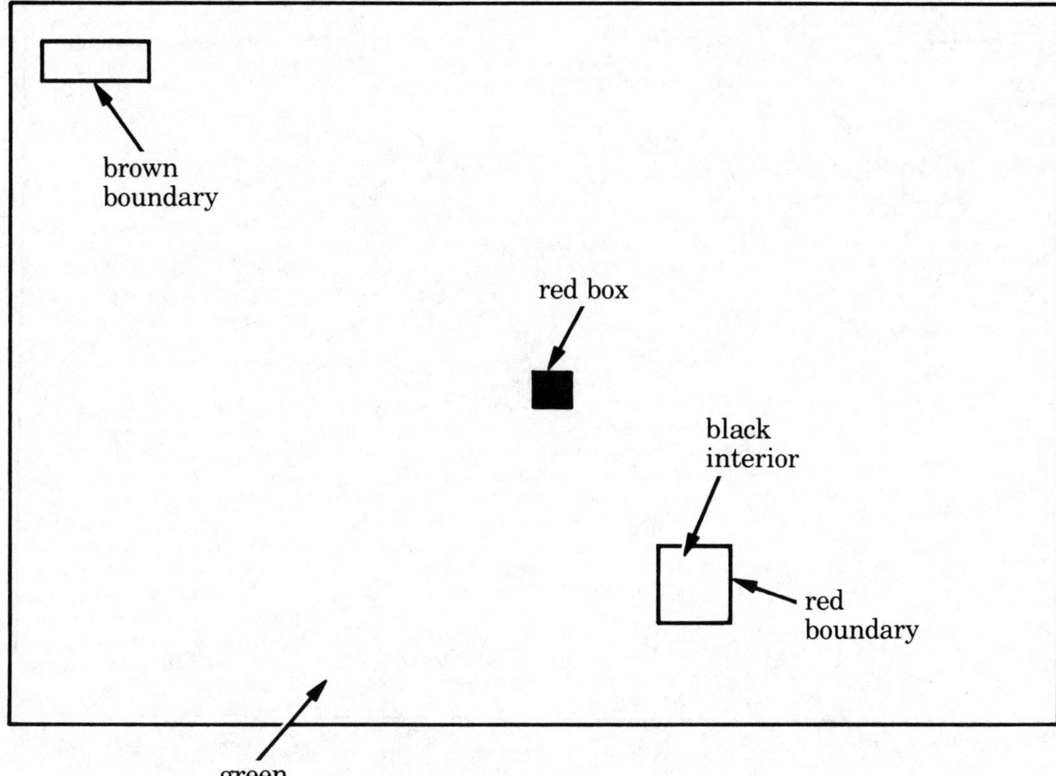

FIG. 5–5. Painting outside the boxes

As another example, suppose we leave line 260 as it was originally, but change the paint command in line 270 so that it paints to a boundary color of brown (3) instead of red (2).

```
270 DRAW "P1,3"
```

Now the program draws and paints the first box, draws the second box, moves to the middle of the second box and paints in green until it finds a brown edge. Since the second box has a border of red, it gets painted right over as the program covers the whole screen with green except for the first box (since it did have a border of brown). After the screen has been covered, the third box is then drawn. The result is shown in Fig. 5–6.

SCALE (S) COMMAND

The S command is used to reduce or enlarge a figure created by relative drawing and movement commands. The scale command takes the following form:

```
S scale-factor
```

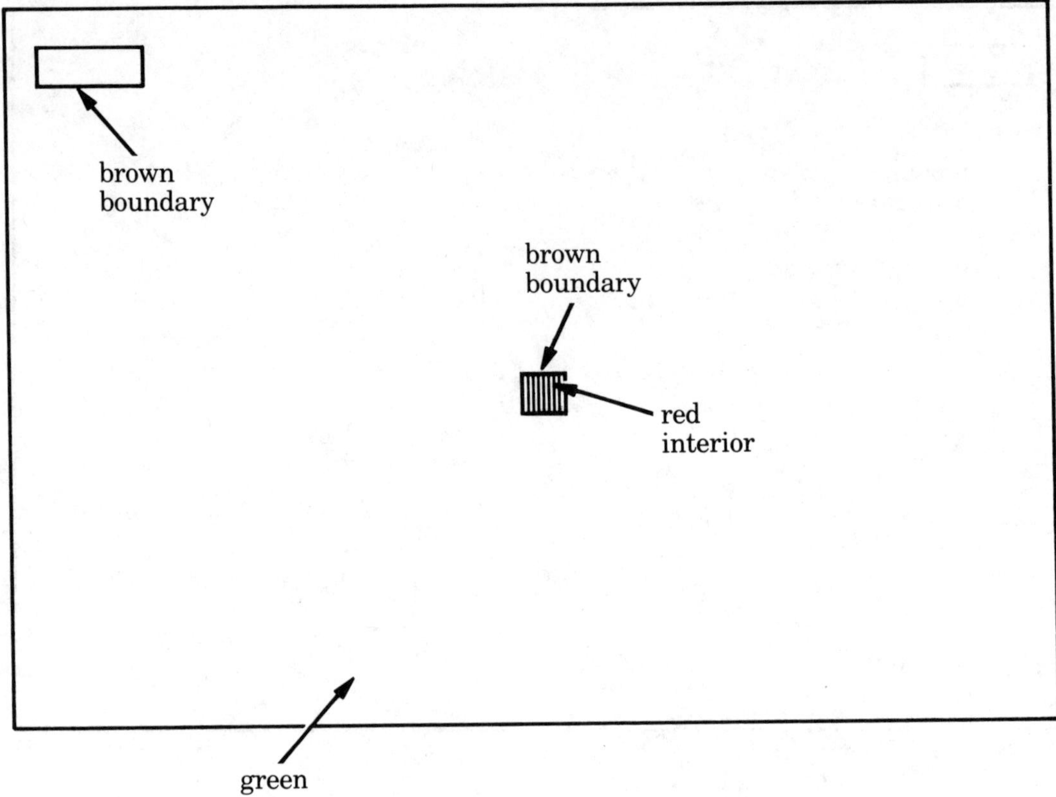

FIG. 5—6. Painting to brown boundaries

where scale-factor is either a number or an equal sign followed by a numeric variable name followed by a semicolon. The scale-factor value must be an integer in the range of 1 through 255.

The scale factor controls the resulting size of the figure: the larger the factor, the larger the figure. The scale factor atuomatically affects every relative draw or movement command executed thereafter, until the scale factor is changed with another S command. The value given for the scale factor is divided by 4 and stored away. Each time that you execute one of the relative commands (U, D, L, R, E, F, G, H, or M with relative coordinates), the distance that you gave in that relative command is multiplied by the scale factor (which has been divided by 4). The resulting distance is then moved or drawn, instead of the original distance given in the relative command.

For example, suppose that the DRAW string "S1 U8 R4 D16 L12" is executed. This has the same effect as the DRAW string "U2 R1 D4 L3" without the S command. The scale command becomes very useful when used with a variable to change the scaling factor.

BASICA automatically sets the scale factor to 4 when a program is run. This means that none of the relative draw or movement commands experience any scaling effect (since the scale factor of 4 is divided by 4, producing a value of 1) until the first S command is executed.

Scaling factors are not cumulative: the DRAW string "S4 S8" has the same effect as the string "S8". The scale factor of 4 is simply overwritten by the new factor of 8. Another important thing to consider when using the scale command is that you have a limited number of scaling factors. Since the scale factor can only be an integer from 1 through 255, which then gets divided by 4, the actual scaling values that we have to work with are 1/4 (0.25) through 255/4 (63.75). This means that there are many large values available to scale your figure to a bigger size, but few smaller values for reducing. Therefore, you should try to draw your original figure as small as possible before scaling it.

For example, suppose that you want to put a box on the screen that is 16 positions long and 16 positions tall. You then want to be able to both enlarge and reduce this box considerably. If you had a "normal" scaling factor of 4 (preset by BASICA), you could create the box with the string

```
DRAW "U16 R16 D16 L16"
```

This allows many possibilities for enlargement, since you can still scale it from 5 to 255 with the addition of an S command to the DRAW string. However, there are only three (1, 2, and 3) values available for reduction. You would only be able to reduce the figure to 1/4 of its original size. This may be fine, but suppose you wanted to reduce the figure further. A better way to do this would be to draw the box very small in the first place, making it perhaps only 2 positions long and 2 positions high. Even though the DRAW string commands only deal with something 2 positions long, you can still make the box *appear* to be 16 positions long *on the screen* by choosing a "normal" scaling factor of 32 instead of 4:

```
DRAW "S32 U2 R2 D2 L2"
```

There are still many factors available for enlargement (33 through 255), but now there are also many more available to reduce the same figure (1 through 31).

The scale command is most useful when a variable is used to control the scaling factor. A program loop can be set up to draw the same figure in different places on the screen using different scaling values to increase and decrease the size. Another application might be a graphics editor where a user designs a figure and then inputs scaling values to increase or decrease the size of the object he or she has created on the screen.

The program of Listing 5–5 demonstrates the first application: looping and placing objects of different sizes on the screen. The program draws 2 rows of boxes on the screen. The bottom row is generated by lines 200 through 240. Each box is drawn with a different scale factor, ranging from 1 through 56. Since the FOR loop has a step value of 8, the actual factors generated are 1, 9, 17, 25, 33, 41, and 49. The DRAW string makes the box with relative draws of length 4, followed by a blank right move of length 8. As the scale factor increases, the boxes and the space in between them get bigger. If we had let the FOR loop run from 1 through 255, we would not be able to see any more than 7 boxes that result from our program because they would all be generated at coordinates that are off the screen.

Lines 300 through 340 of our program generate another row of boxes, this time changing the scale factor from 64 through 120. This produces 8 boxes (factors of 64, 72, 80, 88, 96, 104, 112, and 120). These boxes do not increase in size as quickly as the previous ones because we have used relative draw commands with length 2 rather than 4. Also, because the blank right move at the end of the string is now only of length 1 rather than 8, the boxes overlap each other as they are drawn on the screen. Figure 5–7 shows the result.

LISTING 5–5. Scaling Boxes

```
100 REM * set screen *
110 SCREEN 1,0: KEY OFF
120 COLOR 0,0: CLS
199 '
200 REM * do first row of boxes *
210 DRAW "BM 0,199"              'position for first row
220 FOR X = 1 TO 56 STEP 8       'X controls scale factor
230   DRAW "S=X; U4 R4 D4 L4 BR8" 'make a box and move right
240 NEXT X
299 '
300 REM * do second row of boxes *
310 DRAW "BM 0,100"
320 FOR X = 64 TO 120 STEP 8
330   DRAW "S=X; U2 R2 D2 L2 BR1"  'make a smaller box and move right
340 NEXT X
350 GOTO 350                      'loop
```

FIG. 5–7. Scaling boxes

Note: The TA command is available only in BASICA Version 2.0 or higher.

As we mentioned earlier, there are only 8 basic drawing directions: up, down, left, right, and the 4 diagonals. Suppose that you want to draw a line on the screen that goes in some other direction. This is very easy to do if you are using BASICA's LINE statement. All you have to do is specify the start and end points and it draws a line for you. You can do the same thing using the M command of the DRAW statement.

However, suppose that you knew the direction in which you wanted to move in terms of the number of degrees from the origin. To use LINE or M, you would have to calculate the end point of the line based on the number of degrees and the desired length. The A (ANGLE) and TA (TURN ANGLE) commands of the graphics definition language take care of this for you. These commands rotate the eight-direction drawing axis to a particular orientation, based on the value that you give them. This provides a very convenient way to rotate figures on the screen in much the same way that you scaled them earlier.

The A command, available in all versions of BASICA, allows you to rotate the axis to 1 of 4 orientations, each 90 degrees apart. The TA command, which is available in BASICA Version 2.0 and higher, allows you to rotate the axis to any 1 of 360 orientations, each 1 degree apart.

Consider the 8 possible movement directions as being relative to an axis where "up" is toward the top of the screen:

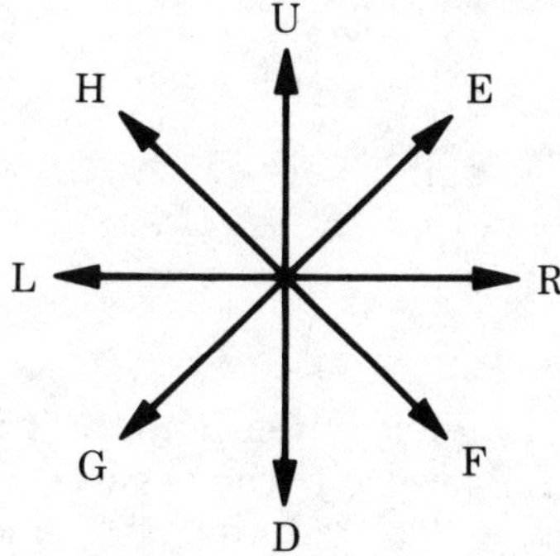

The function of the A and TA commands is to rotate this axis relative to the top-of-screen direction.

The A (Angle) Command

With the A command, the axis can be rotated 0, 90, 180, or 270 degrees from "up." When the axis is changed, the directions represented by the relative commands U, D, L, R, E, F, G, and H change as well. Rotation by 0 degrees has no effect—"up" remains "up." This is the initial angle set up by BASICA so that none of the normal movement commands are rotated. The 4 axis rotations and the resulting direction orientations are shown here:

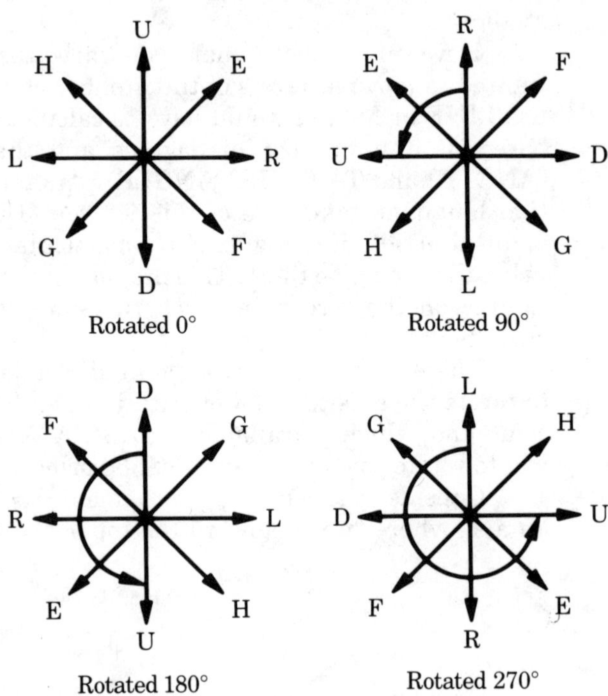

Thus, it is very easy to flip your figures upside-down or right-left. The form that the A command takes is as follows:

```
A angle
```

where angle is either a numeric integer value 0 through 3, or an equal sign followed by the name of a numeric variable followed by a semicolon. The values 0, 1, 2, and 3 represent angles of 0, 90, 180, and 270 degrees, respectively. Like the scale command described earlier, the angle set with the A command stays in effect until another A (or TA) command is given. The angle values are not cumulative.

The program in Listing 5–6 demonstrates the A command. The figure used in this example is a simple house of 5 sides. The house is rotated through all 4 orientations by changing the angle for the A command with a program loop. The variable P is used to position each

```
100 REM * set screen *
110 SCREEN 1,0: KEY OFF
120 COLOR 0,0: CLS
199 '
200 REM * draw house in each orientation *
210 FOR X = 0 TO 3
220   P = X * 50                         'P = x-coordinate for house
230   DRAW "BM =P;,100"                   'position corner of house
240   DRAW "A=X; U10 E5 F5 D10 L10"       'draw house at angle X
250 NEXT X
260 GOTO 260                              'loop
```

house in a different place on the same line of the screen. The result is shown in Fig. 5—8.

FIG. 5—8. Rotated houses

Automatic Scaling for Rotation

You may have noticed that sometimes figures appear to be "taller" in the vertical direction than they are "wide" in the horizontal direction, even though the lengths for the GDL commands are the same. Since there are more dots on the screen horizontally (320) than there are vertically (200), a line drawn vertically with 10 dots will appear to be longer than a line drawn horizontally with 10 dots.

One way of looking at this is that the horizontal points are "squeezed" closer together so that more can fit across the screen. This is even more apparent in the high-resolution mode, where there are 640 dots horizontally but still only 200 vertically. If you put a figure on the screen and rotated it either 90 or 270 degrees, causing the horizontal and vertical lines to be exchanged, the figure would look shorter in the horizontal direction than it was before in the vertical direction.

The A and TA commands compensate for this effect by scaling everything by a predefined factor. The result is that the figure appears to be the same size no matter which way it is rotated.

The program in Listing 5—7 demonstrates this effect. First, three lines are drawn on the screen, all with the same length parameters. Then we rotate the figure by 90 degrees, not by using the A command, but rather by changing which relative draw commands we use. This creates a figure whose lines appear to be different lengths. Next to this, we place the same figure, but we create it by using the A command to rotate (and automatically scale) the original figure. The results are

```
100 REM * set screen *
110 SCREEN 1,0: KEY OFF
120 COLOR 0,0: CLS
199 '
200 REM * show different directions *
210 DRAW "BM 60,100 NU20 NL20 NR20"      'draw original figure
220 DRAW "BM 140,100 NU20 ND20 NL20"     'rotate using new draws
230 DRAW "BM 220,100 A1 NU20 NL20 NR20"  'rotate using A
240 GOTO 240
```

shown in Fig. 5–9. Comparing these three objects, you can see that the rotated version resembles the original much more closely than does the version done with different draw commands.

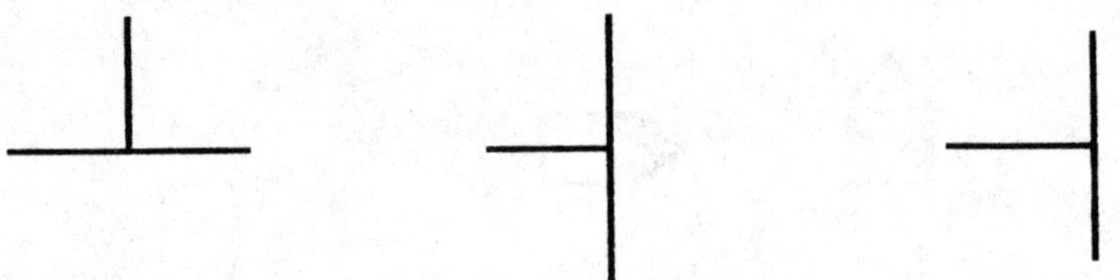

FIG. 5—9. Uneven rotations

The TA (Turn Angle) Command

The A command is fine if you only wish to rotate your figures through 4 existing directions (standard up, down, left, and right). However, you might want to go further than this. The TA command lets you rotate into orientations that are not available on the standard eight-direction axis. The TA command takes the form

```
TA turn-angle
```

where turn-angle is either a numeric integer value ranging from 0 through 360, or an equal sign followed by a numeric variable name followed by a semicolon. The turn angle specifies the number of degrees to rotate the axis from the top-of-screen direction. Notice that the direction of rotation is to the left (counterclockwise).

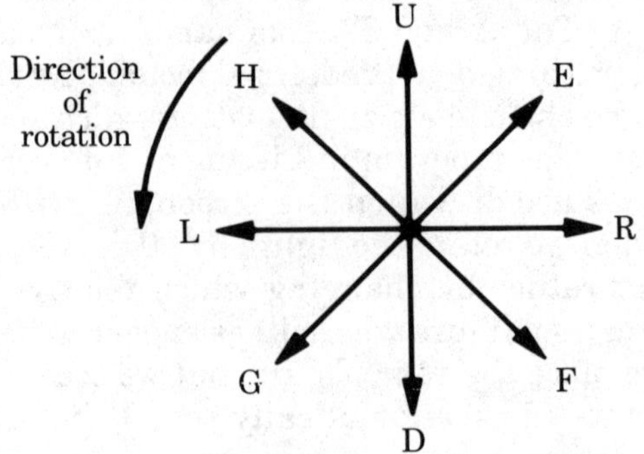

It is important to remember that when you rotate the axis, you still have only the 8 basic directions to draw in. The difference is that now those directions are based on a new orientation relative to the "standard." The TA command provides us not only with an easy way to rotate whole figures, but also with a convenient method of creating a figure with precise angles.

Suppose that you want to draw a particular right triangle on the screen. You want one of the angles to be 35 degrees, making the other 55 degrees. Suppose also that you want the hypotenuse (the side opposite the right angle) to have a length of 30. Rather than calculating the triangle vertices from this information and drawing the sides using the M command or LINE statement, it is possible to create the triangle using a combination of TA and relative draw commands. The triangle is shown here. It will be necessary to calculate the lengths of the sides as well. The results are rounded up to the nearest integer.

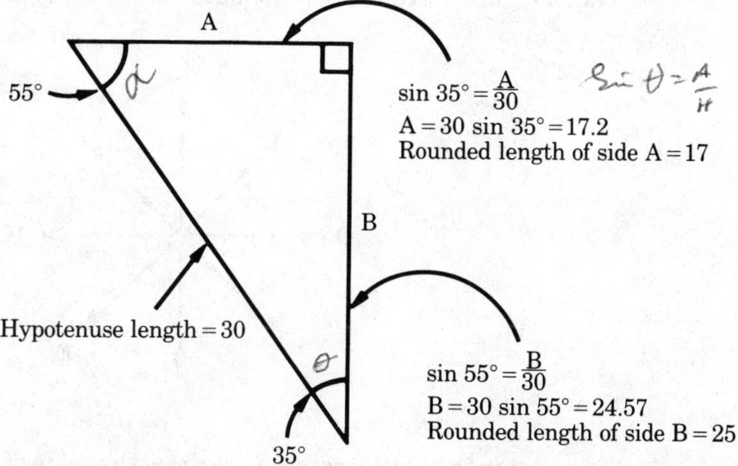

The program in Listing 5–8 carries out the steps necessary to create this triangle on the screen. First of all, a blank move is used to position the triangle at the center of the screen. This point will be the location of the vertex of the angle that is 35 degrees. Now we rotate the axis by 35 degrees via the DRAW string "TA35". The axis orientation is as shown here:

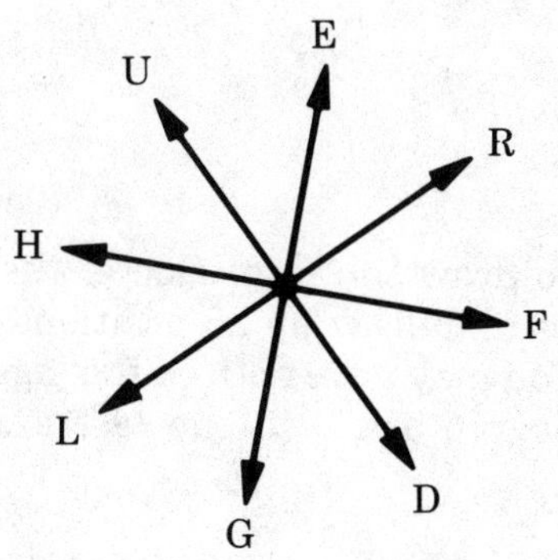

Next, the DRAW string "U30" creates the hypotenuse of the triangle, 30 positions long, rotated by 35 degrees from the top-of-screen direction.

Now we wish to draw the side of the triangle that is 17 units long. We do this by first rotating the axis to an orientation of 270 degrees, causing "up" to refer to what used to be "right" on the standard axis.

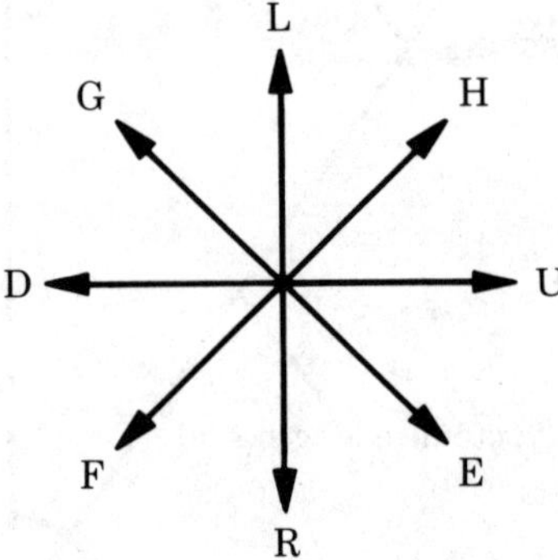

After the axis is rotated, we draw that side of the triangle with the DRAW string "U17".

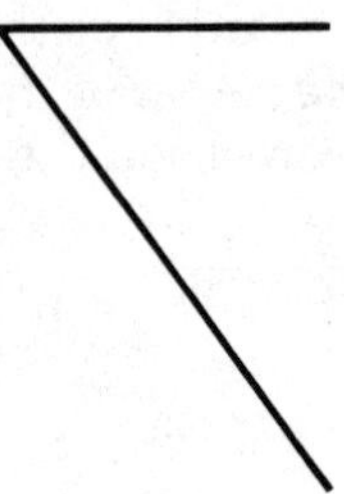

To draw the final side of the triangle, we rotate the axis to 180 degrees and draw up 25 positions. The result is shown in Fig. 5–10.

You may have noticed the jaggedness of the line that was drawn at a 35-degree angle in the last example. It is not possible to draw a

LISTING 5–8. Right Triangle

```
100 REM * set screen *
110 SCREEN 1,0: KEY OFF
120 COLOR 0,0: CLS
199 '
200 REM * draw triangle *
210 DRAW "BM 60,100"
220 DRAW "TA35 U30"      'rotate to 35 degrees and draw up 30
230 DRAW "TA270 U17"     'rotate to 270 degrees and draw up 17
240 DRAW "TA180 U25"     'rotate to 180 degrees and draw up 25
250 GOTO 250
```

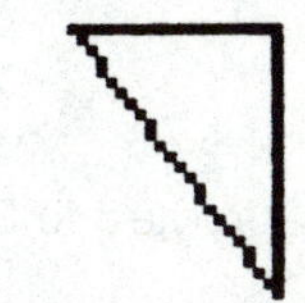

FIG. 5–10. Right triangle

perfect line at all angles because there are not enough dots available on the IBM screen (in either medium-resolution or high-resolution modes) to make the line appear to be straight. The jagged lines do look better in the high-resolution mode, but they are not perfect.

The program shown in Listing 5–9 rotates a simple figure (a revised version of the house we used earlier) through a complete 360-degree circle, 1 degree at a time. Each time the house is rotated, the degree to which it is rotated is shown in the lower-left corner of the screen. Notice the angles at which the figure is most jagged and those where it is most nearly perfect. Figures 5–11, 5–12, and 5–13 illustrate the results of rotating the house to a few selected angles.

LISTING 5–9. Rotating House with Angles

```
100 REM * set screen *
110 SCREEN 1,0: KEY OFF
120 COLOR 0,0: CLS
199 '
200 REM * show figure at all angles *
210 FOR X = 0 TO 360
220   DRAW "TA=X;"                          'X controls turn angle
230   DRAW "BM 150,100 R20 U20 H10 G10 D20" 'move and draw house
240   LOCATE 23,1
250   PRINT X;                              'locate angle of rotation
299   '
300   REM * wait in between drawing at different angles *
310   FOR W = 1 TO 1000: NEXT W
320   CLS
330 NEXT X
```

3

FIG. 5–11. House rotated to 3 degrees

180

FIG. 5–12. House rotated to 180 degrees

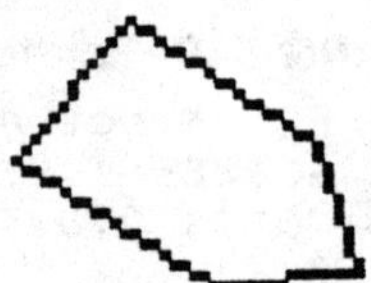

234

FIG. 5–13. House rotated to 234 degrees

At this point, we have covered all but one of the GDL commands available in the DRAW statement. We have seen how to move, draw lines, change colors, paint, scale, and rotate our figures. The last GDL command, X, does not actually change our drawings on the screen, but it is rather useful. It allows you to execute one DRAW string from within another. It takes the form

```
X string-variable-name ;
```

where string-variable-name contains the name of the variable that holds the inner DRAW string. The semicolon after the variable name is required.

The execute command has several uses. Suppose that you have a favorite figure that you want to use many times in your program. Say that the GDL commands used to create this figure are stored in a string variable called FIG$. We will use our house from earlier as an example.

```
FIG$ = "R20 U20 H10 G10 D20"
```

Whenever you want to make a house appear on the screen in your program, all you have to do is add the X command to the current DRAW statement.

```
DRAW "U10 R15 BM 100,100 XFIG$; R10"
```

Using X is like calling a subroutine to draw the house. First the U, R, and BM commands are executed, then the R, U, H, G, and D commands in the string FIG$ are executed, then the R command is executed.

At first glance, using X seems to have the same effect as simply adding the FIG$ to the DRAW string.

```
DRAW "U10 R15 BM 100,100+ "FIG$+ "R10"
```

There is, however, another advantage to using X other than the fact that it makes the DRAW statement look nicer without those extra quotes and addition signs. The maximum string length in BASICA is 255 characters. If we had many long strings that we wished to include in our DRAW statement, their combined length might exceed the 255-character limit if we simply concatenated the strings together as above.

The X command gets around this problem easily. When an execute command is encountered, BASICA stops processing the current DRAW statement, finds and executes the contents of the X string, then returns to processing the DRAW statement. This way, the characters in the strings "called" by X commands do not count toward the total string space available for any one DRAW statement.

If you had four strings, A$, B$, C$, and D$, each 255 characters long, it would be possible to execute them all with only one DRAW:

```
DRAW "XA$; XB$; XC$; XD$;"
```

even though their combined length is greater than the maximum string length.

A WORD ABOUT ASPECT RATIO

In the rotation section, we pointed out that equal-distance parameters do not always provide lines that appear to be the same length on the screen.

Since there are more points horizontally on the screen than vertically (320 versus 200), a DRAW statement such as

```
DRAW "U50 R50 D50 L50"
```

produces a rectangle rather than a perfect square.

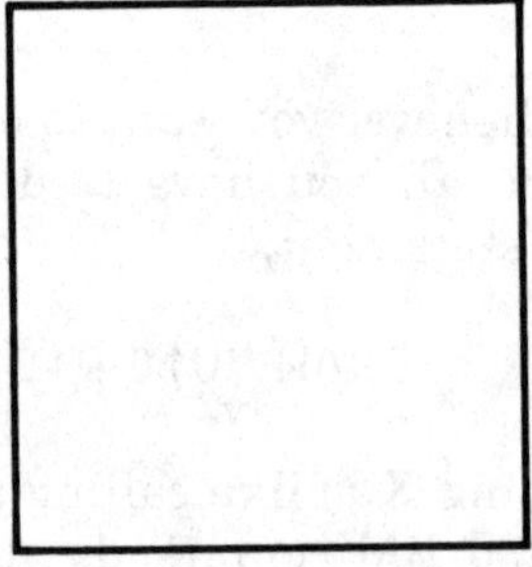

Since 320 is to 200 as 8 is to 5, there must be 8 dots horizontally for every 5 vertically, right? Not so. Most computer screens are manufactured so that they have an "aspect ratio" of 4 to 3. This means that they are 4/3 as long horizontally as they are vertically. We must take this factor into account also when computing the ratio of horizontal to vertical dots on the screen. There would be 8 horizontal dots for every 5 vertical dots if the physical screen had equal horizontal and vertical dimensions. Such a screen would have an aspect ratio of 1 to 1. Since that is not the case for the standard screen, we must multiply the number of vertical points by the new aspect ratio before arriving at the final ratio.

$$\frac{(\#\ of\ horizontal\ dots\ on\ screen)}{(aspect\ ratio) \times (\#\ of\ vertical\ dots)} = \frac{\#\ of\ horizontal\ dots\ that}{are\ equal\ to\ 1\ vertical\ dot}$$

Notice that we have actually done this when we illustrated an aspect ratio of 1 to 1; the denominator remains the same when multiplied by an aspect ratio of 1.

Using the medium-resolution mode and a standard size screen, we have:

$$\frac{(320)}{(4/3)(200)} = \frac{24\ \text{horizontal}}{20\ \text{vertical}} = 1.2$$

Therefore, 24 horizontal dots are equal to 20 vertical dots. In order to make a square square, we must multiply the horizontal lengths in our DRAW statement by 1.2.

```
DRAW "U50 R60 D50 L60"
```

produces the following figure:

This method also works for the high-resolution mode where the screen is organized as 640 by 200 dots.

$$\frac{(640)}{(4/3)(200)} = \frac{48\ \text{horizontal}}{20\ \text{vertical}} = 2.4$$

Again we multiply the horizontal distances by the new ratio.

```
DRAW "U50 R120 D50 L120"
```

SUMMARY

In this chapter we have explained all the commands of the graphics definition language.

- Relative lines can be drawn in the eight standard directions using the U, D, L, R, E, F, G, and H commands.

```
DRAW "U16 R8 D16 L8"
```

- A line can be drawn from the current position to an absolute or relative position using M.

```
DRAW "M 10,10"
```

- A move can be made without leaving a line using B.

        DRAW "BM 160,100"

- A return to the starting position after drawing a line can be performed using N.

        DRAW "NU10"

- The draw color can be changed using C.

        DRAW "C3"

- The interior of figures can be painted using P.

        DRAW "P 1,3"

- Drawings can be scaled using S.

        DRAW "S10 U30 R20 D40"

- Figures can be rotated using A or TA.

        DRAW "A3 U5 R10"
        DRAW "TA270 U5 R10"

- DRAW strings can be executed from within another using X.

        DRAW "XA$; XB$; XC$;"

- Regular variables can be used as command arguments.

        DRAW "U=V1; BM =V2; ,=V3;"

- Finally, we have shown how to make objects appear to have the same dimensions on the screen, regardless of the number of dots available horizontally or vertically.

6
SIMPLE ANIMATION

Graphics Statements, Functions,
and Terms Introduced

**WINDOW
WINDOW SCREEN
coordinate systems**

The objective of this chapter is to teach you various ways to move objects about the screen. Animation makes heavy use of the DRAW statement discussed in Chapter 5. You will also learn to control the size and placement of "windows" that are displayed on the screen. Rotary, as well as linear, movement is discussed.

BASIC statements and terms that are explained are WINDOW, WINDOW SCREEN, and coordinate systems.

Animation of an object on the video screen is achieved by creating the illusion of motion. Think of a movie film composed of thousands of frames composed of single "still" pictures. The "moving" picture is created by displaying the frames rapidly in sequence. Objects in the sequence of pictures are placed in slightly different positions in each frame. The eye is tricked into believing that it sees a single frame in which the objects move.

A similar technique is used in producing animation by the computer. However, the technique described in this chapter has only one frame, the video screen, with which to perform its trickery.

DRAW, ERASE, MOVE...

The simplest form of animation involves a repeated performance of a series of actions. First an object is drawn at a specified position. A time delay follows to allow the eye to observe the object. The object is then erased and drawn at a new position. The cycle repeats over and over to create the illusion of motion.

This technique is effective when working with a single, small moving object. The effectiveness is determined by two major factors: the length of the time delay and the distance the object is moved to each new position.

We will use two drawing methods for comparison. Our moving object will be a single colored rectangle. The first method uses the LINE statement with the BLOCK-FILL option and the PAINT statement. The second method uses DRAW and PAINT statements.

The animation is controlled by a FOR-NEXT loop, which provides horizontal movement across the screen. A red-filled box is drawn by line 240, held on the screen by line 250, and erased by line 230.

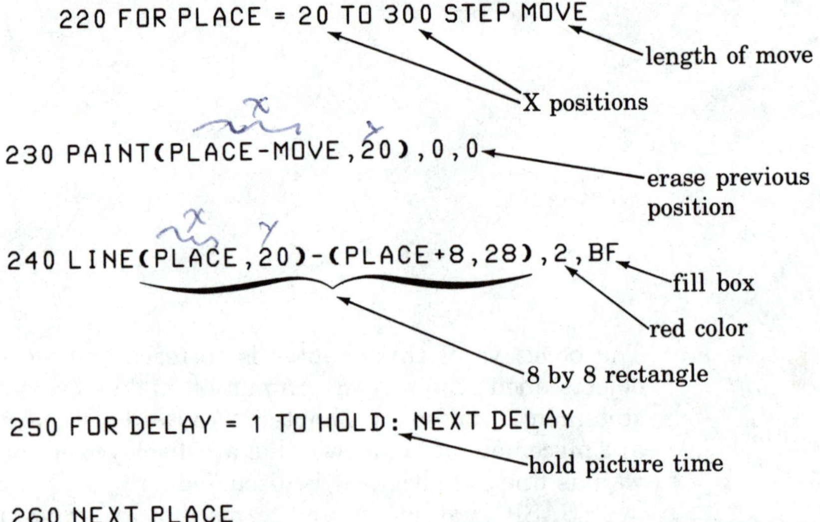

The action in the FOR-NEXT loop is controlled by the variables HOLD and MOVE. The HOLD variable controls how long the object stays on the screen at a given position. The MOVE variable controls the distance the object is moved each time the loop is executed. The PAINT statement uses the background color to erase the previous object.

Listing 6–1 provides an opportunity to input values for the HOLD and MOVE variables so that you can test several combinations to find the most desirable for effective movement. The erasure begins at the upper-left corner of the object painting with the background color to the background border as shown in Fig. 6–1.

The object is erased by painting from an X,Y position that trails the current X value (PLACE) by the amount of the MOVE. The new object is then drawn at the current X position (PLACE). Thus, regardless of the magnitude of the move chosen, the computer "finds" the last position of the object that must be erased.

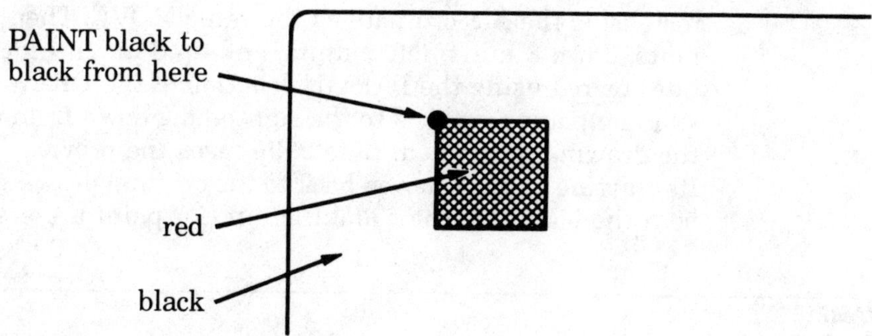

FIG. 6–1. Erasing the object

LISTING 6–1. Move by LINE

```
100 REM * get variable values *
110 SCREEN 0,0: KEY OFF
120 WIDTH 40: CLS
130 INPUT"Time delay =";HOLD
140 INPUT"Move increment =";MOVE
199 '
200 REM * erase, draw, delay *
210 SCREEN 1,0:COLOR 0,0
220 FOR PLACE = 20 TO 300 STEP MOVE
230   PAINT(PLACE-MOVE,20),0,0
240   LINE(PLACE,20)-(PLACE+8,28),2,BF
250   FOR DELAY = 1 TO HOLD: NEXT DELAY
260 NEXT PLACE
299 '
300 REM * repeat *
310 GOTO 110
```

Run the program with several combinations of HOLD and MOVE to see if you can find an effective combination. You will notice considerable flicker and jerkiness as the red object moves across the screen.

The second method uses a DRAW statement in the FOR-NEXT loop to draw and to erase the object. Change and add lines of Listing 6–1 to

```
220 MOVE$ = STR$(MOVE)              ⟵——— change MOVE to string
230 START$ = STR$(20-MOVE)          ⟵——— for first draw
240 DRAW "BM" + START$ + ",20"
250 FOR PLACE = 20 TO 300 STEP MOVE
260   DRAW "C3;BM+" + MOVE$ + ",0 R8 D8 L8 U8;"
270   DRAW "BM+2,+; P2,3"
280   FOR DELAY = 1 TO HOLD: NEXT DELAY
290   DRAW "BM-2,-2; P0,0"
300 NEXT PLACE
```

Line 220 defines the move value as a string variable so that it can be used in the DRAW statement. The DRAW statement in line 260 defines the color as 3 (brown). It uses a relative blank move (BM)

increasing the X-coordinate by the value MOVE. Then it draws right 8 units, down 8 units, left 8 units, and up 8 units. Line 270 paints the interior red using the P (PAINT) option of the DRAW statement. The starting paint point is 2 to the right and 2 down from the point where the drawing originated. Line 290 erases the previously drawn object. Its starting point is moved back to the original drawing's origin so that both the boundary color and the interior paint are erased.

For painting:

```
PLACE = 20
DRAW "BM+2,+2; P2,3"
```

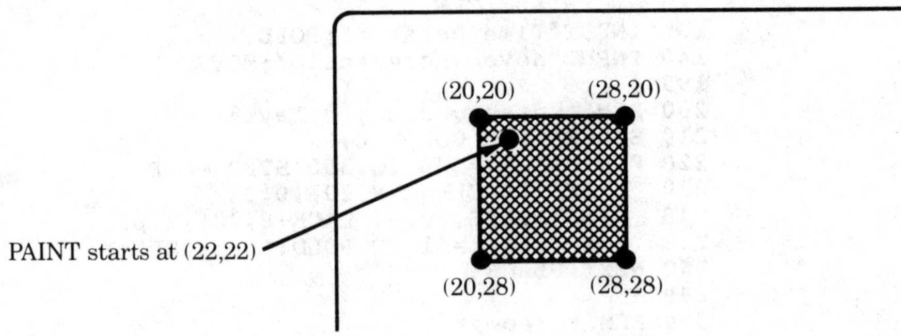

For erasing:

```
DRAW "BM-2,-2; P0,0"
```

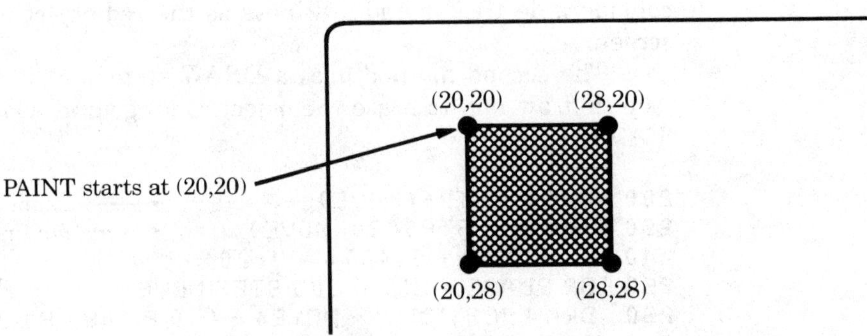

The complete listing for the revised program is given in Listing 6–2.

When you run the revised program, you will also notice the flicker of the screen and the jerky motion. Therefore, you can see that the method of draw, erase, move, and redraw is not entirely satisfactory for animating objects in a linear motion.

```
100 REM * get variable values *
110 SCREEN 0,0: KEY OFF
120 WIDTH 40: CLS
130 INPUT"Time delay =";HOLD
140 INPUT"Move increment =";MOVE
199 '
200 REM * erase, draw, paint, delay *
210 SCREEN 1,0: COLOR 0,0
220 MOVE$=STR$(MOVE)
230 START$=STR$(20-MOVE)
240 DRAW "BM " + START$ + ",20"
250 FOR PLACE = 20 TO 300 STEP MOVE
260   DRAW "C3; BM+" + MOVE$ + ",0 R8 D8 L8 U8"
270   DRAW "BM +2,+2;P2,3"
280   FOR DELAY = 1 TO HOLD: NEXT DELAY
290   DRAW "BM -2,-2;P0,0"
300 NEXT PLACE
399 '
400 REM * repeat *
410 GOTO 110
```

TWO-DIMENSIONAL COORDINATE SYSTEMS

As was pointed out in Chapter 4, the coordinate system used for the IBM PC is not the same as that normally used to describe two-dimensional objects. To conform with IBM PC notation, we will use the term *screen coordinates* to describe that used by its video screen. We will use the term *natural coordinates* to describe the system normally used to describe two-dimensional space in nature (also referred to as the Cartesian coordinate system). Figure 6–2 displays the differences in the two systems.

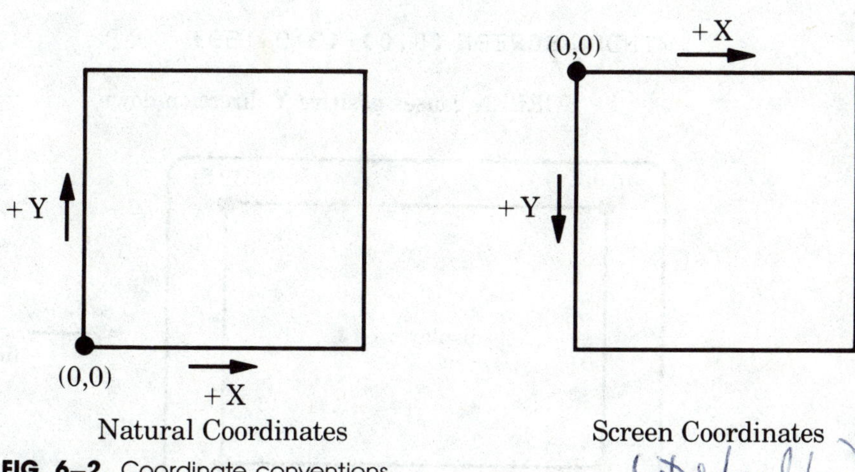

FIG. 6–2. Coordinate conventions

The WINDOW statement of BASICA (not available on versions earlier than 2.0) can be used to control the positive direction of the Y-axis to make a video display conform to the natural coordinate system. WINDOW can also be used to fill the screen with minimum and maximum programmed coordinates, thus "clipping" off areas that would normally be displayed.

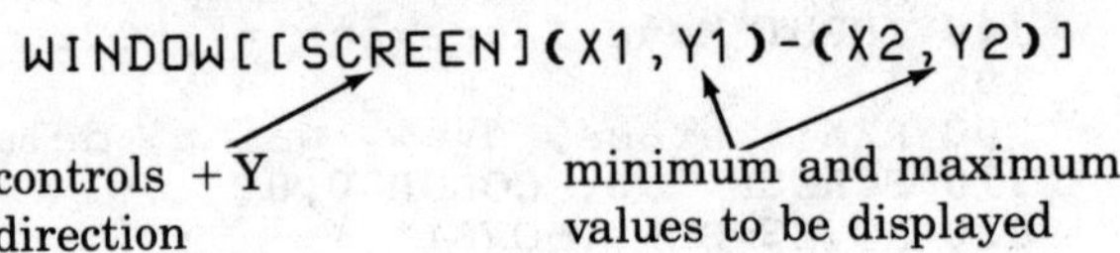

EXAMPLES

WINDOW (0,0)-(319,199)

SCREEN is omitted; therefore, positive Y direction is up; Xmin = 0; Ymin = 0; Xmax = 319; Ymax = 199

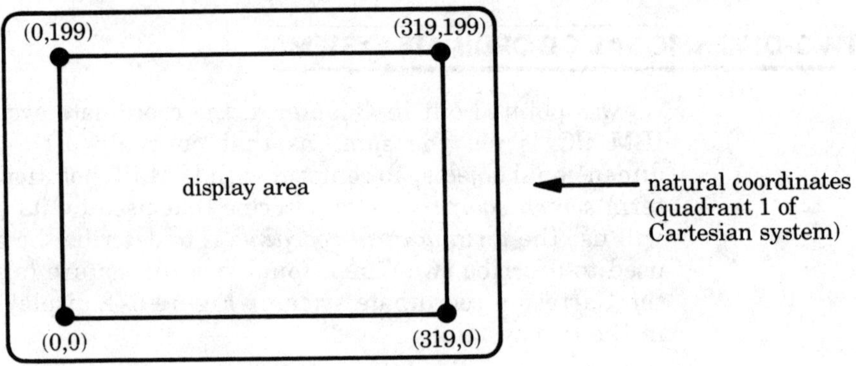

WINDOW SCREEN (0,0)-(319,199)

SCREEN causes positive Y direction down

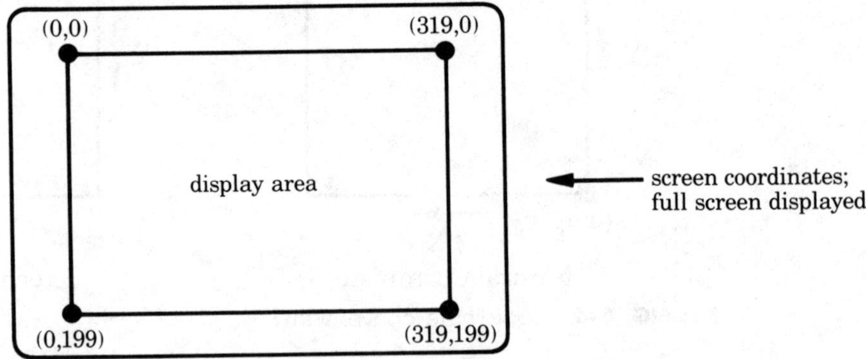

```
WINDOW (160,0)-(319,199)
```

SCREEN omitted—positive Y up; screen will be filled by area
enclosed by minimum and maximum values of X and Y

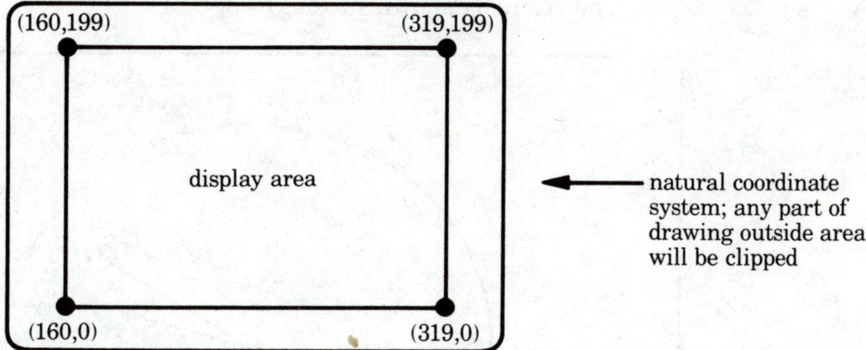

The program of Listing 6–3 demonstrates the capability of the
WINDOW statement. Imagine a clock face with hour and minute
hands.

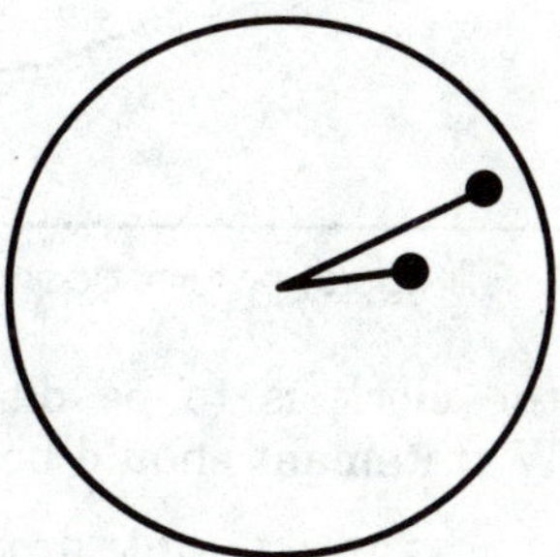

The center of the face is located at (160,100) near the center of the
screen. The hands are drawn using natural coordinates by the following program lines.

```
1000 REM * clock subroutine *
1010 CIRCLE(160,100),90
1020 LINE(160,100)-(200,110)
1030 CIRCLE(200,110),5,2
1040 LINE (160,100)-(215,130)
1050 CIRCLE(215,130),5,2
1060 LINE(0,0)-(319,199),,B
1070 FOR DELAY = 1 TO 500: NEXT DELAY
1080 RETURN
```

—— face of clock

—— hour hand

—— minute hand
—— rectangle around
screen edge

If the clock is to be displayed using the normal coordinate system, the WINDOW statement is

```
220 WINDOW(0,0)-(319,199)
```

The result is shown in Fig. 6–3.

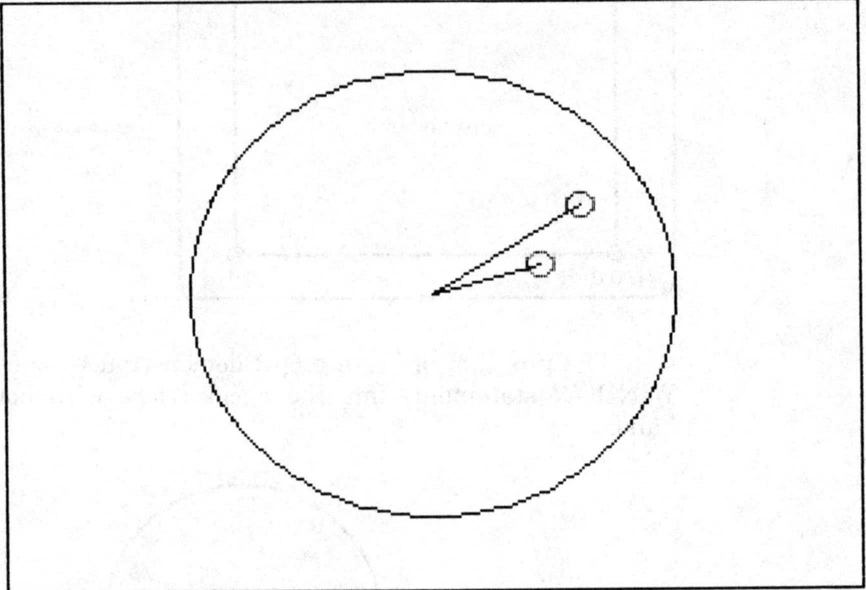

FIG. 6–3. Full figure, natural coordinates

If the clock is to be displayed using screen coordinates, the WINDOW statement should be

```
320 WINDOW SCREEN(0,0)-(319,199)
```

The result is shown in Fig. 6–4.

A portion of the figure can be clipped and the balance enlarged with the WINDOW statement by changing the minimum and maximum values of the coordinates. Suppose you wish to show the quarter of the screen containing the clock hands of Figs. 6–3 and 6–4. The appropriate WINDOW statements would be

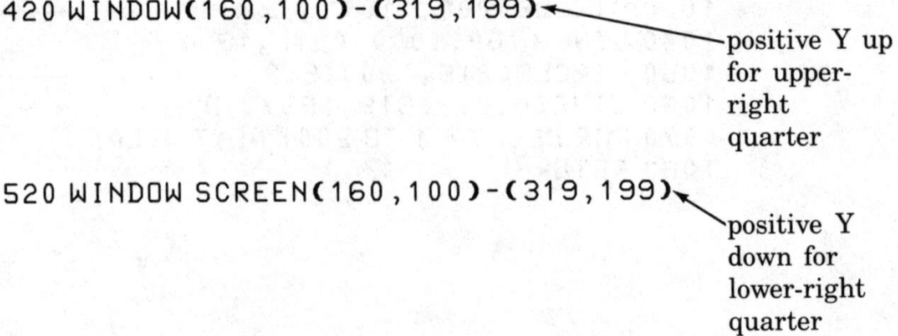

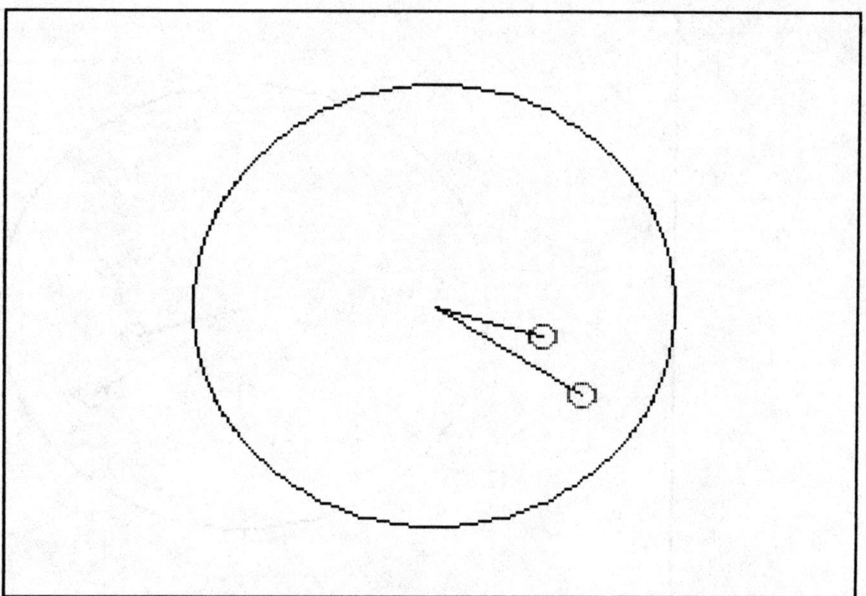

Listing 6–3 demonstrates the four pictures of Fig. 6–5 using the previous examples. A time delay holds each figure on the screen for a short time.

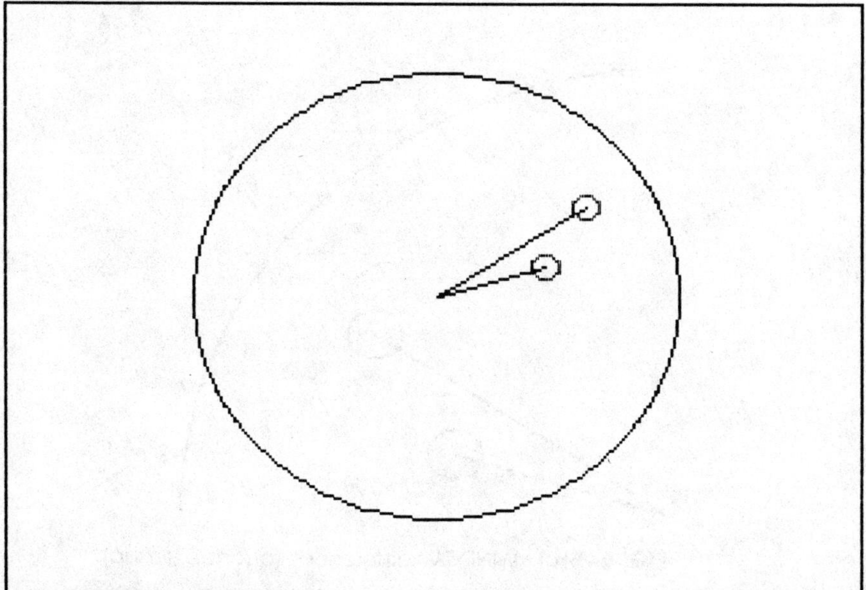

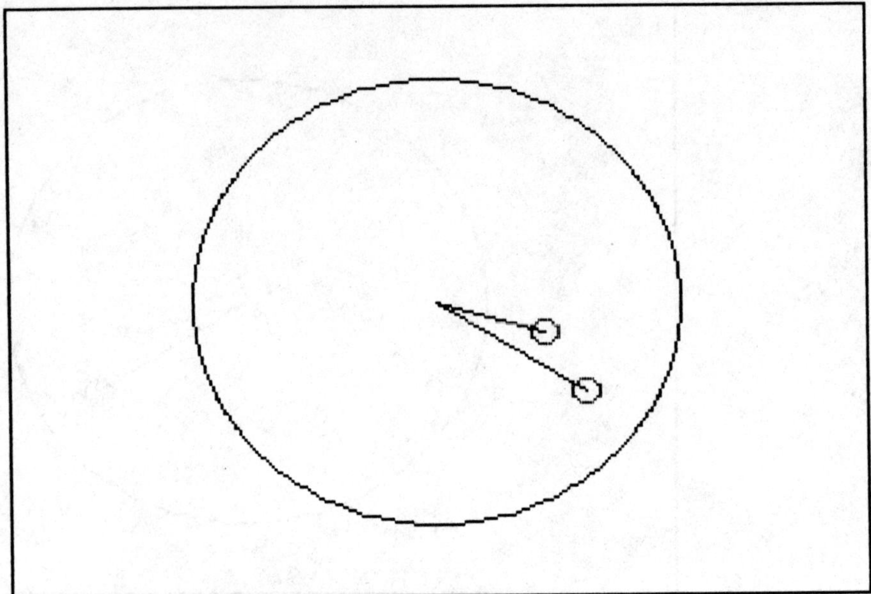

FIG. 6–5(b). WINDOW differences (full, +Y down)

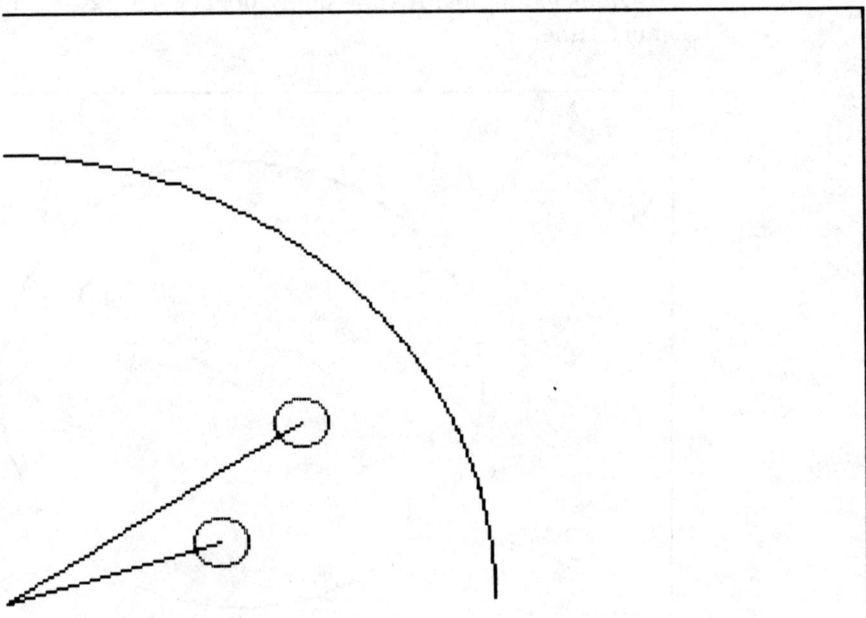

FIG. 6–5(c). WINDOW differences (quarter, +Y up)

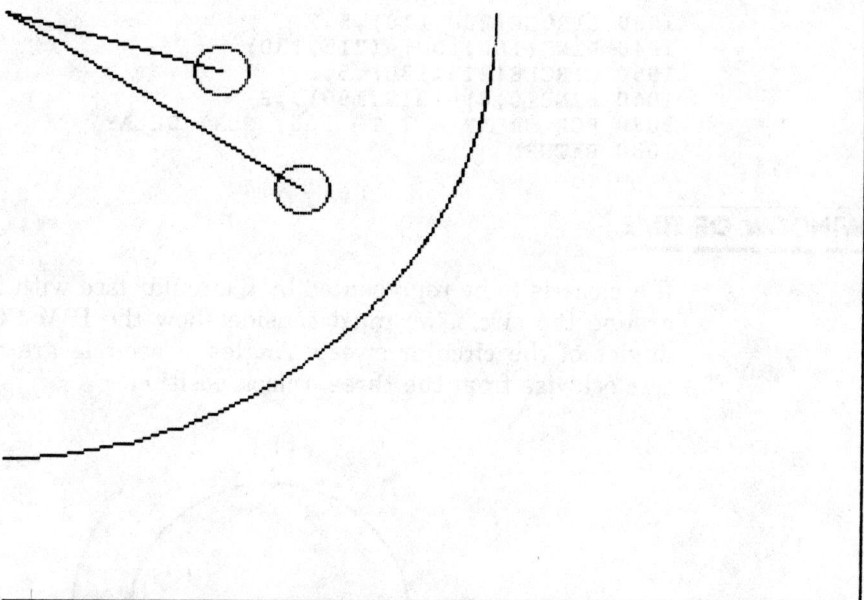

FIG. 6–5(d). WINDOW differences (quarter, +Y down)

LISTING 6–3. WINDOW Demonstration

```
100 REM * set screen *
110 SCREEN 1,0: KEY OFF
120 COLOR 0,0
130 '
200 REM * all screen, positive up *
210 CLS
220 WINDOW (0,0)-(319,199)
230 GOSUB 1010
299 '
300 REM * all screen, positive down *
310 CLS
320 WINDOW SCREEN (0,0)-(319,199)
330 GOSUB 1010
399 '
400 REM * upper quarter, positive up *
410 CLS
420 WINDOW (160,100)-(319,199)
430 GOSUB 1010
499 '
500 REM * lower quarter, positive down *
510 CLS
520 WINDOW SCREEN (160,100)-(319,199)
530 GOSUB 1010
599 '
990 END
999 '
1000 REM * clock subroutine *
1010 CIRCLE(160,100),90
1020 LINE(160,100)-(200,110)
```

```
1030 CIRCLE(200,110),5,2
1040 LINE(160,100)-(215,130)
1050 CIRCLE(215,130),5,2
1060 LINE(0,0)-(319,199),,B
1070 FOR DELAY = 1 TO 500: NEXT DELAY
1080 RETURN
```

WINDOW OF TIME

If a clock is to be represented by a circular face with hands sweeping around the circle, we must consider how the IBM PC measures the angles of the circular sweep. Angles of a circle are measured counterclockwise from the three o'clock position.

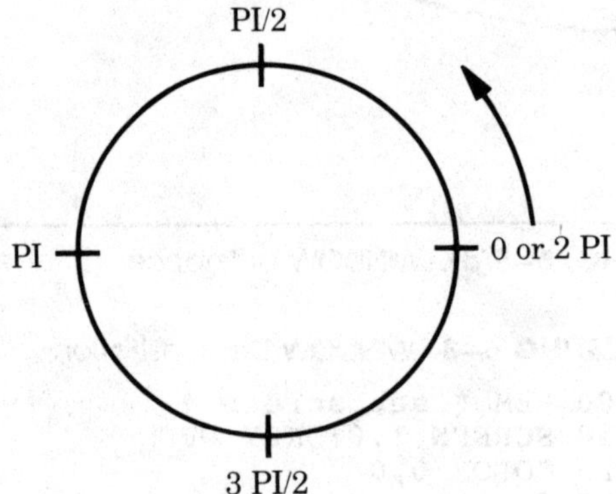

A problem arises when we try to simulate a hand on the clock that moves clockwise starting at the twelve o'clock position.

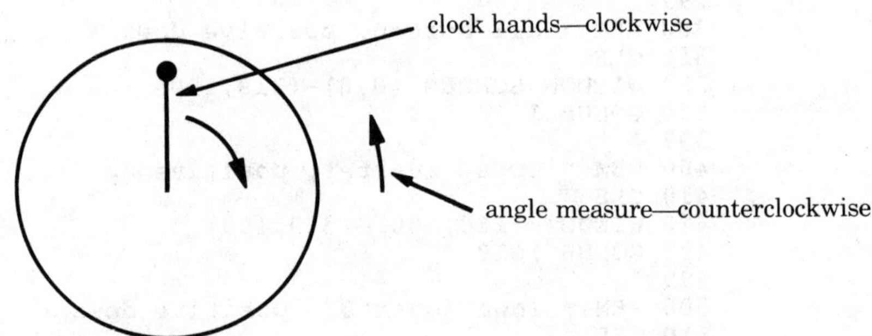

We want to use the following equations:

```
X = 160 + 75*COS(ANGLE)
Y = 100 + 75*SIN(ANGLE)
```

where 160,100 is the clock face center and 75 is the length of the hand

For each sweep of the clock face, the angle of the clock hand is to move in turn from PI/2 to 0 to PI*3/2 to PI and back one step larger than PI/2. A FOR statement for a step of -PI/6 would be

```
FOR ANGLE = PI/2 TO PI*2/3 STEP -PI/6
```

PI*2/3 is larger than PI/2. The computer will not perform a FOR-NEXT loop with a negative step if the upper limit (PI*2/3) is greater than the lower limit (PI/2). However, we can use negative angles and think of our circle as

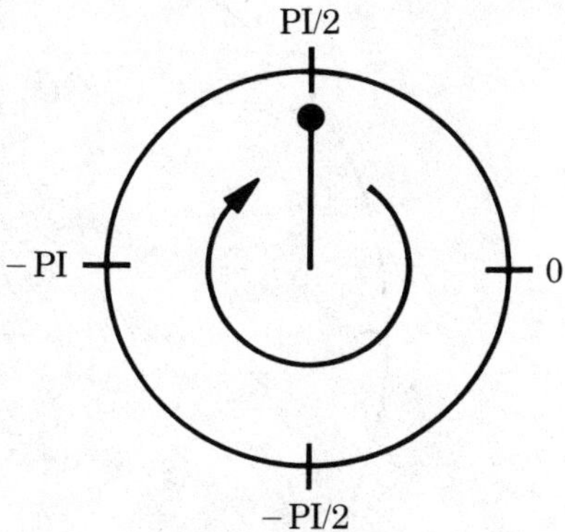

Then our FOR statement would be

```
FOR ANGLE = PI/2 TO -PI*4/3 STEP -PI/6
```

This will move the hands in a clockwise direction as desired. Another part of the problem is solved by using the form of the WINDOW statement that displays the X,Y coordinates in the natural system rather than the screen system.

```
210 WINDOW (0,0)-(319,199)
```

The program in Listing 6–4 steps the minute and hour hands of the clock through a period representing 12 hours. The minute hand moves in increments of PI/12, or 15 degrees. The hour hand moves in increments of PI/6, or 30 degrees. The hour hand moves only when the minute hand has passed through a complete revolution. The action takes place in nested FOR-NEXT loops, which call separate subroutines for each hand. Drawing and erasing actions are controlled by the color variable (KOLOR).

```
310 FOR ALPH=PI/2 TO -PI*4/3 STEP -PI/6      ◄——————hour hand
320   KOLOR = 2: GOSUB 1010
330   FOR BETA = PI/2 TO -PI*17/12 STEP -PI/12
340     KOLOR = 2: GOSUB 1110               ◄——————minute hand
```

```
350     FOR DELAY = 1 TO 200: NEXT DELAY
360     KOLOR = 0: GOSUB 1110          ←—— erase minute
370     KOLOR = 2: GOSUB 1010          ←—— redraw hour
380   NEXT BETA
390   KOLOR = 0: GOSUB 1110            ←—— erase hour
400 NEXT ALPH
```

Figure 6–6 shows the clock at 3:05 when ALPH = PI/3 and BETA = 0.

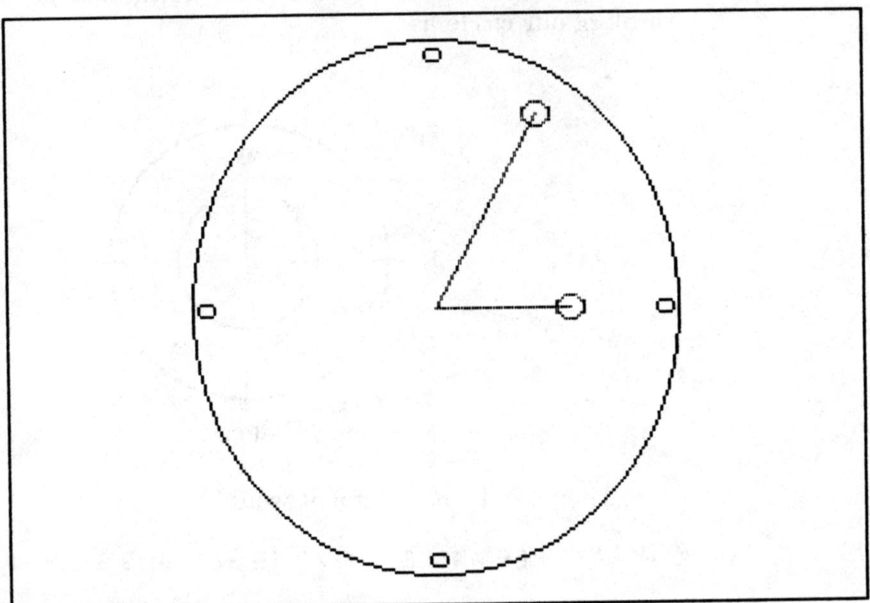

FIG. 6–6. Clock demonstration

LISTING 6–4. Passing Time

```
100 REM * set screen & PI *
110 SCREEN 1,0: KEY OFF
120 COLOR 0,0: CLS
130 PI = 3.141593
199 '
200 REM * clock face *
210 WINDOW(0,0)-(319,199)
220 CIRCLE(160,100),90,,,,1
230 CIRCLE(160,15),3,3: CIRCLE(160,185),3,3
240 CIRCLE(75,100),3,3: CIRCLE(245,100),3,3
299 '
300 REM * move hands *
310 FOR ALPH = PI/2 TO -PI*4/3 STEP -PI/6
320   KOLOR=2: GOSUB 1010
330   FOR BETA = PI/2 TO -PI*17/12 STEP -PI/12
340     KOLOR=2: GOSUB 1110
350     FOR DELAY = 1 TO 200: NEXT DELAY
360     KOLOR=0: GOSUB 1110
370     KOLOR=2: GOSUB 1010
380   NEXT BETA
390   KOLOR=0: GOSUB 1010
```

```
400 NEXT ALPH
499 '
990 END
999 '
1000 REM * hour hand *
1010 U = 160+50*COS(ALPH)
1020 V = 100+50*SIN(ALPH)
1030 LINE(160,100)-(U,V),KOLOR
1040 CIRCLE(U,V),5,KOLOR
1050 RETURN
1099 '
1100 REM * minute hand *
1110 X = 160+75*COS(BETA)
1120 Y = 100+75*SIN(BETA)
1130 LINE(160,100)-(X,Y),KOLOR
1140 CIRCLE(X,Y),5,KOLOR
1150 RETURN
```

ROTATING WITH DRAW

The DRAW statement is much simpler to use when drawing the hands of a clock than the combination LINE and CIRCLE statements used in the previous program. The TA (TURN ANGLE) option of the DRAW statement (available in Version 2.0 of Advanced BASIC) is ideally suited for changing the angle of the clock hands. This means that you can omit the SIN and COS functions of Listing 6–4.

The clock face of Listing 6–4 is duplicated in the program of Listing 6–5. The hand-drawing subroutines are much shorter due to the DRAW statements used. The hands are drawn with arrowheads rather than circles as shown in Fig. 6–7.

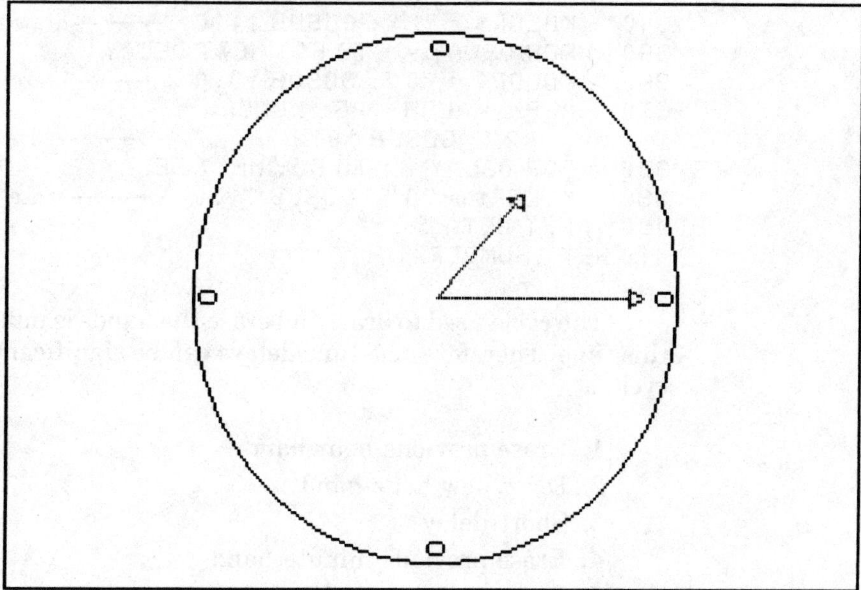

FIG. 6–7. Clock face at 1:15

The hands are drawn by the following subroutines:

```
1000 REM * hour hand *
1010 DRAW"c"+KOLOR$+"bm160,100; ta=alph; u4014e4f414"
1020 RETURN
```

turn angle

hour hand

```
1100 REM * minute hand *
1110 DRAW"c"+KOLOR$+"bm160,100; ta=beta; u6014e4f414"
1120 RETURN
```

turn angle

minute hand

The colors for the hands (red to draw and black to erase) are defined by the variable KOLOR$ in the main program.

In the previous program (Listing 6–4), the minute hand jumped in increments of PI/12 (15 degrees). The hour hand was stationary until the minute hand finished a complete revolution. Then it jumped PI/6 (30 degrees). The hour hand turns a very small amount (¼ of 1 degree) in this program. It moves each time the minute hand moves. The minute hand makes a smaller jump (3 degrees) than before. Therefore, the movement of the clock hands is much more realistic. The movement of the hands is accomplished by the following nested FOR-NEXT loops.

```
300 REM * move hands *
310 ALPH = 360.25                          initialize hour angle
320 FOR NUMBER = 1 TO 12                    repeat for 12 hours
330   FOR BETA = 360 TO 3 STEP -3          minute hand angle
340     KOLOR$ = "2": GOSUB 1110           draw minute hand
350     FOR DELAY = 1 TO 50: NEXT DELAY
360     KOLOR$ = "0": GOSUB 1010           erase hour hand
370     ALPH = ALPH-.25: KOLOR$ =
            "2": GOSUB 1010                draw hour hand
380     FOR DELAY = 1 TO 50: NEXT DELAY
390     KOLOR$ = "0": GOSUB 1110           erase minute hand
400   NEXT BETA
410 NEXT NUMBER
```

The cycle used to draw and erase the hands is much more efficient this time. Therefore, the time delays can be significantly reduced. The cycle is

1. Erase previous hour hand
2. Draw new hour hand
3. Short delay
4. Erase previous minute hand
5. Draw new minute hand

6. Short delay

Repeat over and over.

Each hand is displayed while the other hand is being erased and redrawn in a new position. The complete program is shown in Listing 6–5.

LISTING 6–5. Clock by DRAW

```
100 REM * set screen & PI *
110 SCREEN 1,0: KEY OFF
120 COLOR 0,0: CLS
199 '
200 REM * clock face *
210 CIRCLE(160,100),90,,,,1
220 CIRCLE(160,15),3,3: CIRCLE(160,185),3,3
230 CIRCLE(75,100),3,3: CIRCLE(245,100),3,3
299 '
300 REM * move hands *
310 ALPH=360.25
320 FOR NUMBER = 1 TO 12
330   FOR BETA=360 TO 3 STEP -3
340     KOLOR$="2": GOSUB 1110
350     FOR DELAY = 1 TO 50: NEXT DELAY
360     KOLOR$="0": GOSUB 1010
370     ALPH=ALPH-.25: KOLOR$="2": GOSUB 1010
380     FOR DELAY = 1 TO 50: NEXT DELAY
390     KOLOR$="0": GOSUB 1110
400   NEXT BETA
410 NEXT NUMBER
499 '
500 END
599 '
1000 REM * hour hand *
1010 DRAW"c"+KOLOR$+"bm 160,100;ta=alph;u4014e4f414"
1020 RETURN
1099 '
1100 REM * minute hand *
1110 DRAW"c"+KOLOR$+";bm 160,100;ta=beta;u6014e4f414"
1120 RETURN
```

You may have noticed that the points of the clock hands are slightly distorted when drawn at certain angles. Such distortion becomes more evident when rotated figures are larger and/or more complex.

The program of Listing 6–6 draws and rotates a polygon that has an irregular shape. When drawn at 0, 90, 180, or 270 degree turn angles the sides of the polygon are smooth as shown in Fig. 6–8.

The polygon is drawn from point (140,80) as shown in Fig. 6–9 by the draw commands "...u40 r40 d40 r10 d10 l60 u10 r10".

The figure is rotated by drawing and erasing at angle increments of 15 degrees. The polygon is rotated about the point (140,80). A noticeable distortion occurs at angles other than multiples of 90 degrees. Figure 6–10 shows a typical distortion as seen on the video screen.

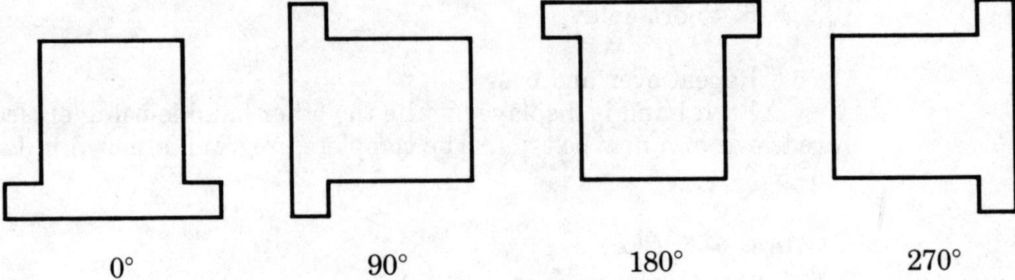

0°   90°   180°   270°

FIG. 6–8. Polygon at 90-degree increments

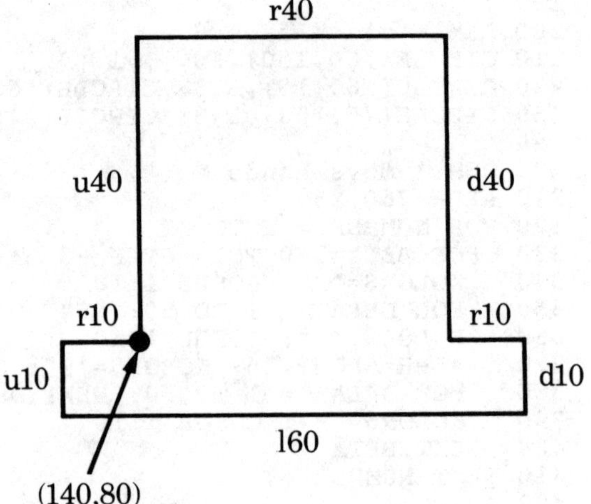

FIG. 6–9. Drawing the polygon

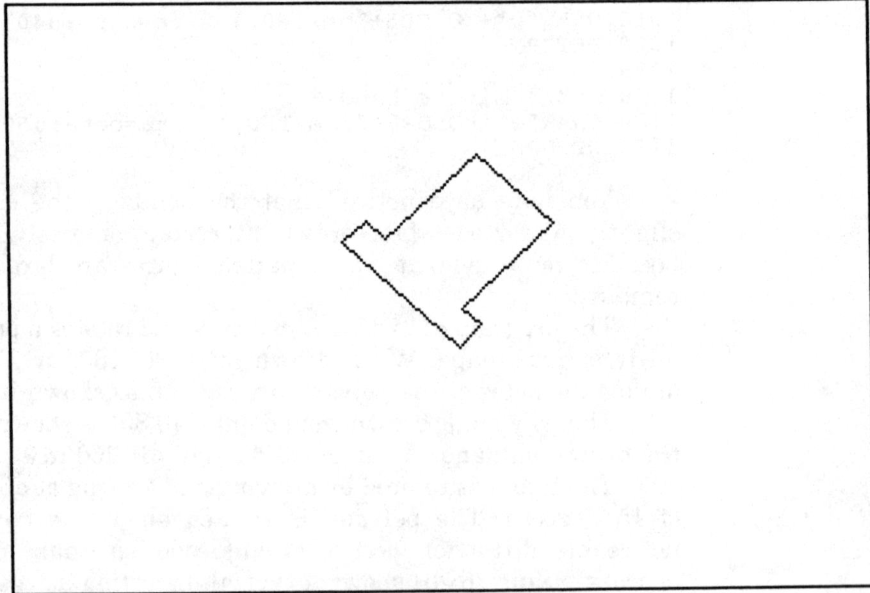

FIG. 6–10. Distortion at an odd angle

The program that performs the rotation is given in Listing 6–6.

LISTING 6–6. Rotating Polygon

```
100 REM * set screen *
110 SCREEN 1,0: KEY OFF
120 COLOR 0,0: CLS
199 '
200 REM * draw polygon *
210 DRAW"c3;bm140,80;u40r40d40r10d10160u10r10"
299 '
300 REM * rotate polygon *
310 FOR ALPH = 360 TO 15 STEP -15
320   BETA=ALPH-15
330   FOR DELAY = 1 TO 200: NEXT DELAY
340   DRAW"c0;bm140,80;ta=alph;u40r40d40r10d10160u10r10"
350   DRAW"c3;bm140,80;ta=beta;u40r40d40r10d10160u10r10"
360 NEXT ALPH
```

SUMMARY

Simple animation was created in this chapter by drawing an object, erasing it, and then redrawing it in a new position.

- Linear motion of a painted object was simulated by using:
  1. LINE with the BOX-FILL option to draw and PAINT to erase
  2. DRAW with the PAINT option and relative moves
- The WINDOW statement was introduced to demonstrate how objects can be placed on the video screen using either the natural (Cartesian) coordinate system or the screen coordinate system.
- Rotary motion of clock hands was simulated by
  1. LINE with the SIN and COS functions
  2. DRAW with the TURN ANGLE (TA) option
- Rotary motion of a polygon was simulated using DRAW with the TURN ANGLE option.

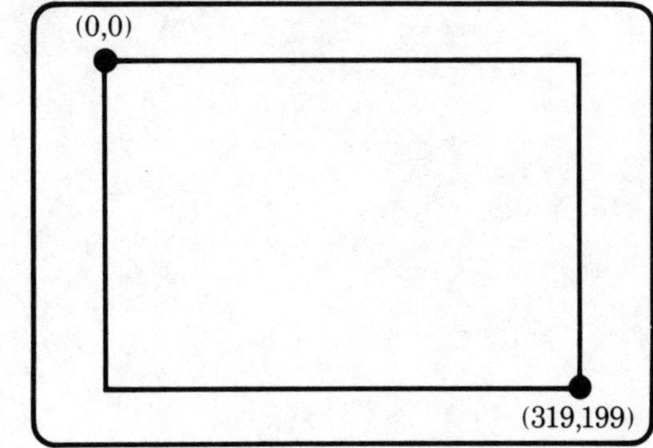


```
WINDOW SCREEN(0,0)-(319,199)
```

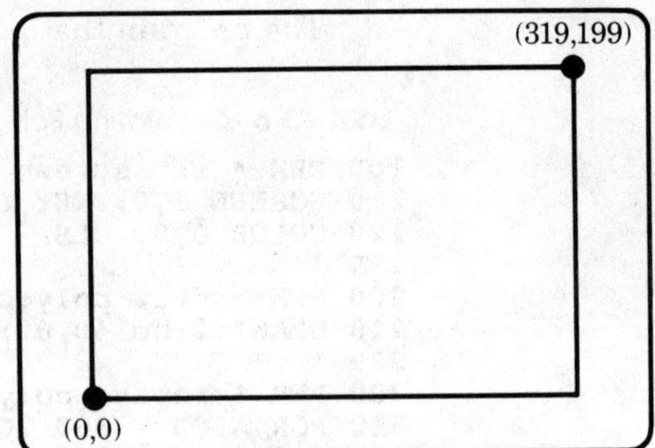

WINDOW (0,0)-(319,199)

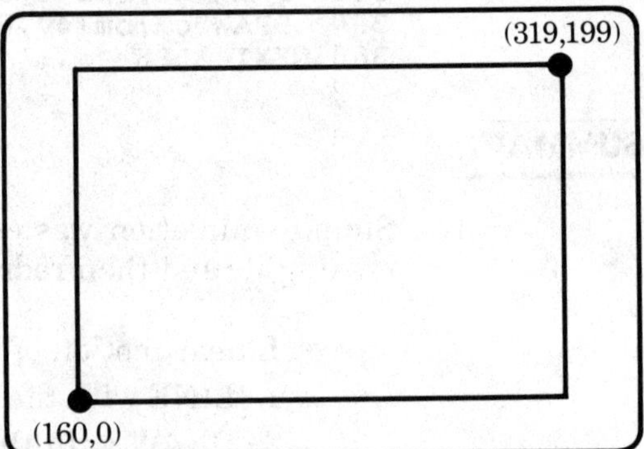

WINDOW (160,0)-(319,199)

7

MORE ANIMATION

Graphics Statements, Functions,
and Terms Introduced

GET
PUT
action
POINT

The objective of this chapter is to teach you more sophisticated methods of producing animation. Rather than moving individual pixels or lines that make up a shape, these new methods will let you move an entire shape.

BASIC statements and terms that we assume you are familiar with are all those of previous chapters, plus arrays, AND, DIM, HEX\$, LPRINT, OR, PEEK, and VARPTR.

BASIC statements and terms that are explained are GET, PUT, action, and POINT.

The movement in earlier animation programs was slow, producing jerky actions. BASICA's GET and PUT commands can be used to produce pictures faster and more easily than previously used methods.

> Note: GET and PUT graphics statements should not be confused with GET and PUT file statements.

GET STATEMENT

The GET statement allows you to store the contents of a rectanglar area of the screen into an array.

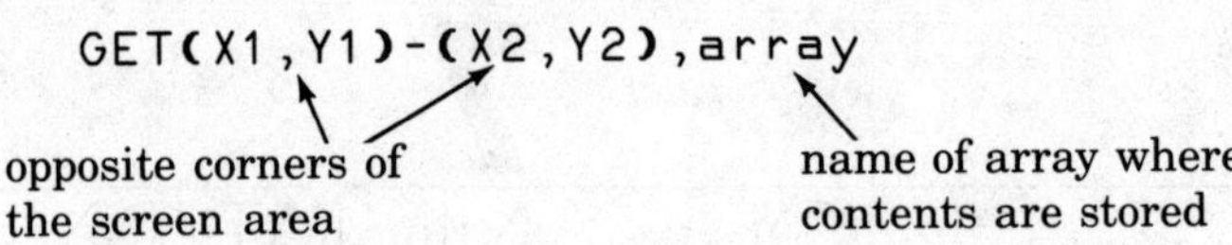

A screen area saved by GET in array A is shown in Fig. 7–1 for the statement

$$GET(40,100)-(55,110),A$$

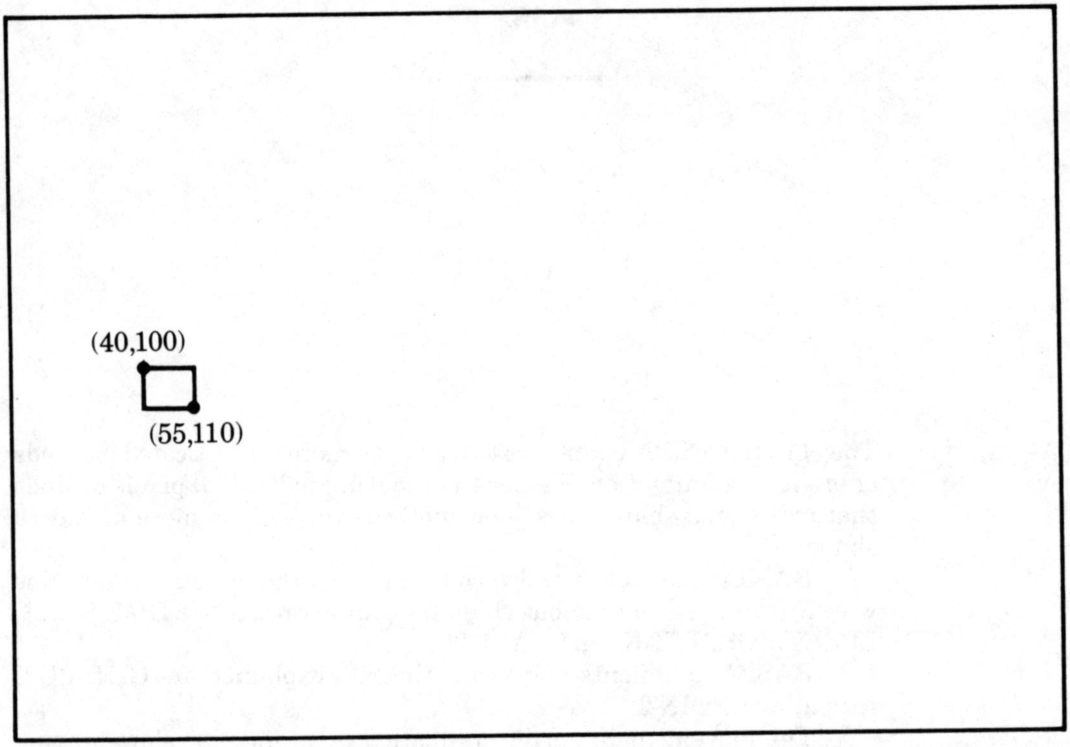

FIG. 7–1. GET array A

Storage is allotted for the array by a DIMENSION statement (DIM). The size to which the array is dimensioned can be determined from

$$BYTES = 4 + INT((X * bitsperpixel + 7) / 8) * Y$$

where X = horizontal length of screen area, Y = vertical length of screen area, bitsperpixel = 2 in medium-resolution, and bitsperpixel = 1 in high-resolution.

For the previous example:

```
X = 55-40 = 15

Y = 110-100 = 10

bitsperpixel = 2

BYTES = 4+INT((15*2+7)/8)*10
      = 4+INT(37/8)*10
      = 4+40
      = 44
```

The bytes per element of an array are 2 for integer, 4 for single precision, and 8 for double precision. Therefore, we must use an array with at least 44/4 (or 11) elements. The dimension statement would be

```
DIM A(11)
```

GET reads the colors of the points within the specified area into the specified array. It is possible to look at the data in the array if an integer array is used. The X dimension is in element 0 of the array, and the Y dimension is in element 1 of the array. Each element occupies 2 bytes of memory. The data for the colored points fill out the balance of the array.

Listing 7–1 draws a rectangle at the outer boundary of the example used for the GET area of Fig. 7–1. It then prints out the values of array A in hexadecimal format. Color values of 1, 2, and 3 are used to draw the rectangle so that you can see the change produced in the data values as shown in Table 7–1. Keep in mind that integers occupy 2 bytes of memory and that they are stored with the low byte of the value first, followed by the high byte.

LOCATION	CONTENT	
4284	20	= X dimension
4285	0	= 020 Hex = 32
4286	B	= Y dimension
4287	0	= 00B Hex = 11

The program of Listing 7–1 draws the rectangle of Fig. 7–1 and sends the hexadecimal contents of array A to a printer. The VARPTR function is used to find the area of memory used to store the array. This function returns the address in memory of the variable A in our program. It assigns the value to N in line 310.

$$N = VARPTR(A(0)) \text{ TO } VARPTR(A(0))+47$$

The values of N and the contents of N are sent to the printer by the LPRINT statement in line 320. Each memory location in the block is accessed by HEX$(PEEK(N)) in line 320. The PEEK function returns the contents of the specified memory location (N). The HEX$ function then converts the decimal value returned by PEEK(N) to a string representation of its hexadecimal equivalent. We printed the values in hexadecimal format as this will be used in Chapter 9 when sending data directly to screen memory. Data is sent to the display screen in much the same way as data is stored in an array's block of memory. A typical printed output is shown in Table 7–1. Your address values may be different.

LISTING 7–1. GET Values

```
100 REM * dimension array and set screen *
110 SCREEN 1: KEY OFF: CLS
120 DIM A(11)
199 '
200 REM * INPUT, draw, and GET *
210 INPUT "color code of rectangle";C:CLS
220 LINE(40,100)-(55,110),C,B
230 GET(40,100)-(55,110),A
299 '
300 REM * print array data *
310 FOR N = VARPTR(A(0)) TO VARPTR(A(0))+47
320   LPRINT N; HEX$(PEEK(N))
330 NEXT N
```

> Note: Both PUT and GET work significantly faster in medium-resolution when X1 MOD 4 is equal to 0 (X1 is evenly divisible by 4), and in high-resolution when X1 MOD 8 is equal to 0.

PUT STATEMENT

There is no reason to save an array with GET unless you intend to access the data later in the program. The array is accessed by the PUT statement, which writes colors onto the specified area of the screen.

$$PUT(X,Y),array [,action]$$

If X dimension in LINE is specified you get X dimension on printout as 2 for Y. If specified as 0 you get Y dimension printed out as 1

TABLE 7–1

GET ARRAY

COLOR CODE 1	COLOR CODE 2	COLOR CODE 3	
4284 20	4284 20	4284 20	} ← X dimension
4285 0	4285 0	4285 0	
4286 B	4286 B	4286 B	} ← Y dimension
4287 0	4287 0	4287 0	
4288 55	4288 AA	4288 FF	← color codes for points
4289 55	4289 AA	4289 FF	
4290 55	4290 AA	4290 FF	
4291 55	4291 AA	4291 FF	
4292 40	4292 80	4292 C0	
4293 0	4293 0	4293 0	
4294 0	4294 0	4294 0	
4295 1	4295 2	4295 3	
4296 40	4296 80	4296 C0	
4297 0	4297 0	4297 0	
4298 0	4298 0	4298 0	
4299 1	4299 2	4299 3	
4300 40	4300 80	4300 C0	
4301 0	4301 0	4301 0	
4302 0	4302 0	4302 0	
4303 1	4303 2	4303 3	
4304 40	4304 80	4304 C0	
4305 0	4305 0	4305 0	
4306 0	4306 0	4306 0	
4307 1	4307 2	4307 3	
4308 40	4308 80	4308 C0	
4309 0	4309 0	4309 0	
4310 0	4310 0	4310 0	
4311 1	4311 2	4311 3	
4312 40	4312 80	4312 C0	
4313 0	4313 0	4313 0	
4314 0	4314 0	4314 0	
4315 1	4315 2	4315 3	
4316 40	4316 80	4316 C0	
4317 0	4317 0	4317 0	
4318 0	4318 0	4318 0	
4319 1	4319 2	4319 3	
4320 40	4320 80	4320 C0	
4321 0	4321 0	4321 0	
4322 0	4322 0	4322 0	
4323 1	4323 2	4323 3	
4324 40	4324 80	4324 C0	
4325 0	4325 0	4325 0	
4326 0	4326 0	4326 0	
4327 1	4327 2	4327 3	
4328 55	4328 AA	4328 FF	
4329 55	4329 AA	4329 FF	
4330 55	4330 AA	4330 FF	
4331 55	4331 AA	4331 FF	

Only the top-left coordinate of the array is needed to place the array data on the screen. The name of the array must be the same as that used to store the data by the GET statement. The action to be performed is selected from

PSET PRESET XOR OR AND

PSET simply stores the data from the array onto the screen, obliterating any color that may be there. The function performed by PUT with the PSET action is the true reverse of the GET statement.

PRESET produces the negative image of PSET. A value of 0 in the array causes that point to have color number 3, and vice versa. A value of 1 in the array causes that point to have color number 2, and vice versa.

XOR (exclusive OR) is effective in producing animation. It causes points on the screen to be inverted where a point exists in the array image. When an image is PUT against a complex background twice, the background is restored to its original color. This allows you to move an object around without destroying the background.

OR is used to superimpose the image of the array onto the existing screen image.

AND is used when you want to transfer an array image of a given color that already exists on the screen.

The effects on screen points using AND, OR, and XOR are given in Table 7–2.

TABLE 7–2

EFFECT OF PUT ACTION

		XOR	OR	AND
		ARRAY COLOR	ARRAY COLOR	ARRAY COLOR
		0 1 2 3	0 1 2 3	0 1 2 3
	0	0 1 2 3	0 1 2 3	0 0 0 0
Screen	1	1 0 3 2	1 1 3 3	0 1 0 1
Color	2	2 3 0 1	2 3 2 3	0 0 2 2
	3	3 2 1 0	3 3 3 3	0 1 2 3

Listing 7–2 is a program that allows you to investigate PUT with any one of XOR, OR, or AND actions. It draws a filled circle and a filled rectangle. You may choose, by input, any of the three specified actions. You may also choose the colors for the rectangle and the circle. By varying the colors and the actions, you may verify the color values given in Table 7–2.

The AND and OR logical operators are used in lines 220 and 420 through 440. The AND operator returns a value of true only when both conditions being compared are true. Thus, in line 220, the IF condition will be true only if all the following are true: A$<>"AND", A$<>"OR", A$<>"XOR", A$<>"and", A$<>"or", and A$<>"xor". When all these conditions are true, a "bad input" has been made, and the THEN statement is executed. If one of the conditions is false, a correct input has been made, and the program continues without executing the THEN statement.

The OR operator returns a true value if either one or both of the compared conditions are true. The OR operations in lines 420, 430, and 440 determine which subroutine is executed.

Notice the array used in this program is designated A%. The percent symbol (%) following the variable A declares that its values are to be integers. Integers use fewer memory locations when stored.

LISTING 7–2. Test AND, OR, and XOR

```
100 REM * dimension array and set screen *
110 DIM A%(24)
120 SCREEN 1: KEY OFF: CLS
199 '
200 REM * input section *
210 INPUT"AND, OR, or XOR";A$
220 IF A$<>"AND" AND A$<>"OR" AND A$<>"XOR"
                AND A$<>"and" AND A$<>"or" AND A$<>"xor"
                            THEN PRINT "bad input": GOTO 210
230 INPUT"Color code of rectangle";R
240 INPUT"Color code of circle";C
299 '
300 REM * draw and paint figures *
310 LINE(40,100)-(55,110),R,BF
320 CIRCLE(290,100),20,C
330 PAINT(290,100),C,C
399 '
400 REM * GET and PUT *
410 GET(40,100)-(55,110),A%
420 IF A$="AND" OR A$="and" THEN GOSUB 1010
430 IF A$="OR" OR A$="or" THEN GOSUB 1110
440 IF A$="XOR" OR A$="xor" THEN GOSUB 1210
499 '
900 END
999 '
1000 REM * AND subroutine *
1010 PUT(265,100),A%,AND
1020 RETURN
1099 '
1100 REM * OR subroutine *
1110 PUT(265,100),A%,OR
1120 RETURN
1199 '
1200 REM * XOR subroutine *
1210 PUT(265,100),A%,XOR
1220 RETURN
```

ANIMATION BY GET AND PUT

When an object is to be animated, it must first be drawn. Its shape and color is then stored in an array by a GET statement. You only need to GET the array once. The object is then moved by a series of PUT statements. As an example, consider the simple car shown in Fig. 7–2.

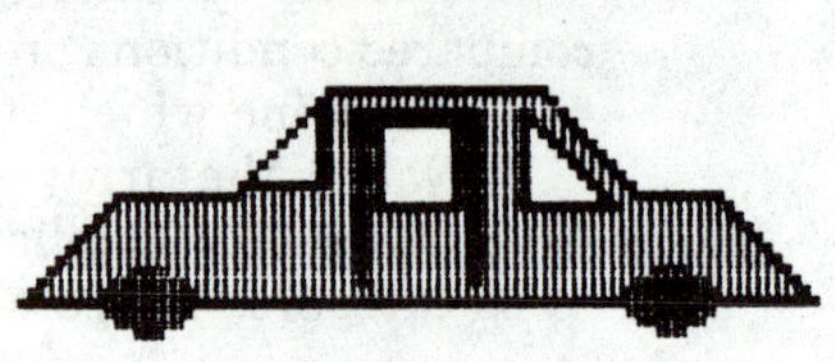

FIG. 7–2. Car

Since the car is facing left, we will place the car near the right side of the screen. The array will be dimensioned for 276 elements. The car is drawn with the following statements:

```
200 REM * draw car *                          ←——————body shape
210 DRAW"bm300,50;h1018h10122g1d818be8g9112g10r82"
220 DRAW"bm253,48;u16r12d16"                   ←—————— door
230 DRAW"bm255,33;r8d818u8"                     ←————— door window
240 DRAW"bm270,41;u9f919"                       ←————— back window
250 PAINT(290,48),1,3                           ←————— paint the body
260 CIRCLE(285,50),4,2: PAINT(285,50),2,2       ←————— back wheel
270 CIRCLE(231,50),4,2: PAINT(231,50),2,2       ←———— front wheel
```

After the car is drawn, it is placed in an array, named A%, by

```
300 REM * store picture *
310 GET(218,30)-(302,54),A%
```

Finally, the car must be moved across the screen. We have chosen steps of 2 in the negative X direction. We must also remember to erase the previous image. In this first attempt, we will merely tack on a blank 2 by 24 area.

A FOR-NEXT loop provides the change in X.

```
400 REM * move car *
410 FOR X = 216 TO 24 STEP -2
420   PUT(X,30),A%,PSET
430   FOR DELAY = 1 TO 50: NEXT DELAY
440 NEXT X
```

The complete program is shown in Listing 7–3. Enter and run the program.

LISTING 7–3. Moving Car

```
100 REM * dimension array & set screen *
110 DIM A%(276)
120 SCREEN 1: KEY OFF: CLS
190 '
200 REM * draw car *
210 DRAW"bm300,50;h1018h10122g1d818be8g9112g10r82"
220 DRAW"bm253,48;ul6rl2dl6"
230 DRAW"bm255,33;r8d818u8"
240 DRAW"bm270,41;u9f919"
250 PAINT(290,48),1,3
260 CIRCLE(285,50),4,2: PAINT(285,50),2,2
270 CIRCLE(231,50),4,2: PAINT(231,50),2,2
290 '
300 REM * store picture *
310 GET(218,30)-(302,54),A%
390 '
400 REM * move car *
410 FOR X = 216 TO 24 STEP -2
420   PUT(X,30),A%,PSET
430   FOR DELAY = 1 TO 50: NEXT DELAY
440 NEXT X
```

The speed of the car can be controlled by the delay at line 430. The speed can also be increased by enlarging the step of the FOR-NEXT loop (line 410). If the step is increased, the blank area at the rear of the car must correspondingly be widened. The DIM statement of line 110 may have to be increased.

EXAMPLE

```
410 FOR X = 214 TO 24 STEP-4

310 GET(218,30)-(304,54)
```
— 4 units beyond car

Adding the trailing blank area at the rear of a moving object works fine when no objects are pictured in the background. However, a problem arises for complex backgrounds. The program of Listing 7–4 is the same as that of Listing 7–3 except that a painted house is placed on the screen so that the image of the car passes in front of the house.

LISTING 7–4. Car Moving Past House

```
100 REM * dimension array & set screen *
110 DIM A%(276)
120 SCREEN 1: KEY OFF: CLS
190 '
200 REM * draw car *
210 DRAW"bm300,50;h1018h10122g1d818be8g9112g10r82"
220 DRAW"bm253,48;u16r12d16"
230 DRAW"bm255,33;r8d818u8"
240 DRAW"bm270,41;u9f919"
250 PAINT(290,48),1,3
260 CIRCLE(285,50),4,2: PAINT(285,50),2,2
270 CIRCLE(231,50),4,2: PAINT(231,50),2,2
290 '
300 REM * store picture *
310 GET(218,30)-(304,54),A%
320 DRAW"bm100,45;u26g5e24f24h5d26138"
330 PAINT(110,40),2,2
390 '
400 REM * move car *
410 FOR X = 216 TO 24 STEP -2
420   PUT(X,30),A%,PSET
430   FOR DELAY = 1 TO 50: NEXT DELAY
440 NEXT X
```

house added to Listing 7–3.

Remember, the PSET action of the PUT statement uses the background color for setting all points that are not actually a part of the image.

EXAMPLE

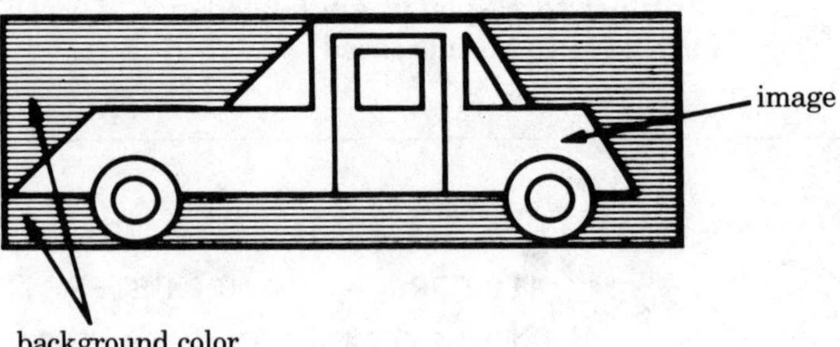

As the car moves in front of the house, the background color of the array erases the house image, as shown in Fig. 7–3.

After the car has passed, the bottom portion of the house has been completely obliterated, as shown in Fig. 7–4.

FIG. 7–3. Car erasing house

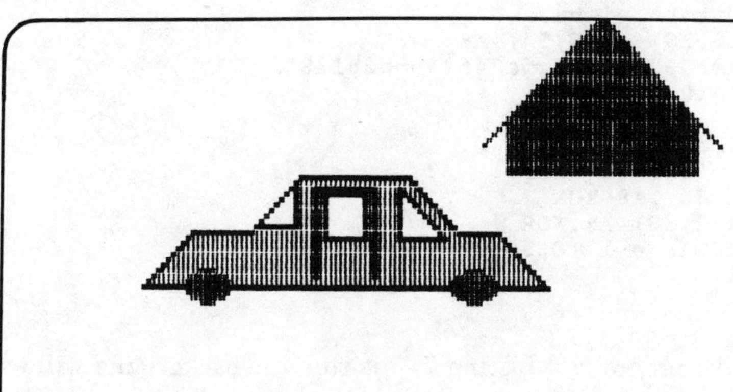

FIG. 7–4. House destroyed

We can turn to the XOR action option of the PUT statement to avoid erasing the house. The program of Listing 7–4 is modified in the following way to accomplish this.

Line 310 is changed to

```
310 GET(216,30)-(300,54),A%
```

The FOR-NEXT loop is changed to

```
410 FOR X = 216 TO 22 STEP-2
420   PUT(X,30),A%,XOR          ← turn off old image
430   PUT(X-2,30),A%,XOR        ← turn on new image
440   FOR DELAY = 1 TO 50: NEXT DELAY
450 NEXT X
```

LISTING 7–5. Moving Car with XOR

```
100 REM * dimension array & set screen *
110 DIM A%(276)
120 SCREEN 1: KEY OFF: CLS
199 '
200 REM * draw car *
210 DRAW"bm300,50;h1018h10122g1d818be8g9112g10r82"
220 DRAW"bm253,48;ul6rl2dl6"
230 DRAW"bm255,33;r8d818u8"
240 DRAW"bm270,41;u9f919"
250 PAINT(290,48),1,3
260 CIRCLE(285,50),4,2: PAINT(285,50),2,2
270 CIRCLE(231,50),4,2: PAINT(231,50),2,2
299 '
300 REM * store picture *
310 GET(216,30)-(300,54),A%
320 DRAW"bm100,45;u26g5e24f24h5d26138"
330 PAINT(110,40),2,2
399 '
400 REM * move car *
410 FOR X = 216 TO 22 STEP -2
420   PUT(X,30),A%,XOR
430   PUT(X-2,30),A%,XOR
440   FOR DELAY = 1 TO 50: NEXT DELAY
450 NEXT X
```

When the program of Listing 7–5 is run, the background will be unchanged when the car moves in front of the house. There is a change in the color of the area where the car and house overlap, as shown in Fig. 7–5.

When the car has passed, the house has been restored to its original shape and color, as seen in Fig. 7–6.

MOTION IN A FIXED AREA

The Moving Car program (Listing 7–3) illustrated a fixed object moving across the screen. The following program demonstrates how to create animation at a fixed area of the screen.

A simple figure, representing a human, is drawn in three different positions. LINE statements are used to draw the figures.

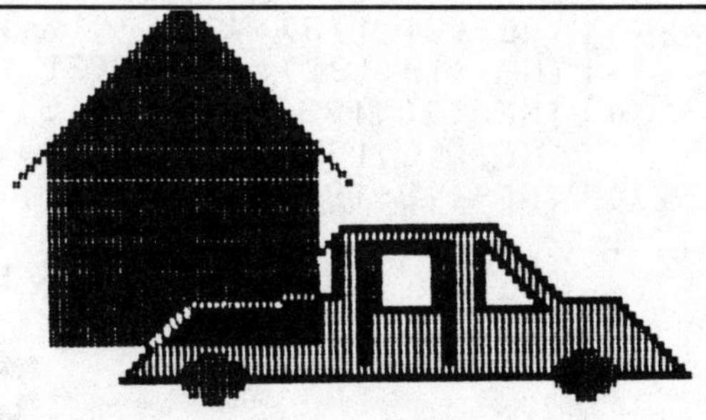

FIG. 7—5. Car and house XORed

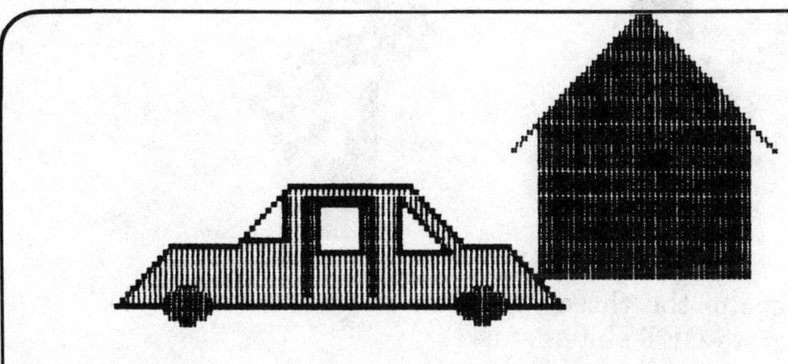

FIG. 7—6. House restored

EXAMPLE

```
200 REM * draw figure 1 *
210 LINE(11,189)-(11,188): LINE-(12,188): LINE-(12,185)
220 LINE-(14,183): LINE-(14,179): LINE-(11,182):
    LINE-(10,181): LINE-(13,178)
230 LINE-(15,178): LINE-(15,177): LINE-(14,176):
    LINE-(14,174): LINE-(17,174)
240 LINE-(17,176): LINE-(16,177): LINE-(16,178):
    LINE-(17,178): LINE-(20,175)
```

```
250 LINE-(21,176): LINE-(17,180): LINE-(17,185):
    LINE-(19,183): LINE-(21,185)
260 LINE-(20,186): LINE-(19,185): LINE-(17,187):
    LINE-(15,185): LINE-(13,186)
270 LINE-(13,189): LINE-(11,189)
```

This is the figure drawn by lines 200–270:

Lines 300–370 and 400–460 draw similar figures:

The images of the three positions are stored in three different arrays by separate GET statements.

```
500 REM * store figures *
510 GET(10,174)-(21,190),A%     ←————image 1
520 GET(25,174)-(36,190),B%     ←————image 2
530 GET(40,174)-(51,190),C%     ←————image 3
```

The images are repeatedly displayed in the sequence ABCB to create the illusion of movement.

```
600 REM * PUT figures for animation *
610 PUT(150,100),A%,PSET
620 FOR DELAY = 1 TO 50: NEXT DELAY
630 PUT(150,100),B%,PSET
640 FOR DELAY = 1 TO 50: NEXT DELAY
650 PUT(150,100),C%,PSET
660 FOR DELAY = 1 TO 50: NEXT DELAY
670 PUT(150,100),B%,PSET
680 FOR DELAY = 1 TO 50: NEXT DELAY
690 GOTO 610
```

The three shapes that are drawn are displayed at the bottom left corner of the screen, as shown in Figs. 7–7(a), 7–7(b), and 7–7(c). The animation occurs near the center of the screen, as shown in the same figures. You'll have to run the program to see the image appear to move. The complete program is given in Listing 7–6.

LISTING 7–6. Moving Man

```
100 REM * dimension arrays & set screen *
110 SCREEN 1: KEY OFF: CLS
120 DIM A%(28),B%(28),C%(28)
199 '
200 REM * draw figure 1 *
210 LINE(11,189)-(11,188): LINE-(12,188): LINE-(12,185)
220 LINE-(14,183): LINE-(14,179): LINE-(11,182): LINE-(10,181): LINE-
(13,178)
230 LINE-(15,178): LINE-(15,177): LINE-(14,176): LINE-(14,174): LINE-
(17,174)
240 LINE-(17,176): LINE-(16,177): LINE-(16,178): LINE-(17,178): LINE-
(20,175)
250 LINE-(21,176): LINE-(17,180): LINE-(17,185): LINE-(19,183): LINE-
(21,185)
260 LINE-(20,186): LINE-(19,185): LINE-(17,187): LINE-(15,185): LINE-
(13,186)
270 LINE-(13,189): LINE-(11,189)
299 '
300 REM * draw figure 2 *
310 LINE(26,189)-(26,188): LINE-(27,188): LINE-(27,185)
320 LINE-(29,183): LINE-(29,179): LINE-(26,182): LINE-(25,181): LINE-
(28,178)
330 LINE-(30,178): LINE-(30,177): LINE-(29,176): LINE-(29,174): LINE-
(32,174)
340 LINE-(32,176): LINE-(31,177): LINE-(31,178): LINE-(33,178): LINE-
(36,181)
350 LINE-(35,182): LINE-(32,179): LINE-(32,189): LINE-(30,189): LINE-
(30,188)
360 LINE-(31,188): LINE-(31,185): LINE-(29,185): LINE-(28,186): LINE-
(28,189)
370 LINE-(26,189)
399 '
400 REM * draw figure 3 *
410 LINE(45,189)-(45,188): LINE-(46,188): LINE-(46,185): LINE-(45,185
): LINE-(45,183)
420 LINE(46,185)-(45,186): LINE-(44,186): LINE-(44,180): LINE-(40,176
): LINE-(41,175)
430 LINE-(44,178): LINE-(45,178): LINE-(45,177): LINE-(44,176): LINE-
(44,174)
440 LINE-(47,174): LINE-(47,176): LINE-(46,177): LINE-(46,178): LINE-
(48,178)
450 LINE-(51,181): LINE-(50,182): LINE-(47,179): LINE-(47,184): LINE-
(48,183)
460 LINE-(49,184): LINE-(50,183): LINE-(48,181): LINE-(47,182): LINE-
(47,189): LINE-(45,189)
499 '
500 REM * store figures *
510 GET(10,174)-(21,190),A%
520 GET(25,174)-(36,190),B%
```

```
530 GET(40,174)-(51,190),C%
599 '
600 REM * put figures for animation *
610 PUT(150,100),A%,PSET
620 FOR DELAY=1 TO 50: NEXT DELAY
630 PUT(150,100),B%,PSET
640 FOR DELAY = 1 TO 50: NEXT DELAY
650 PUT(150,100),C%,PSET
660 FOR DELAY = 1 TO 50: NEXT DELAY
670 PUT(150,100),B%,PSET
680 FOR DELAY = 1 TO 50: NEXT DELAY
690 GOTO 610
```

FIG. 7–7(a). Moving man (image 1)

FIG. 7–7(b). Moving man (image 2)

FIG. 7–7(c). Moving man (image 3)

TWO-WAY MOTION

In the program of Listing 7–5, we moved a fixed object across the screen. Then we produced a moving object at a fixed location in the program of Listing 7–6. Now, we'll combine the two types of movement by having our moving man cross the screen.

The moving man is created and stored in the same way as in the previous program. However, the PUT and GET statements are changed. After the images are stored, the screen is cleared to erase the original drawings.

```
500 REM * store figures *
510 GET(10,174)-(24,190),A%     GET statements
520 GET(25,174)-(39,190),B%     changed to include
530 GET(40,174)-(54,190),C%     blank area
540 CLS                         erases original images
```

The PUT statements are changed so that the man will move across the screen. The sequence of PUTs and moves is

B, move, A, B, move, C, B, move, A, B, move, C, B, etc.

```
600 REM * PUT figures for animation *
610 PUT(299,100),B%,PSET            start with image B
620 FOR DELAY = 1 TO 50: NEXT DELAY
630 FOR X = 296 TO 16 STEP-6
640   PUT(X,100),A%,PSET            move, then image A
650   FOR DELAY = 1 TO 50: NEXT DELAY
660   PUT(X,100),B%,PSET            image B
670   FOR DELAY = 1 TO 50: NEXT DELAY
680   PUT(X-3,100),C%,PSET          move, then image C
```

```
690  FOR DELAY = 1 TO 50: NEXT DELAY
700  PUT(X-3,100),B%,PSET              ——image B
710  FOR DELAY = 1 TO 50: NEXT DELAY
720 NEXT X
```

Figure 7–8 shows the original images drawn at the bottom-left corner of the screen as in the previous program.

FIG. 7–8. Images for animated man

Figures 7–9(a), 7–9(b), 7–9(c), and 7–9(d) show the animated positions as the image moves across the screen from right to left. The complete program is given in Listing 7–7.

FIG. 7–9(a). Animated man (array C%)

FIG. 7–9(b). Animated man (array B%)

FIG. 7–9(c). Animated man (array A%)

FIG. 7–9(d). Animated man (end of run)

```
100 REM * dimension arrays & set screen *
110 SCREEN 1: KEY OFF: CLS
120 DIM A%(36),B%(36),C%(36)
190 '
200 REM * draw figure 1 *
210 LINE(11,189)-(11,188): LINE-(12,188): LINE-(12,185)
220 LINE-(14,183): LINE-(14,179): LINE-(11,182): LINE-(10,181): LINE-
(13,178)
230 LINE-(15,178): LINE-(15,177): LINE-(14,176): LINE-(14,174): LINE-
(17,174)
240 LINE-(17,176): LINE-(16,177): LINE-(16,178): LINE-(17,178): LINE-
(20,175)
250 LINE-(21,176): LINE-(17,180): LINE-(17,185): LINE-(19,183): LINE-
(21,185)
260 LINE-(20,186): LINE-(19,185): LINE-(17,187): LINE-(15,185): LINE-
(13,186)
270 LINE-(13,189): LINE-(11,189)
299 '
300 REM * draw figure 2 *
310 LINE(26,189)-(26,188): LINE-(27,188): LINE-(27,185)
320 LINE-(29,183): LINE-(29,179): LINE-(26,182): LINE-(25,181): LINE-
(28,178)
330 LINE-(30,178): LINE-(30,177): LINE-(29,176): LINE-(29,174): LINE-
(32,174)
340 LINE-(32,176): LINE-(31,177): LINE-(31,178): LINE-(33,178): LINE-
(36,181)
350 LINE-(35,182): LINE-(32,179): LINE-(32,189): LINE-(30,189): LINE-
(30,188)
360 LINE-(31,188): LINE-(31,185): LINE-(29,185): LINE-(28,186): LINE-
(28,189)
370 LINE-(26,189)
399 '
400 REM * draw figure 3 *
410 LINE(45,189)-(45,188): LINE-(46,188): LINE-(46,185): LINE-(45,185
): LINE-(45,183)
420 LINE(46,185)-(45,186): LINE-(44,186): LINE-(44,180): LINE-(40,176
): LINE-(41,175)
430 LINE-(44,178): LINE-(45,178): LINE-(45,177): LINE-(44,176): LINE-
(44,174)
440 LINE-(47,174): LINE-(47,176): LINE-(46,177): LINE-(46,178): LINE-
(48,178)
450 LINE-(51,181): LINE-(50,182): LINE-(47,179): LINE-(47,184): LINE-
(48,183)
460 LINE-(49,184): LINE-(50,183): LINE-(48,181): LINE-(47,182): LINE-
(47,189): LINE-(45,189)
499 '
500 REM * store figures *
510 GET(10,174)-(24,190),A%
520 GET(25,174)-(39,190),B%
530 GET(40,174)-(54,190),C%
540 CLS
599 '
600 REM * put figures for animation *
610 PUT(299,100),B%,PSET
620 FOR DELAY=1 TO 50: NEXT DELAY
630 FOR X = 296 TO 16 STEP -6
640   PUT(X,100),A%,PSET
650   FOR DELAY = 1 TO 50: NEXT DELAY
```

```
660   PUT(X,100),B%,PSET
670   FOR DELAY = 1 TO 50: NEXT DELAY
680   PUT(X-3,100),C%,PSET
690   FOR DELAY = 1 TO 50: NEXT DELAY
700   PUT(X-3,100),B%,PSET
710   FOR DELAY = 1 TO 50: NEXT DELAY
720 NEXT X
```

ANIMATION BY DECISION

Sometimes you may wish for certain types of animation to occur at specific times, or when specific events take place. The Hurdler program of Listing 7–8 demonstrates that situation.

The animation sequence changes when a specified letter on the keyboard is pressed. A different kind of action takes place when the keyboard letter is not pressed at certain times during a run of the program.

Images used in the program are shown in Fig. 7–10. The three "running" images of previous programs are drawn at the lower-left corner of the screen as before. A fourth image, the runner in a hurdling position, is added along with a hurdle that has been knocked down. The runner images are drawn in white (color 3, palette 1), and the hurdle is drawn in magenta (color 2).

FIG. 7–10. PUT figures

After the images are drawn in the lower-left corner, the arrays are stored by GET statements, and the screen is cleared. An additional blank array (F%) is also stored. This will be used to erase small areas of the screen during the animation.

```
600 REM * store figures *
610 GET(10,174)-(24,190),A%
620 GET(25,174)-(39,190),B%        ←——— 3 previous figures
630 GET(40,174)-(54,190),C%
640 GET(55,168)-(69,184),D%        ←——— hurdler position
650 GET(70,185)-(74,190),E%        ←——— hurdle down
660 GET(85,168)-(99,184),F%        ←——— blank area
670 CLS
```

Three upright hurdles, uniformly spaced, are then drawn as shown in Fig. 7–11. The hurdles are drawn in magenta (color 2).

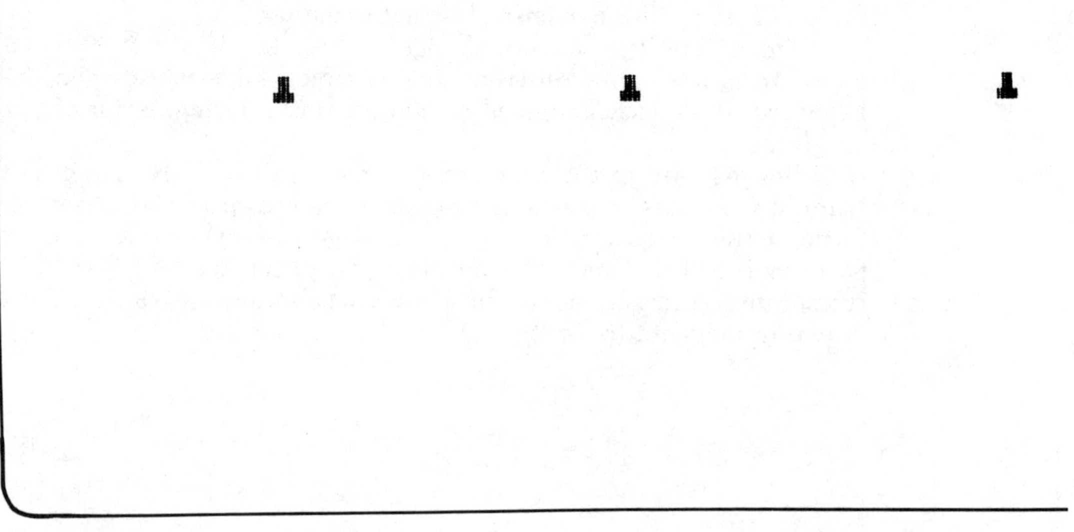

FIG. 7–11. Hurdles

The running sequence is similar to that of Listing 7–7. However, a test is performed after each image of the sequence is drawn. The test is made in a subroutine (beginning at line 2000) to see if the runner and a standing hurdle occupy the same area. If they do, the hurdle will be knocked down. The standing hurdle and the runner will be erased. The standing hurdle is replaced by the fallen hurdle, and the runner's position is moved ahead 18 spaces.

EXAMPLE

```
830 PUT(X,100),A%,XOR
840 GOSUB 2010: IF Q=1 THEN GOTO 1010
    .                           ↖
    .                            hurdle was hit if Q=1
    .
2000 REM * test points *
```

```
2010 IF POINT(X+3,115)=1 OR POINT(X+4,115)=1
     OR POINT(X+1,112)=1 OR POINT(X+2,112)=1
     OR POINT(X+3,112)=1 OR POINT(X+10,112)=1
     THEN PUT(X-2,100),F%,PSET:
     PUT(X-2,115),E%,PSET: X=X-18: Q=1
2020 RETURN
```

When the runner and the hurdle occupy the same space, a combination of colors 3 (the runner) and 2 (the hurdle) occurs. Since the runner's image is created with PUT's XOR action, the color displayed when color 2 and 3 are XORed is color 1 (see Table 7–2). This condition indicates a hit and is detected by the POINT function, which has the format

$$POINT(X,Y)$$

screen position

This function returns the color code of the specified point on the screen. In medium-resolution valid return values are 0, 1, 2, and 3. In high-resolution only 0 and 1 are valid.

Points tested in the subroutine are:

(X+3,115) and
(X+4,115) at the hurdle's base; and
(X+1,112),
(X+2,112),
(X+3,112), and
(X+10,112) at the top of the hurdle.

All these points are tested because of the many ways the possible hurdler's positions may intersect a standing hurdle.

During each sequence of the three running positions, the keyboard is scanned to see if the letter *j* (j for jump) has been pressed. To successfully clear a hurdle, the *j* key must be pressed when the runner's image is near a hurdle. If the key is pressed when the runner is too far away, the runner will come down on the hurdle in his descent. If the key is not pressed soon enough, the runner will hit the hurdle before the jump. The jump is accomplished in a subroutine (line 3000).

```
850 IF INKEY$ = "j" THEN GOSUB 3010
```

lowercase letter *j*

```
3000 REM * hurdle subroutine *
3010 PUT(X,100),F%,AND
3020 FOR N = 0 TO 21 STEP 3
3030   PUT(X-N,94),D%,XOR
```

```
3040   FOR DELAY = 1 TO 50: NEXT DELAY
3050   PUT(X-N,94),D%,XOR
3060 NEXT N
3070 X = X-24
3080 PUT(X,100),A%,XOR
3090 RETURN
```

The runner is shown clearing hurdle 1 in Fig. 7–12. A runner hits a hurdle in Fig. 7–13, and the hurdle that was knocked down is shown in Fig. 7–14. The complete program is given in Listing 7–8.

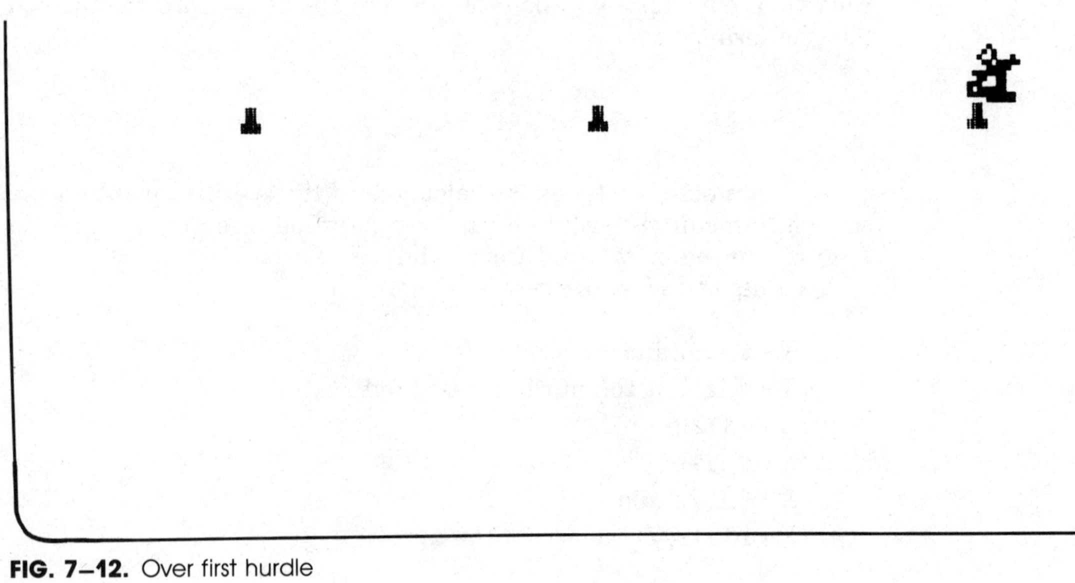

FIG. 7–12. Over first hurdle

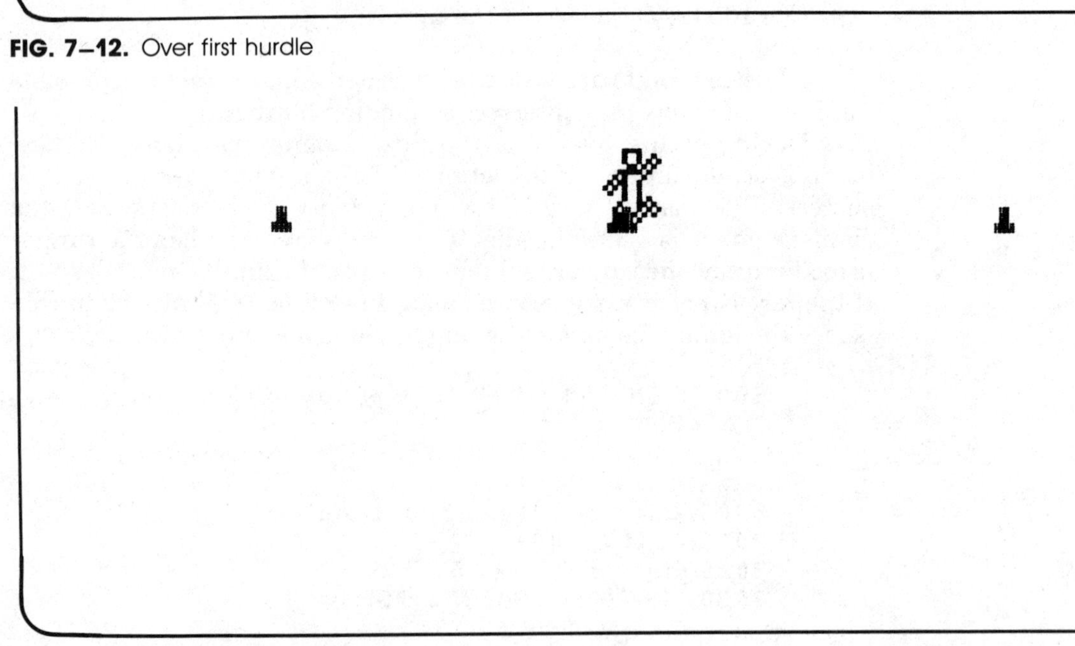

FIG. 7–13. Hurdler hits hurdle

FIG. 7–14. Hurdle down

LISTING 7–8. Hurdler

```
100 REM * dimension arrays & set screen *
110 SCREEN 1: KEY OFF: CLS
120 DIM A%(36),B%(36),C%(36),D%(36),E%(12),F%(36)
199 '
200 REM * draw figure 1 *
210 LINE(11,189)-(11,188): LINE-(12,188): LINE-(12,185)
220 LINE-(14,183): LINE-(14,179): LINE-(11,182): LINE-(10,181): LINE-
(13,178)
230 LINE-(15,178): LINE-(15,177): LINE-(14,176): LINE-(14,174): LINE-
(17,174)
240 LINE-(17,176): LINE-(16,177): LINE-(16,178): LINE-(17,178): LINE-
(20,175)
250 LINE-(21,176): LINE-(17,180): LINE-(17,185): LINE-(19,183): LINE-
(21,185)
260 LINE-(20,186): LINE-(19,185): LINE-(17,187): LINE-(15,185): LINE-
(13,186)
270 LINE-(13,189): LINE-(11,189)
299 '
300 REM * draw figure 2 *
310 LINE(26,189)-(26,188): LINE-(27,188): LINE-(27,185)
320 LINE-(29,183): LINE-(29,179): LINE-(26,182): LINE-(25,181): LINE-
(28,178)
330 LINE-(30,178): LINE-(30,177): LINE-(29,176): LINE-(29,174): LINE-
(32,174)
340 LINE-(32,176): LINE-(31,177): LINE-(31,178): LINE-(33,178): LINE-
(36,181)
350 LINE-(35,182): LINE-(32,179): LINE-(32,189): LINE-(30,189): LINE-
(30,188)
360 LINE-(31,188): LINE-(31,185): LINE-(29,185): LINE-(28,186): LINE-
(28,189)
370 LINE-(26,189)
399 '
400 REM * draw figure 3 *
410 LINE(45,189)-(45,188): LINE-(46,188): LINE-(46,185): LINE-(45,185
): LINE-(45,183)
```

```
420 LINE(46,185)-(45,186): LINE-(44,186): LINE-(44,180): LINE-(40,176
): LINE-(41,175)
430 LINE-(44,178): LINE-(45,178): LINE-(45,177): LINE-(44,176): LINE-
(44,174)
440 LINE-(47,174): LINE-(47,176): LINE-(46,177): LINE-(46,178): LINE-
(48,178)
450 LINE-(51,181): LINE-(50,182): LINE-(47,179): LINE-(47,184): LINE-
(48,183)
460 LINE-(49,184): LINE-(50,183): LINE-(48,181): LINE-(47,182): LINE-
(47,189): LINE-(45,189)
499 '
500 REM * draw hurdler position & downed hurdle *
510 DRAW"bm63,185;ul14ulbr317u2r2dlr5ulbdlbllu3"
520 LINE(61,178)-(57,180): LINE-(56,179): LINE-(60,178)
530 DRAW"hlllhle2fldlflrl"
540 LINE(62,177)-(64,176): LINE-(65,177): LINE-(62,178)
550 DRAW"buld6r2d2ll"
560 LINE(71,190)-(70,189),2: LINE-(73,188),2: LINE-(73,187),2: LINE-(
74,187),2
570 LINE-(74,190),2: LINE-(73,190),2: LINE-(73,189),2: LINE-(71,190),
2
599 '
600 REM * store figures *
610 GET(10,174)-(24,190),A%
620 GET(25,174)-(39,190),B%
630 GET(40,174)-(54,190),C%
640 GET(55,168)-(69,184),D%
650 GET(70,185)-(74,190),E%
660 GET(85,168)-(99,184),F%
670 CLS
699 '
700 REM * draw hurdles *
710 DRAW"bm83,115;c2r3ulllu3lld3ll  "
720 DRAW"bm155,115;r3ulllu3lld3lldl"
730 DRAW"bm233,115;r3ulllu3lld3lldl"
750 LINE(0,0)-(319,199),,B
799 '
800 REM * put figures for animation *
810 FOR DELAY=1 TO 50: NEXT DELAY
820 FOR X = 302 TO 16 STEP -6
830  PUT(X,100),A%,XOR
840  GOSUB 2010: IF Q=1 THEN GOTO 980
850  IF INKEY$="j" THEN GOSUB 3010
860  GOSUB 2010: IF Q=1 THEN GOTO 980
870  FOR DELAY = 1 TO 50: NEXT DELAY
880  PUT(X,100),A%,XOR
890  PUT(X,100),B%,XOR
900  FOR DELAY = 1 TO 50: NEXT DELAY
905  GOSUB 2010: IF Q=1 THEN GOTO 980
910  PUT(X,100),B%,XOR
920  PUT(X-3,100),C%,XOR
930  FOR DELAY = 1 TO 50: NEXT DELAY
935  GOSUB 2010: IF Q=1 THEN GOTO 980
940  PUT(X-3,100),C%,XOR
950  PUT(X-3,100),B%,XOR
960  FOR DELAY = 1 TO 50: NEXT DELAY
965  GOSUB 2010: IF Q=1 THEN GOTO 980
970  PUT(X-3,100),B%,XOR: GOTO 980
```

```
980   Q=0
990  NEXT X
1000 END
1999 '
2000 REM * test points *
2010 IF POINT(X+1,112)=1 OR POINT(X+2,112)=1 OR POINT(X+3,112)=1 OR
     POINT(X+10,112)=1 THEN PUT(X-2,100),F%,PSET: PUT(X-2,115),E%,
     PSET: X=X-18: Q=1
2020 RETURN
2999 '
3000 REM * hurdle subroutine *
3010 PUT(X,100),F%,AND
3020 FOR N = 0 TO 21 STEP 3
3030   PUT(X-N,94),D%,XOR
3040   FOR DELAY = 1 TO 50: NEXT DELAY
3050   PUT(X-N,94),D%,XOR
3060 NEXT N
3070 X = X-24
3080 PUT(X,100),A%,XOR
3090 RETURN
```

SUMMARY

In this chapter, we explored animation by GET and PUT statements.
GET and PUT produce pictures faster and more easily than previously
introduced methods.

- The GET statement allows you to store images from screen
  areas into arrays in memory.

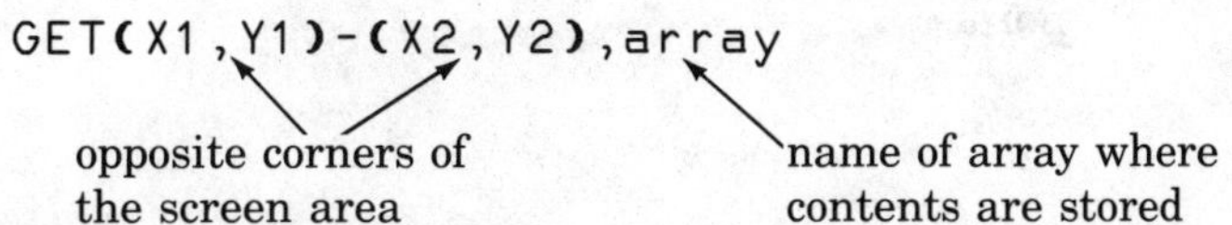

- Arrays for GET data are allotted storage space by a DIMEN-
  SION (DIM) statement using

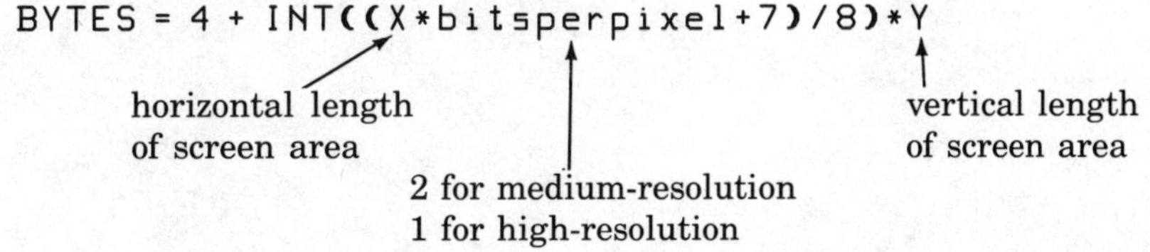

Bytes per element of an array are two for integer, four for single
precision, and eight for double precision.

- The PUT statement transfers data from an array to the display
  screen.

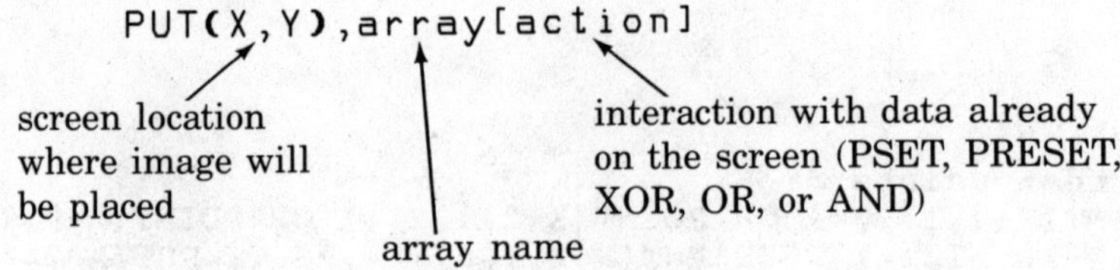

- Table 7–2 shows color interactions for the action option of PUT statements for XOR, OR, and AND.
- Three types of animation were demonstrated:
  1. Fixed object at changing locations
  2. Moving object at a fixed location
  3. A combination of 1 and 2
- The POINT function returns the color code of a specified point on the screen.

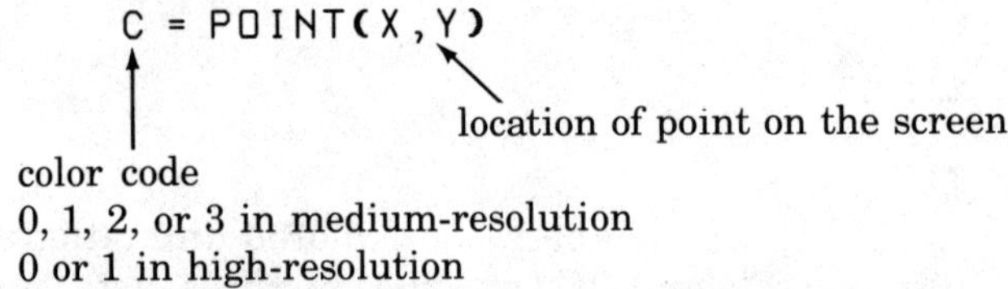

- The use of the POINT function was demonstrated in the Hurdler program. It caused a standing hurdle to be replaced by a fallen hurdle when the hurdler and the hurdle occupied the same screen area (causing a change in color of the screen at that point).

8
GRAPHS AND CHARTS

Graphics Statements, Functions,
and Terms Introduced

SCREEN 2
MOD
VIEW
high-resolution

The objective of this chapter is to show you how to use what you have learned to produce some practical applications in graphical form. Charts and graphs are discussed. High-resolution graphics are used. The VIEW statement is used to show how to put one or more "viewports" on the screen.

BASIC statements that we assume you are familiar with include all those of previous chapters, plus MID\$, ON...GOSUB, RESTORE, SPC, and VAL.

BASIC statements that are explained are MOD, SCREEN 2, and VIEW.

Information displayed in graphical form can provide a much more powerful impact than tables of raw data. The use of graphics for this purpose is widespread, especially in business applications. The three most popular graphics display types are bar graphs (or histograms), line graphs, and pie charts (or circle graphs). Each of these forms is discussed in this chapter.

BAR GRAPHS

The bar graph is perhaps the simplest and easiest form to display. Data presented in this form should be readily divided into a relatively small number of distinct units (such as months in a given year, items of inventory, individual productivity of sales force members, etc.). Too many units will overcrowd the display or present an overly complex picture. A second concern is scaling the graph to reasonably fill the screen while including both the maximum and minimum values.

Remember, the IBM PC has three screen modes: text, medium-resolution graphics, and high-resolution graphics. We will first consider the text mode. It has the capability to produce block graphics, which may be sufficient for producing bars. It also provides the largest number of usable colors for constructing the bars. It's true that the text screen resolution is much lower than the graphics modes, but extreme detail is usually unnecessary when constructing bar graphs.

We will demonstrate the difference in the three screen modes in the first three programs of this chapter. The data used in all three programs is given in Table 8–1. It represents the monthly income of a corporation over one year's time.

TABLE 8–1

INCOME OF BAR, INC.

MONTH	INCOME (THOUSANDS)
Jan	50
Feb	54
Mar	58
Apr	64
May	72
Jun	88
Jul	86
Aug	84
Sep	80
Oct	74
Nov	66
Dec	56

We must remember that we have a maximum of 25 lines for the display in the text mode, SCREEN 0. Some lines will be needed to label the graph, say 5. That leaves a maximum of 20 lines for the bars. Each graphic block in this mode occupies 1 line. Therefore, the number of blocks for each month can be calculated by

```
NUMBER = 20*INCOME/MAX
```

where INCOME = the current month's income and MAX = the maximum scale value.

Since the largest income value to be plotted is 88, we'll set the maximum scale value at 100. Therefore,

```
NUMBER = 20*INCOME/100 = INCOME/5
```

FOR JANUARY   FOR JULY

NUMBER = 50/5 = 10   NUMBER = 86/5 = 17.2

Since the number of blocks must be integer, the formula is modified to

$$\text{NUMBER} = \text{INT(INCOME/5+.5)}$$

EXAMPLES

FOR JANUARY   FOR JULY

```
NUMBER = INT(50/5 +.5)     NUMBER = INT(86/5 +.5)
       = INT(10.5)                = INT(17.7)
       = 10                       = 17
```

The bar graph program shown in Listing 8–1 draws and labels a bar for each month of the year in a different color. The data (lines 210–230) is entered by the READ statement in line 330. A more sophisticated program would be able to accept data from several sources such as the keyboard, a disk file, another program, a modem, etc. However, we have used DATA statements to keep the program simple and to focus on the use of graphics.

The program outputs the data to the video screen. Output to other devices such as a plotter, a printer, or disk storage could also be provided by additions to the program.

The bars are drawn in a subroutine by means of nested FOR-NEXT loops. The color code is varied, and the number of blocks is calculated in the outside loop.

```
1010 FOR NUMBER = 1 TO 12
1020   COLOR NUMBER                        ⟵——————— color specified
1030   BLOCKS = INT(INCOME(NUMBER)/5+.5)
     .
                                                      block calculation
     .
1080 NEXT NUMBER
```

The bars are displayed in the inner loop.

```
1040 FOR BAR = BLOCKS-1 TO 0 STEP -1 ⟵
1050   LOCATE 21-BAR,2*NUMBER+8            start at top
1060   PRINT CHR$(219);              ⟵———— solid block
1070 NEXT BAR
```

The months are spelled vertically by lines 420–470.

```
420 FOR ROW = 1 TO 3
430  FOR NUMBER = 1 TO 12
440   LOCATE ROW+22,2*NUMBER+8            ◄────── lines 23–25
450   PRINT MID$(MONTH$(NUMBER),ROW,1);
460  NEXT NUMBER                     ◄─ pick appropriate letter
470 NEXT ROW
```

The MID$ function in line 450 returns a part of the string MONTH$(NUMBER). It picks one letter for the specified month at the position in the month's name that is specified by ROW.


```
                 For the month of jan (NUMBER=1)

      When ROW=1, MID$(MONTH$(NUMBER),ROW,1) =
              MID$(jan,1,1) = the letter j

      When ROW=2, MID$(MONTH$(NUMBER),ROW,1) =
              MID$(jan,2,1) = the letter a

      When ROW=3, MID$(MONTH$(NUMBER),ROW,1) =
              MID$(jan,3,1) = the letter n
```

The scale is marked along the left of the bars by lines 510–580. CHR$(221) is a vertical line one character high. The underline character is used to provide a "tick" every other line. Each tick represents ten thousand dollars.

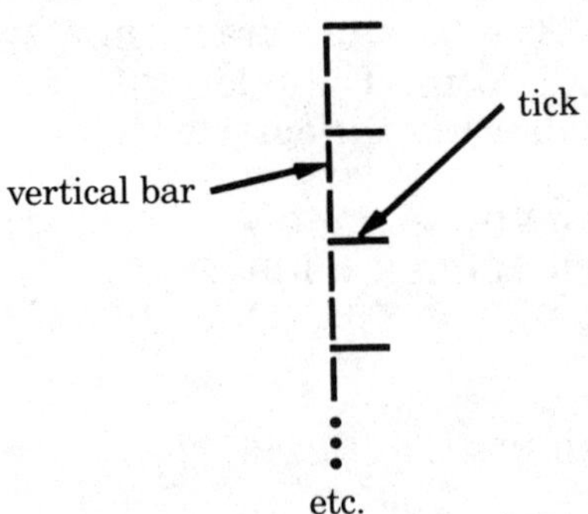


```
510 FOR NUMBER = 1 TO 20 STEP 2
520  LOCATE NUMBER,7
530   PRINT CHR$(221); "_";        ◄────── bar and tick
540  LOCATE NUMBER +1,7
550   PRINT CHR$(221);             ◄────── bar only
560 NEXT NUMBER
570 LOCATE NUMBER,7
580 PRINT CHR$(221); "_";          ◄────── final bar and tick
```

The complete program is given in Listing 8–1. Enter and run the program. Study the display carefully. Compare the bar lengths of February and December, April and November, and July and August. Notice that the lengths of the pairs of bars are the same even though the income values were not equal.

LISTING 8–1. Bar Graph in Text Mode

```
100 REM * dimension arrays and set screen *
110 SCREEN 0,0: KEY OFF: CLS
120 DIM MONTH$(12),INCOME(12)
130 WIDTH 40
199 '
200 REM * data to be graphed *
210 DATA jan,50,feb,54,mar,58,apr,64
220 DATA may,72,jun,88,jul,86,aug,84
230 DATA sep,80,oct,74,nov,66,dec,56
299 '
300 REM * read in data *
310 FOR NUMBER = 1 TO 12
320   READ MONTH$(NUMBER),INCOME(NUMBER)
330 NEXT NUMBER
399 '
400 REM * draw graph then label months *
410 GOSUB 1010
420 FOR ROW = 1 TO 3
430   FOR NUMBER = 1 TO 12
440     LOCATE ROW+22,2*NUMBER+8
450     PRINT MID$(MONTH$(NUMBER),ROW,1);
460   NEXT NUMBER
470 NEXT ROW
499 '
500 REM * draw income scale *
510 FOR NUMBER = 1 TO 20 STEP 2
520   LOCATE NUMBER,7
530   PRINT CHR$(221); "_";
540   LOCATE NUMBER+1,7
550   PRINT CHR$(221);
560 NEXT NUMBER
570 LOCATE NUMBER,7
580 PRINT CHR$(221); "_";
599 '
900 END
999 '
1000 REM * draw in text mode *
1010 FOR NUMBER = 1 TO 12
1020   COLOR NUMBER
1030   BLOCKS = INT(20*INCOME(NUMBER)/100+.5)
1040   FOR BAR = BLOCKS-1 TO 0 STEP -1
1050     LOCATE 21-BAR,2*NUMBER+8
1060     PRINT CHR$(219);
1070   NEXT BAR
1080 NEXT NUMBER
1090 RETURN
```

Because of the low resolution of the block graphics of the text mode, the display shows the following pairs of months to be the same:

February 54 and December 56
April 64 and November 66
June 88 and July 86

This is due to the fact that each block represents five thousand dollars and the number of blocks printed must be an integer. Round-off errors cause an inaccurate display. Therefore, it seems that the text mode is not always accurate, even for bar graphs.

The program of Listing 8–2 is a modification of the text-mode program. It makes use of the medium-resolution graphics mode, using the LINE statement to draw the income scale. Lines 510–580 of the previous listing become:

```
510 LINE(46,6)-(46,166)        ←—— vertical line
520 FOR NUMBER = 1 TO 21 STEP 2
530   LOCATE NUMBER,7
540   PRINT "_";               ←—— scaling tick
550 NEXT NUMBER
```

The LINE statement with the BOX-FILL (BF) option is used to draw the bars. We used 12 different colored bars in the text mode, but we must be satisfied with 3 colors for the bars in medium-resolution. Our bar-drawing subroutine is now

```
1010 FOR NUMBER = 1 TO 12                        ←——calculate height of each bar
1020   HEIGHT = INT(160*INCOME(NUMBER)/100)
1030   START = 16*NUMBER +56                     ←—— starting X coordinate
1040   LINE(START,168-HEIGHT)-(START+8),NUMBER MOD 3+1,BF
1050 NEXT NUMBER
1060 RETURN
```

The complete bar-graph program for medium-resolution is shown in Listing 8–2, and a screen dump of the resulting display is shown in Fig. 8–1. Notice that each bar is now a distinct length. The round-off errors of the text-mode program have been eliminated.

LISTING 8–2. Medium-Resolution Bar Graph

```
100 REM * dimension arrays and set screen*
110 SCREEN 1,0: KEY OFF: CLS
120 DIM MONTH$(12),INCOME(12)
199 '
200 REM * data to be graphed *
210 DATA jan,50,feb,54,mar,58,apr,64
220 DATA may,72,jun,88,jul,86,aug,84
230 DATA sep,80,oct,74,nov,66,dec,56
299 '
300 REM * read in data *
310 FOR NUMBER = 1 TO 12
320   READ MONTH$(NUMBER),INCOME(NUMBER)
```

```
330 NEXT NUMBER
399 '
400 REM * draw graph then label months *
410 GOSUB 1010
420 FOR ROW = 1 TO 3
430   FOR NUMBER = 1 TO 12
440     LOCATE ROW+22,2*NUMBER+8
450     PRINT MID$(MONTH$(NUMBER),ROW,1);
460   NEXT NUMBER
470 NEXT ROW
499 '
500 REM * draw income scale *
510 LINE(46,6)-(46,166)
520 FOR NUMBER =1 TO 21 STEP 2
530   LOCATE NUMBER,7
540   PRINT "_";
550 NEXT NUMBER
599 '
900 END
999 '
1000 REM * draw in medium resolution *
1010 FOR NUMBER = 1 TO 12
1020   HEIGHT = INT(160*INCOME(NUMBER)/100)
1030   START = 16*NUMBER+56
1040   LINE(START,168-HEIGHT)-(START+8,168),(NUMBER) MOD 3+1,BF
1050 NEXT NUMBER
1090 RETURN
```

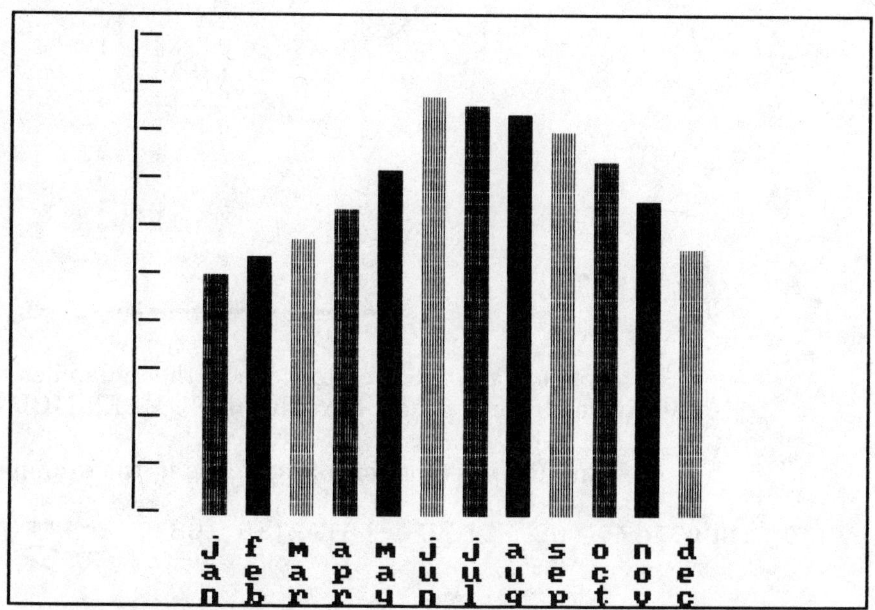

FIG. 8–1. Bar graph medium-resolution mode

Notice the use of the MOD arithmetic operator in line 1040. This operator has the following format:

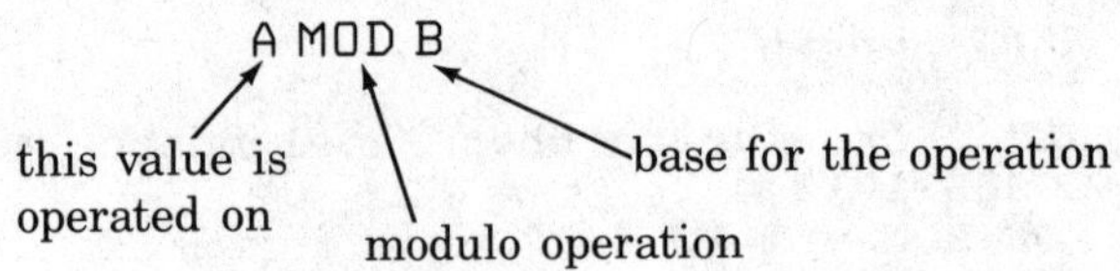

MOD produces an integer value that is the remainder of an integer division.

EXAMPLE

```
110 FOR NUMBER = 1 TO 12
120   X = NUMBER MOD 3
130   Y = NUMBER MOD 3+1
140 PRINT X;Y
150 NEXT NUMBER
```

Running this example prints the X and Y values shown in Table 8–2.

TABLE 8–2

VALUES FOR NUMBER MOD 3

NUMBER	X	Y
1	1	2
2	2	3
3	0	1
4	1	2
5	2	3
6	0	1
7	1	2
8	2	3
9	0	1
10	1	2
11	2	3
12	0	1

Notice that, in each case, X equals the remainder when NUMBER is divided by 3. Y equals the value of NUMBER MOD 3 with 1 added.

Line 140 uses the form that Y has in the example.

```
140 LINE(START,168-HEIGHT)-(START+8,168), NUMBER MOD 3+1 ,BF
```

this yields the color codes used to draw the bars in the sequence: 2, 3, 1, 2, 3, 1, 2, 3, 1, 2, 3, 1

An interesting three-dimensional effect can be achieved by

adding a few lines to Listing 8–2. Line 1045 is added to call a new subroutine (lines 1100–1150) that provides the three-dimensional shading.

Add these lines to Listing 8–2 and run the revised program. The graph is shown in Fig. 8–2.

```
1045 GOSUB 1110

1100 REM * 3-D color bars *
1110 KOLOR = NUMBER MOD 3+2          ←————gives 3, 4, 2, etc.
1120 TOP = 168-HEIGHT
1130 IF KOLOR = 4 THEN KOLOR = 1     ←———— changes to 3, 1, 2, etc.
1140 DRAW "C=KOLOR;BM=START;,=TOP;E4R8NG4D=HEIGHT;
     G4U=HEIGHT;L8"
1150 PAINT(START+10,160),KOLOR,KOLOR
1160 RETURN
```

Notice the use of variables in the DRAW statement in line 1140. These are permissible, as discussed in Chapter 5. The equal sign (=) is a signal to the computer that the following expression is a variable. An alternative method is to convert numeric values to string form and concatenate the results.

AN ALTERNATIVE EXAMPLE

```
1140 DRAW "C"+STR$(KOLOR)+"BM"+STR$(START)+","+STR$(TOP)+
     "E4R8NG4D"+STR$(HEIGHT)+"G4U"+STR$(HEIGHT)+"L8"
```

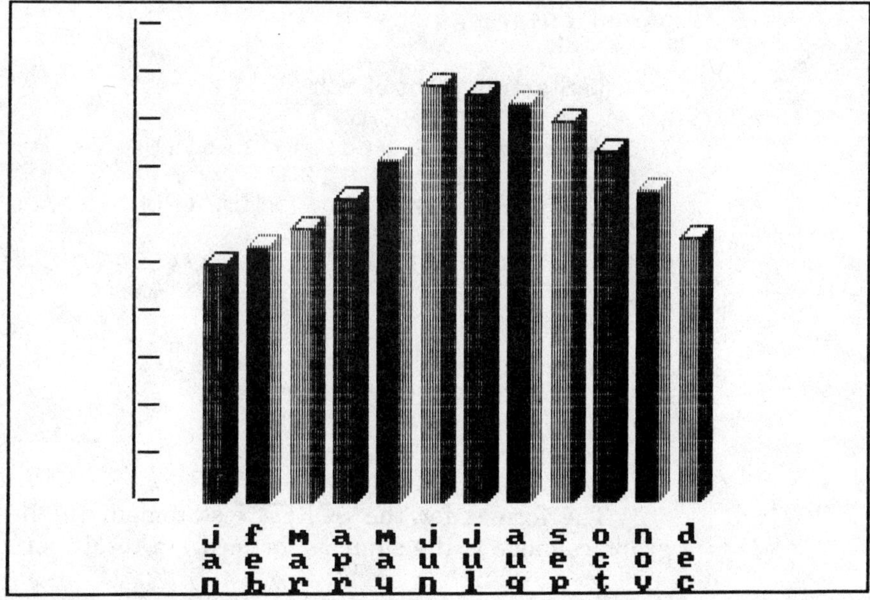

FIG. 8–2. 3-D bar graph

The high-resolution mode can be used for bar graphs also. We have used medium-resolution in most of the graphics displays up to this point. Since high-resolution allows only the use of two colors, its use is usually reserved for occasions where its finer resolution is necessary or when 80-character per line text is needed.

Listing 8–3 draws a bar graph in the high-resolution mode using the same data of the previous bar-graph programs. The listing is similar to that used for medium-resolution and produces the display shown in Fig. 8–3. The following changes were made to the previous listing.

1. Location of names of the months:

```
410 GOSUB 1010
420 FOR ROW = 1 TO 3
430   FOR NUMBER = 1 TO 12
440     LOCATE ROW+22,4*NUMBER+16          ◄──────── this line changed
450     PRINT MID$(MONTH$(NUMBER),ROW,1);
460   NEXT NUMBER
470 NEXT ROW
```

2. Scale line and ticks:

```
510 LINE(98,7)-(98,167)                    ◄──────── line changed
520 FOR NUMBER = 1 TO 21 STEP 2
530   LOCATE NUMBER,14                      ◄──────── tick changed
540   PRINT "_";
550 NEXT NUMBER
```

3. Starting point of bar:

```
1000 REM * draw in medium-resolution *     ◄────── REM changed
1010 FOR NUMBER = 1 TO 12
1020   HEIGHT = INT(160*INCOME(NUMBER)/100)
1030   START = 32*NUMBER+120               ◄──────── start point changed
1040   LINE(START,168-HEIGHT)-(START+8,168),,BF
1050 NEXT NUMBER
1060 RETURN                                no color needed
```

4. Accessing high-resolution:

```
110 SCREEN 2: KEY OFF: CLS                 ◄──────── SCREEN changed
```

The format for the SCREEN statement in the high-resolution graphics mode is the same as for medium-resolution.

```
SCREEN [mode][,burst]
```

Mode 2 selects high-resolution. Since only two colors are available in high-resolution, turning the color burst off has no noticeable effect. Therefore, the SCREEN statement becomes simply

SCREEN 2

The high-resolution mode provides twice as many horizontal pixels as medium-resolution. There are 640 horizontal points (columns) with the same number of vertical points (199 rows).

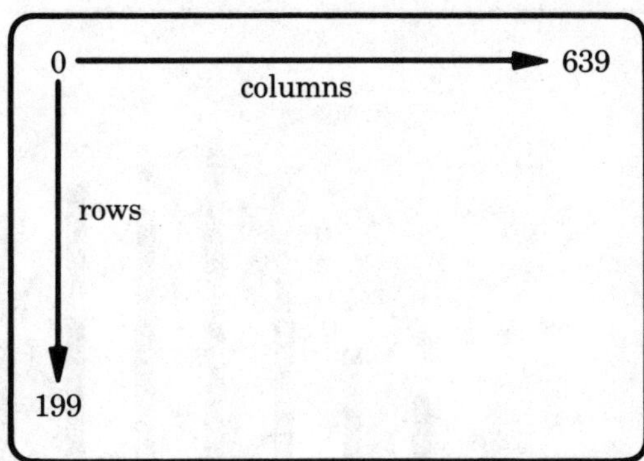

Because of this change in horizontal resolution, the lines that draw the bars and the spacing between bars were changed for the high-resolution mode.

LISTING 8–3. High-Resolution Bar Graph

```
110 SCREEN 2,0: KEY OFF: CLS
120 DIM MONTH$(12),INCOME(12)
199 '
200 DATA jan,50,feb,54,mar,58,apr,64
210 DATA may,72,jun,88,jul,86,aug,84
220 DATA sep,80,oct,74,nov,66,dec,56
299 '
310 MAX=0
320 FOR NUMBER = 1 TO 12
330   READ MONTH$(NUMBER),INCOME(NUMBER)
350 NEXT NUMBER
399 '
410 GOSUB 1010
420 FOR ROW = 1 TO 3
430   FOR NUMBER = 1 TO 12
440     LOCATE ROW+22,4*NUMBER+16
450     PRINT MID$(MONTH$(NUMBER),ROW,1);
460   NEXT NUMBER
470 NEXT ROW
499 '
510 LINE(98,7)-(98,167)
520 FOR NUMBER =1 TO 21 STEP 2
530   LOCATE NUMBER,14
540   PRINT "_";
550 NEXT NUMBER
```

```
590 GOTO 590
599 '
990 END
999 '
1000 REM * draw in high resolution *
1010 FOR NUMBER = 1 TO 12
1020   HEIGHT = 160*INCOME(NUMBER)/100
1030   START = 32*NUMBER+120
1040   LINE(START,168-HEIGHT)-(START+8,168),,BF
1050 NEXT NUMBER
1090 RETURN
```

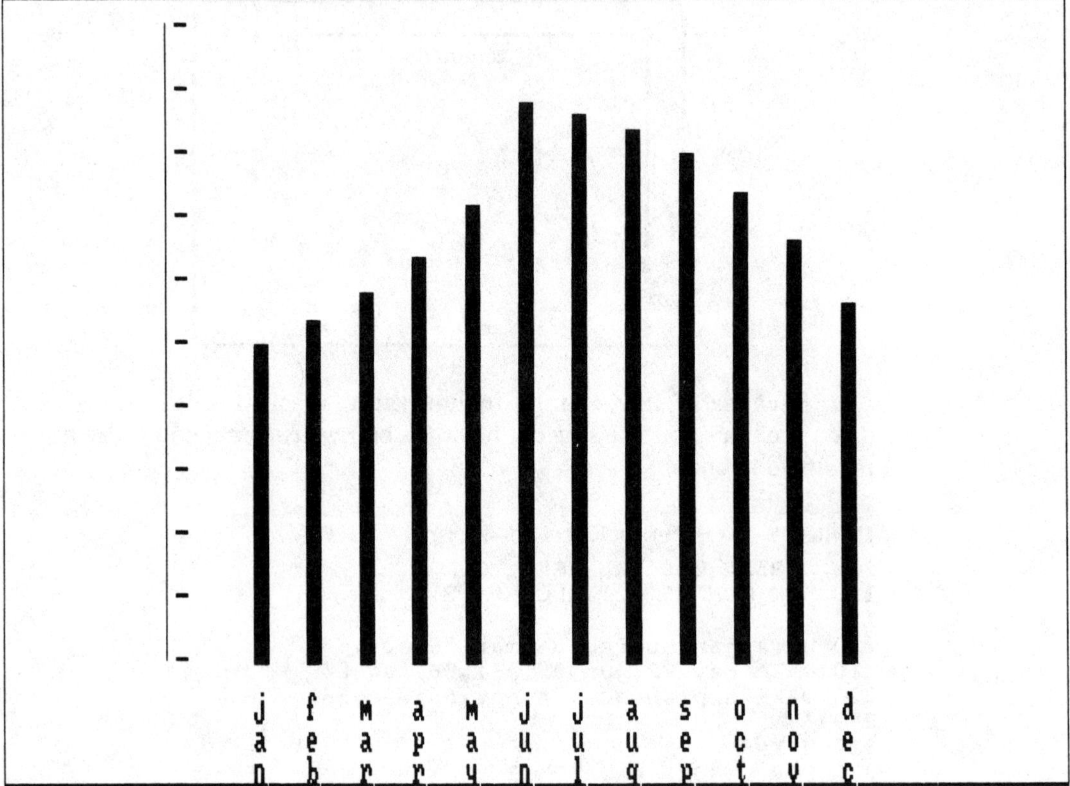

FIG. 8–3. Bar graph high-resolution mode

CIRCLE GRAPHS

Circle graphs were drawn in Chapter 4 by the programs of Listings 4–4 and 4–5. Each program drew a graph for specific data. We would now like to develop a more general program with a menu that will be helpful in preparing the final form of the graph.

Menus used within a program serve a dual purpose. They not only provide for ease of program use, but they also aid the programmer in writing a program that is structured by the menu selections.

In planning a program and its main menu, you must consider how the data will be entered, how the data will be manipulated, and how the results may be used. Items on the menu should appear in the order of use whenever possible. When a selection is made from the menu, control is passed to the selected section of the program. After the necessary chores are performed in that section, a return to the main menu should be provided.

You know that specific information will be needed to draw the graph. Therefore, the first menu item might be

```
1. INPUT INFORMATION
```

This section will accept the information that you provide. It will also calculate and set up the necessary parameters for drawing the graph. It will return you to the main menu.

Another section that might be desirable would be a preliminary drawing that uses the information provided in section 1. You might decide upon changes after looking at the preliminary graph.

```
2. PRELIMINARY DRAWING
```

After viewing the preliminary drawing, a return would be made to the main menu. If changes are needed to your original information, you would select item 1 again to make those changes.

After you have the graph drawn to your satisfaction, you may have choices as to what to do with the results, such as send to screen, send to printer, save information on disk or tape, etc. Therefore, we add a third section.

```
3. OUTPUT RESULTS
```

Finally, although we could use CONTROL BREAK to stop, we add a fourth section (QUIT), which ends the program.

```
4. QUIT
```

Some of us cannot sit down and plan out a program in one sitting. The temptation to begin is just too strong. So we will stop at this point and decide how to program the main menu. The options for the menu placement on the screen are almost endless. Since our menu items are short and simple, we will use the text mode with the 40-column width. The main background color is black with a brown border. The title is printed in a different color than the selections. The enter prompt is displayed on a distinct background color with blinking end markers.

This part of the program can be entered and tested.

```
100 REM * set screen *
110 SCREEN 0,1: KEY OFF
120 WIDTH 40
```

```
130 CLS
199 '
200 REM * print menu *
210 COLOR 7,0,6: LOCATE 2,13
220 PRINT "PIE GRAPH MENU"
230 COLOR 3: LOCATE 5,10
240 PRINT "1. INPUT INFORMATION"
250 LOCATE 7,10
260 PRINT "2. PRELIMINARY DRAWING"
270 LOCATE 9,10
280 PRINT "3. OUTPUT RESULTS"
290 LOCATE 11,10
300 PRINT "4. QUIT"
310 COLOR 26,12: LOCATE 22,2
320 PRINT CHR$(219);
330 COLOR 10
340 PRINT " PRESS NUMBER OF SELECTION DESIRED";
350 COLOR 26,12
360 PRINT CHR$(219);
370 COLOR 7,0
```

Feel free to experiment with the color selections and placement of text on the screen. Our menu resembles that shown in Fig. 8–4.

We now need a method to access subroutines from the menu. We'll use the INKEY$ function.

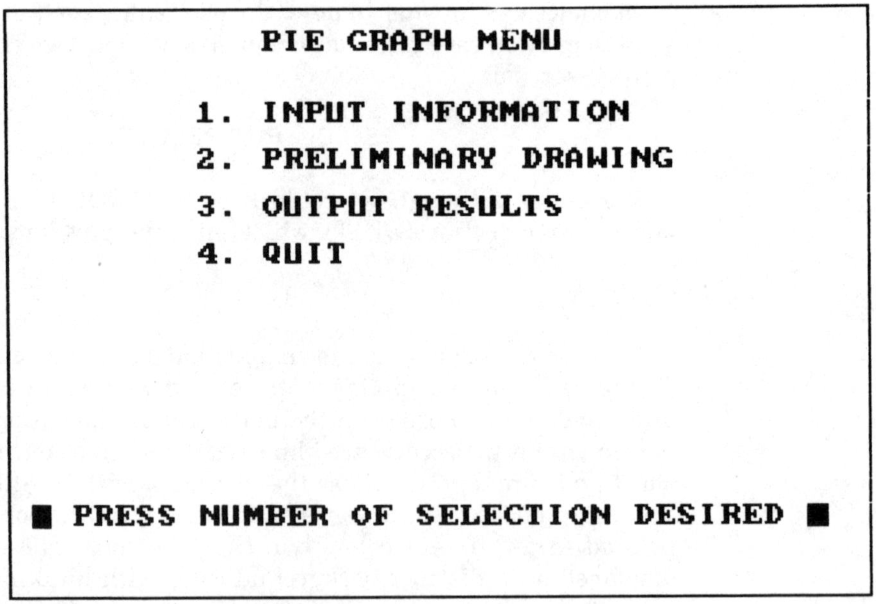

FIG. 8–4. Menu selection

```
400 REM * item selection *
410 ITEM$ = INKEY$
420 IF ITEM$ = "" THEN 410
430 ON VAL(ITEM$) GOSUB 1010,2010,3010,510
440 IF VAL (ITEM$)<1 OR VAL(ITEM$)>4 THEN 410
450 GOTO 110
460 '
510 CLS: END
```

The item number is selected by INKEY$ in line 410. Therefore, it is in string form. We want to go to the correct subroutine determined by the item number. Therefore, the value of the item number must be obtained. The VAL function is used in line 430. It returns the numerical value of the specified string. Once this value is obtained by VAL(ITEM$), it is used to select the correct subroutine by the statement

```
ON VAL(ITEM$) GOSUB 1010,2010,3010,510
```

If VAL(ITEM$) = 1, subroutine 1010 is called

If VAL(ITEM$) = 2, subroutine 2010 is called

If VAL(ITEM$) = 3, subroutine 3010 is called

If VAL(ITEM$) = 4, subroutine 510 is called

Now that the main program is finalized, we can move on to the subroutines. We must decide what information is needed to draw a circle graph. We know that we can draw a circle with the statement

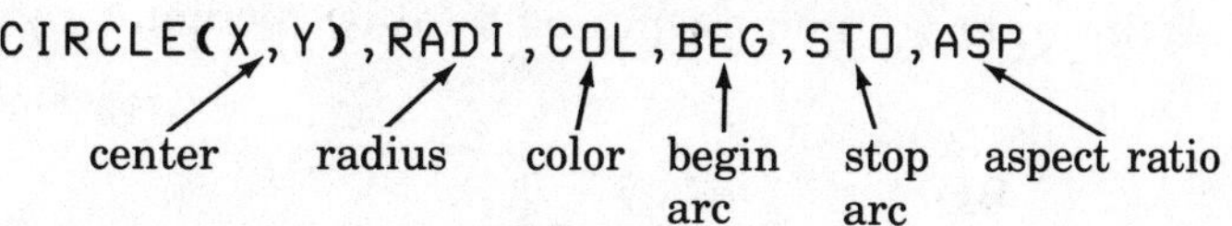

We also know we must provide the number of sections into which the circle is to be divided. We also need the X and Y values for the center of the circle.

```
1000 REM * input information *
1010 CLS
1020 INPUT "NUMBER OF SECTIONS";NUMBER
1030 INPUT "CENTER OF CIRCLE (X,Y)";X(0),Y(0)
1040 INPUT "RADIUS OF CIRCLE";RADIUS
```

We must now find a way to divide the circle into sections of the correct size. How do we locate the points (X1,Y1), (X2,Y2), etc. in order to draw the lines that separate the circle into sections?

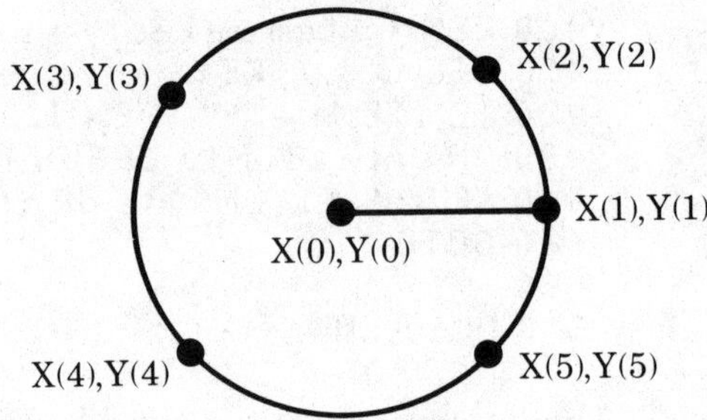

All these X(N),Y(N) values can be found by the equations

```
X(N) = X(0) + COS(A)*RADIUS
Y(N) = Y(0) - SIN(A)*RADIUS
```

where A is the angle formed between the line from X(0),Y(0) to X(1),Y(1) and the line from X(0),Y(0) to X(N),Y(N)

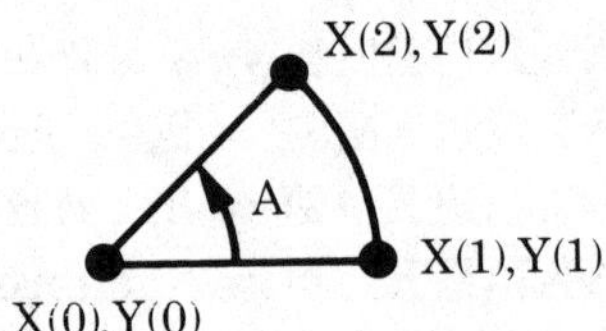

Therefore, we must provide for entering the amount of each item, calculate the percent each item is of the total, and calculate the angle for the end point of each section's arc. The amount of each item is placed in an array, and a running total is calculated by

```
1050 P(0) = 0: A(0) = 0        zero element where total will be
1060 FOR Z = 1 TO NUMBER
1070   PRINT "AMOUNT OF ITEM";Z;
1080   INPUT A(Z): A(0) = A(0)+A(Z)   enter amount and running total
1090 NEXT Z
```

The percent (P) of each item is calculated and added to a running percent total P(Z). Each X,Y coordinate is then calculated.

```
1100 FFOR Z = 1 TO NUMBER
1110   P = A(Z)*100/A(0)         percent for each item
1120   P(Z) = P(Z-1)+P           running percent
1130   A(Z) = P(Z-1)*3.14159/50  angle
1140   X(Z) = X(0)+RADIUS*COS(A(Z))
1150   Y(Z) = Y(0)-RADIUS*SIN(Z(Z))   X,Y coordinates
1160 NEXT Z
1170 RETURN
```

When all entries have been made, control is returned to the main program where the menu is displayed again.

The second choice on the main menu, PRELIMINARY DRAWING, must now be written. Assuming you have already completed the input information, the circle's vital parameters are stored in the computer.

One color is used to draw the graph, and a second color is used for the background. The simplest way to color the sections would be to use the other two colors alternately to paint consecutive sections of the graph. However, if there are an odd number of sections (3, 5, 7, etc.), you will find that the first and last sections will have the same color.

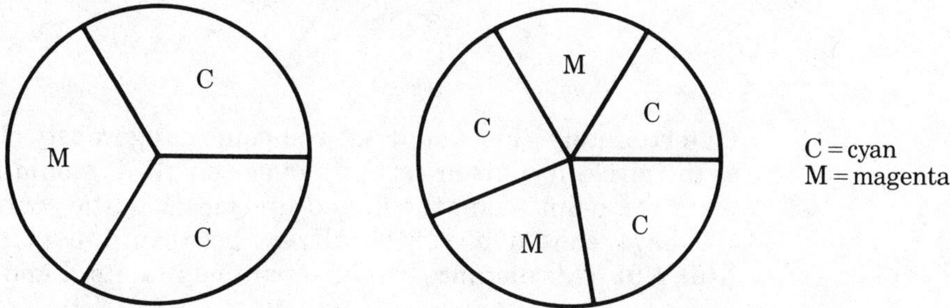

Like adjacent colors can be avoided by painting the last section with the color used to draw the graph (white in our example).

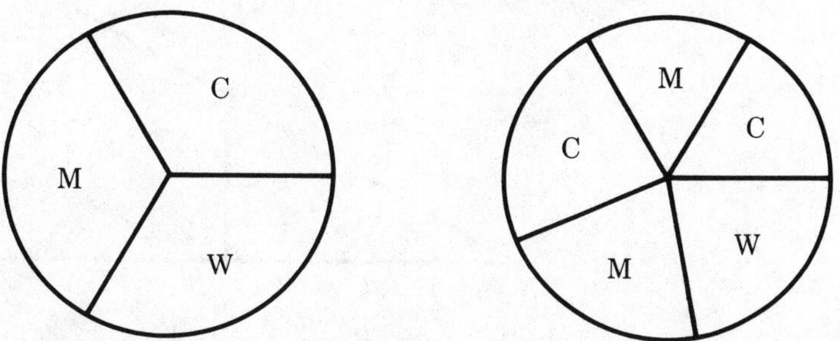

At what point should the PAINT action for each section originate? These points will change depending on the number and size of the sections of each unique graph. If you examine a typical section, you may get some clues as to where the PAINT starting points might be placed.

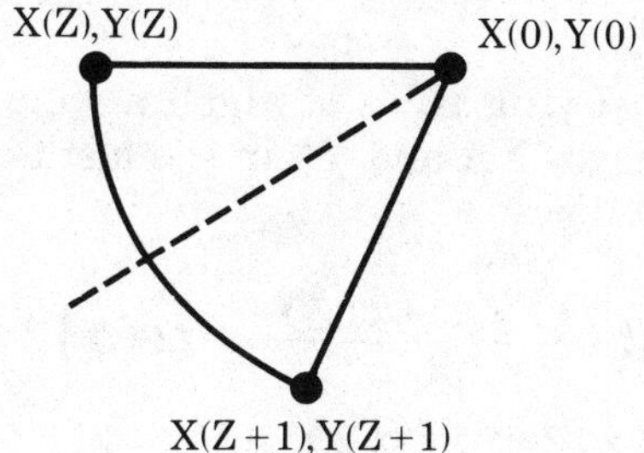

A safe place to put the point would be somewhere on the dotted line. The simplest point to calculate is the average of points $X(Z+1),Y(Z+1)$ and $X(Z),Y(Z)$. This would be

$$XA = (X(Z+1)+X(Z))/2$$
$$YA = (Y(Z+1)+Y(Z))/2$$

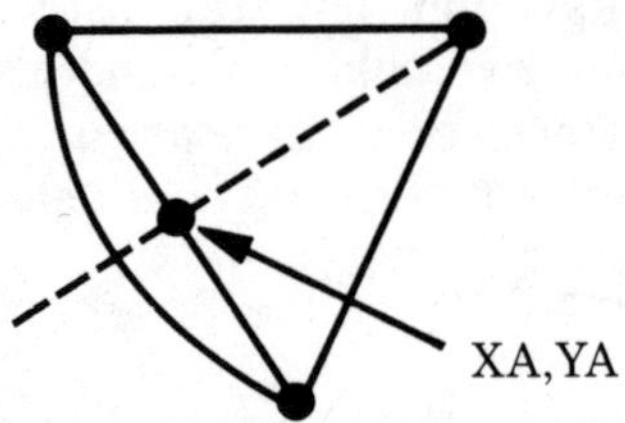

Unfortunately, this would put the point dangerously close to the edge of the circle if a given section is very small. It would seem logical to move the point along the dotted line closer to the center of the circle. We have chosen a point halfway between the point XA,YA and X(0),Y(0). This distance can be separated into its X and Y components.

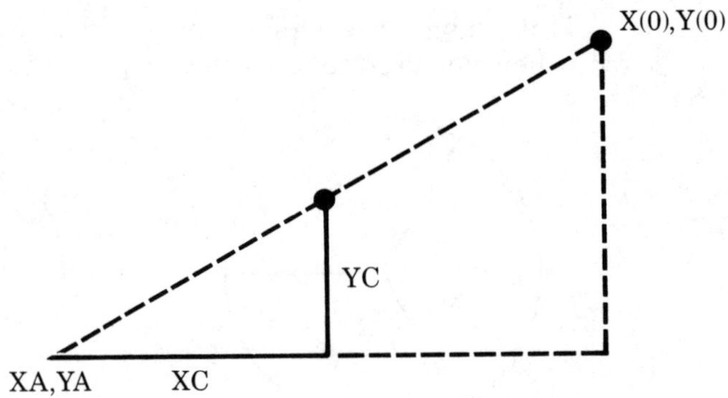

You can see that the X component is

$$XC = (XA-X(0))/2$$

and the Y component is

$$YC = (YA-Y(0))/2$$

Using rules of algebra, you can substitute the previous expressions for XA and YA in the last two equations and combine the results as follows:

$$XC = \left(\frac{X(Z+1)+X(Z)}{2} - X(0)\right)/2 = (X(Z+1)+X(Z)-2*X(0))/4$$

$$YC = (Y(Z+1)+Y(Z)-2*Y(0))/4$$

Remember, the values XC and YC are the distance components that must be added to the values of the center of the circle. The PAINT statement becomes

```
PAINT(X(0)+XC,Y(0)+YC),KOLOR,3
```

The complete drawing subroutine is

```
2000 REM * preliminary drawing *
2010 SCREEN 1: CLS
2020 CIRCLE(X(0),Y(0)),RADIUS,3,,,1          <--draw circle
2030 FOR Z = 1 TO NUMBER
2040  LINE(X(0),Y(0))-(X(Z),Y(Z))           <--section lines
2050 NEXT Z
2060 KOLOR = 1
2070 FOR Z = 1 TO NUMBER
2080  IF Z = NUMBER THEN LAST=1:KOLOR=3 ELSE LAST=Z+1
2090  XC = (X(Z)+X(LAST)-2*X(0))/4
2100  YC = (Y(Z)+Y(LAST)-2*Y(0)/4
2110  PAINT(X(0)+XC,Y(0)+YC),KOLOR,3
2120  KOLOR = KOLOR+1: IF KOLOR=3 THEN KOLOR=1
2130 NEXT Z
2140 A$ = INKEY$          }
2150 IF A$ = "" THEN 2140 } <--wait here to study the picture
2160 RETURN
```

The output section (the third choice on the main menu) will largely depend on the equipment that you are using with your computer. Typical output options are shown in Fig. 8–5.

```
                 OUTPUT OPTIONS

            1. OUTPUT GRAPH TO SCREEN
            2. DATA USED FOR GRAPH
            3. RETURN TO MAIN MENU




■ PRESS NUMBER OF SELECTION DESIRED ■
```

FIG. 8–5. Output menu

The first selection of the output options would pass control to the drawing subroutine at line 2010. The second selection would pass control to a subroutine that would present the menu shown in Fig. 8–6. The third section would pass control back to the main menu.

```
        OUTPUT DATA


   1. TO PRINTER

   2. TO SCREEN

   3. TO DISK

   4. TO CASSETTE

   5. RETURN TO OUTPUT OPTIONS

   6. RETURN TO MAIN MENU



 ■ PRESS NUMBER OF SELECTION DESIRED ■
```

FIG. 8–6. Output options menu

Items 1 through 4 shown on the Output Data menu would pass control to subroutines that output selected data in tabular form to the appropriate device. Items 5 and 6 would return control to previous menus.

Listing 8–4 provides the main program with its menu (lines 100–510), the input subroutine (lines 1000–1170), and the drawing subroutine. The output routines are left as an exercise for you to develop.

Typical screen dumps of sample graphs are given in Figs. 8–7 and 8–8.

LISTING 8–4. Circle Graphs

```
100 REM * set screen *
110 SCREEN 0,1: KEY OFF
120 WIDTH 40
130 CLS
199 '
200 REM * print menu *
210 COLOR 7,0,6: LOCATE 2,13
220 PRINT "PIE GRAPH MENU"
230 COLOR 3: LOCATE 5,10
```

```basic
240 PRINT "1. INPUT INFORMATION"
250 LOCATE 7,10
260 PRINT "2. PRELIMINARY DRAWING"
270 LOCATE 9,10
280 PRINT "3. OUTPUT RESULTS"
290 LOCATE 11,10: PRINT "4. QUIT"
310 COLOR 26,12: LOCATE 22,2
320 PRINT CHR$(219);
330 COLOR 10
340 PRINT " PRESS NUMBER OF SELECTION DESIRED ";
350 COLOR 26,12
360 PRINT CHR$(219);
370 COLOR 7,0
399 '
400 REM * item selection *
410 ITEM$=INKEY$
420 IF ITEM$="" THEN 410
430 ON VAL(ITEM$) GOSUB 1010,2010,3010,510
440 IF VAL(ITEM$)<1 OR VAL(ITEM$)>3 THEN 410
450 GOTO 110
499 '
500 REM * end of program *
510 CLS: END
599 '
1000 REM * input information *
1010 CLS
1020 INPUT "NUMBER OF SECTIONS";NUMBER
1030 INPUT "CENTER OF CIRCLE (X,Y)";X(0),Y(0)
1040 INPUT "RADIUS OF CIRCLE";RADIUS
1050 P(0) = 0: A(0) = 0
1060 FOR Z = 1 TO NUMBER
1070   PRINT "AMOUNT FOR ITEM";Z;
1080   INPUT A(Z): A(0) = A(0)+A(Z)
1090 NEXT Z
1100 FOR Z = 1 TO NUMBER
1110   P = A(Z)*100/A(0)
1120   P(Z) = P(Z-1)+P
1130   A(Z) = P(Z-1)*3.14159/50
1140   X(Z) = X(0)+RADIUS*COS(A(Z))
1150   Y(Z) = Y(0)-RADIUS*SIN(A(Z))
1160 NEXT Z
1170 RETURN
1199 '
2000 REM * preliminary drawing *
2010 SCREEN 1: CLS
2020 CIRCLE(X(0),Y(0)),RADIUS,3,,,1
2030 FOR Z = 1 TO NUMBER
2040   LINE(X(0),Y(0))-(X(Z),Y(Z))
2050 NEXT Z
2060 KOLOR = 1
2070 FOR Z = 1 TO NUMBER
2080   IF Z = NUMBER THEN LAST = 1:KOLOR = 3 ELSE LAST = Z+1
2090   XC = (X(Z)+X(LAST)-2*X(0))/4
2100   YC = (Y(Z)+Y(LAST)-2*Y(0))/4
2110   PAINT(X(0)+XC,Y(0)+YC),KOLOR,3
2120   KOLOR = KOLOR+1: IF KOLOR = 3 THEN KOLOR = 1
2130 NEXT Z
2140 A$ = INKEY$
```

```
2150 IF A$ = "" THEN 2140
2160 RETURN
2999 '
3000 REM * output options *
3010 PRINT "This subroutine is left for you"
3020 A$ = INKEY$
3030 IF A$ = "" THEN 3020
3040 RETURN
```

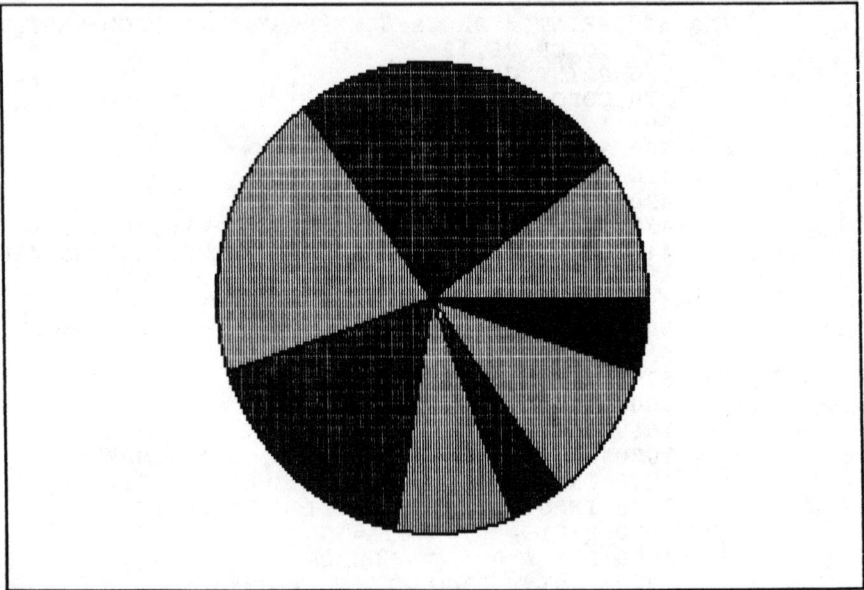

FIG. 8–7. Circle graph 1

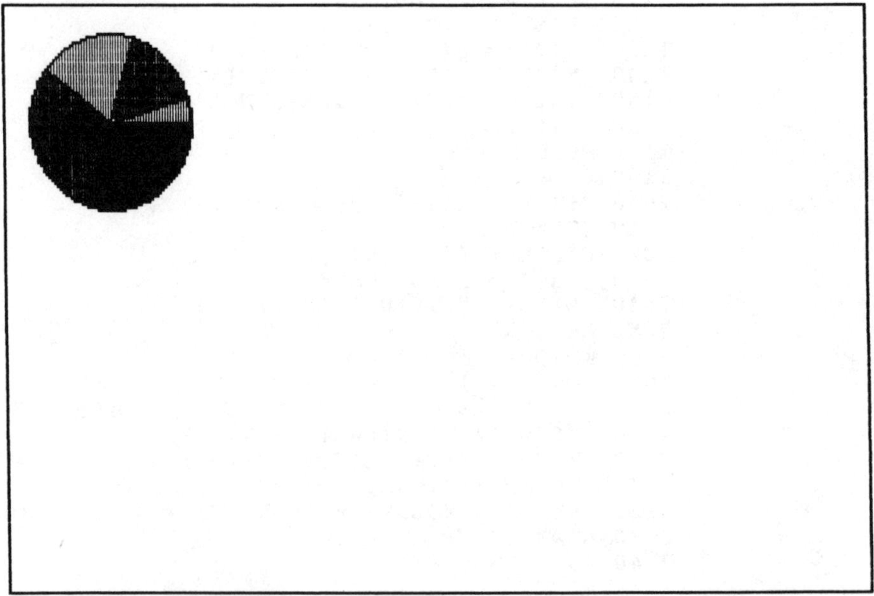

FIG. 8–8. Circle graph 2

Line graphs are usually used to represent data that is continuously changing as a function of some variable.

Temperature as a function of time
Output of a device as a function of input
Seismic activity as a function of time
The sine of an angle as a function of the angle

Measuring devices are not always continuous in nature. They may measure at specific intervals. Therefore, line graphs may consist of gentle curves or may consist of a series of connected straight lines.

Graphs of some trigonometric and other mathematical functions, such as those shown in Chapter 3, are continuous. Therefore, their graphs, as shown in Fig. 3–7, consist of a series of points that appear to form a smooth curve. The points were plotted by selecting a very small (.05 radians) increment for the change of angle size. If each of the points were connected in order, a line graph would be formed. To illustrate this, a plot of the sine function is drawn by the program of Listing 8–5.

Lines 310 through 360 of this program plot one cycle of sine values using an increment of 0.21 radians in angle size. The program halts to allow you to study the pattern of dots at lines 420 and 430. Line 410 displays a prompt to tell you to press a key to connect the points. The points are shown in Fig. 8–9(a).

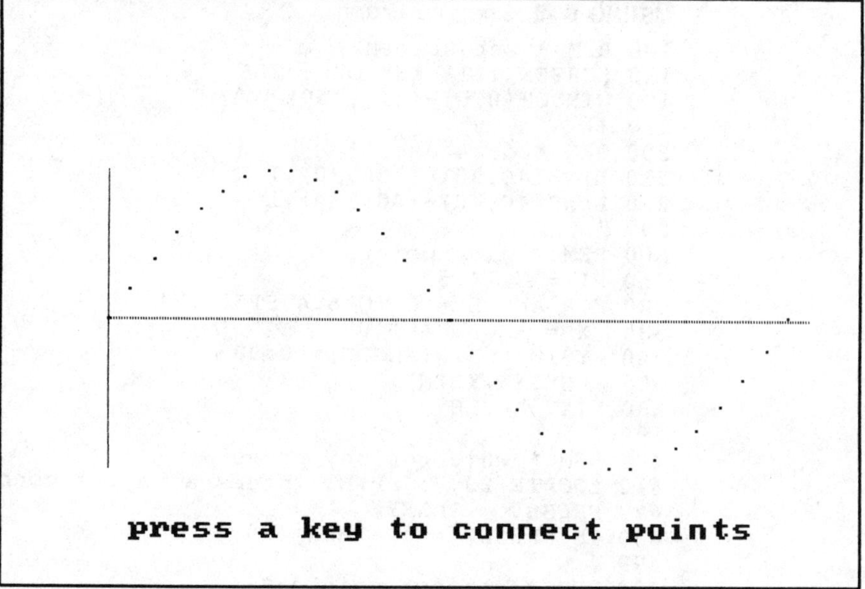

FIG. 8–9(a). Points for sine line graph

When you press a key, the dots are connected, forming the line graph shown in Fig. 8–9(b).

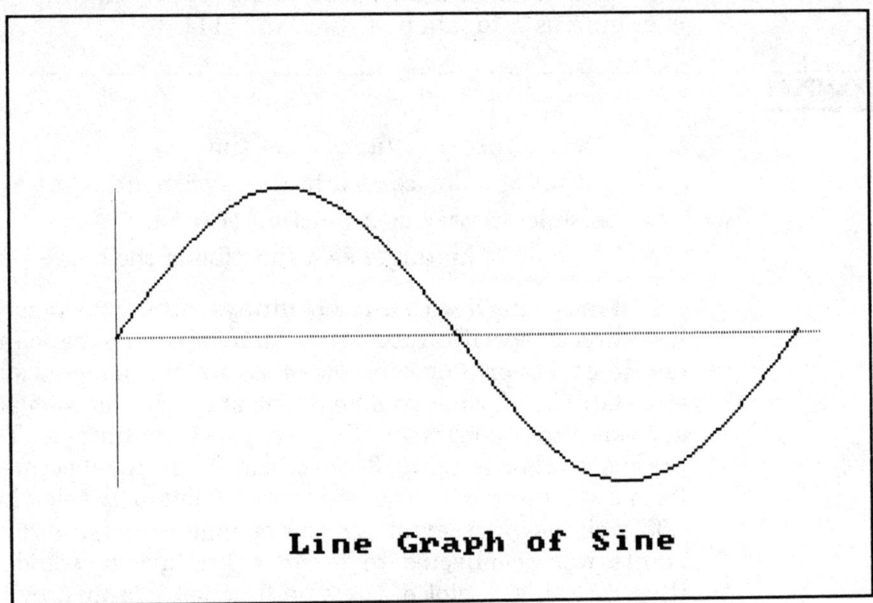

FIG. 8–9(b). Sine line graph

The connecting lines are drawn by lines 510 through 570 of the program. Line 610 places the title below the graph, and centers the title by using the SPC function to skip spaces.

LISTING 8–5. Sine Line Graph

```
100 REM * set screen *
110 SCREEN 1,1: KEY OFF: CLS
120 WINDOW(0,0)-(319,199)
199 '
200 REM * draw axes *
210 LINE(40,90)-(300,90),1
220 LINE(40,40)-(40,140),1
299 '
300 REM * plot points *
310 PI = 3.14159
320 FOR ANGLE = 0 TO 6.4 STEP .21
330   X = ANGLE*40+40
340   YSIN = SIN(ANGLE)*50+90
350   PSET(X,YSIN),2
360 NEXT ANGLE
399 '
400 REM * wait for key press *
410 LOCATE 23,7: PRINT "press a key to connect points"
420 PRESS$ = INKEY$
430 IF PRESS$ = "" THEN 420
499 '
500 REM * connect points *
510 XOLD = 40: YOLD = 90
```

```
520 FOR ANGLE = .21 TO 6.4 STEP .21
530   XNEW = ANGLE*40+40
540   YNEW = SIN(ANGLE)*50+90
550   LINE(XOLD,YOLD)-(XNEW,YNEW),3
560   XOLD = XNEW: YOLD = YNEW
570 NEXT ANGLE
599 '
600 REM * title *
610 LOCATE 23,7: PRINT SPC(7);"Line Graph of Sine";SPC(7);
620 GOTO 620
```

Line graphs are also used to plot the progress of stock prices. Daily prices at the close of stock markets are quite often used. The program of Listing 8–6 plots the fictional daily prices of a corporation over a one-month period.

Line 110 selects high-resolution graphics and clears the screen.

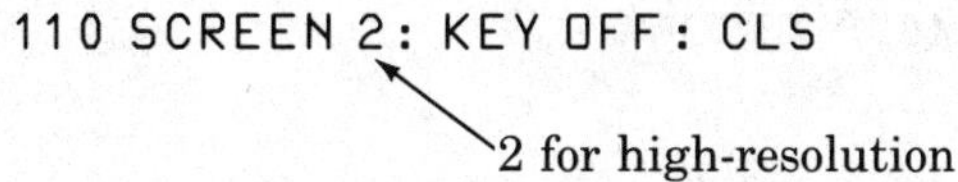

The block of two hundred numbers is not used. We have reserved them for a future modification of the program. Lines 310, 320, and 330 call subroutines that print labels, print scales, and draw the lines between daily prices. Data used for prices is given in lines 1010, 1020, 1030, and 1040. These values are read at line 4020 in the plotting subroutine. The values are scaled to fit the screen in lines 4030 and 4040. Lines are drawn between points by line 4040.

The line graph is shown in Fig. 8–10, and the complete program is given in Listing 8–6.

LISTING 8–6. Closing Stock Prices

```
100 REM * set screen *
110 SCREEN 2: KEY OFF: CLS
120 WINDOW(0,0)-(639,199)
199 '
310 GOSUB 2010
320 GOSUB 3010
330 GOSUB 4010
340 START$ = INKEY$
350 IF START$ = "" THEN 340 ELSE END
399 '
1000 REM * data for graph *
1010 DATA 27.5,26.1,24.6,22.4,23.8
1020 DATA 23.8,22.6,22,24.4,22.5
1030 DATA 24,23.1,23.4,23,23
1040 DATA 23.8,23.4,23.1,21.1,22,21.4,21.5
1999 '
2000 REM * print title and lable *
2010 LOCATE 2,2: PRINT"DATA-STREAM, INC."
2020 LOCATE 3,5: PRINT"Daily Prices"
2030 PRICE = 32
2040 FOR ROW = 5 TO 19 STEP 2
```

```
2050    LOCATE ROW,75: PRINT "-";PRICE;
2060    PRICE = PRICE-2
2070 NEXT ROW
2080 RETURN
2999 '
3000 REM * draw scale lines *
3010 LINE(595,170)-(595,40)
3020 LINE(25,40)-(595,40)
3030 RETURN
3999 '
4000 REM * plot graph *
4010 FOR COLUMN = 25 TO 570 STEP 25
4020    READ PRICE
4030    IF COLUMN = 25 THEN YOLD = PRICE*8-95: XOLD = COLUMN
4040    YNEW = PRICE*8-95: XNEW = COLUMN
4050    LINE(XOLD,YOLD)-(XNEW,YNEW)
4060    LINE(COLUMN,37)-(COLUMN,43)
4070    YOLD = YNEW: XOLD = XNEW
4080 NEXT COLUMN
4090 RETURN
```

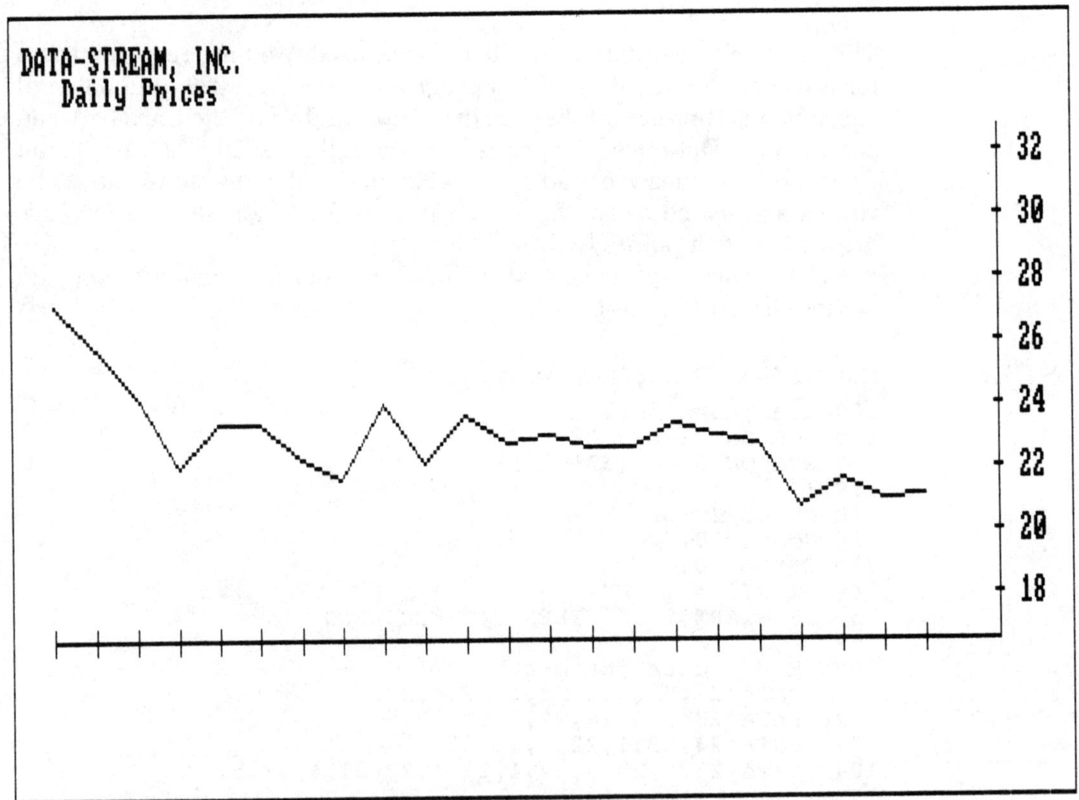

FIG. 8—10. Line graph

A mixture of graph types is often used to present a clearer picture
of complex data than can be presented with a simple line or bar graph.
For instance, the movement of stock prices can be more completely

described by three different data values: the highest value reached, the lowest value reached, and the closing value for a given day. This is often shown by a vertical line from the high value to the low value with a short horizontal line at the closing value.

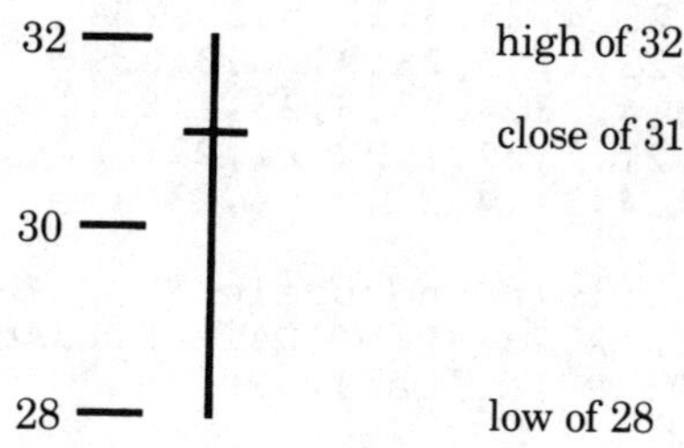

A series of such values for a complete five-day week might look like this:

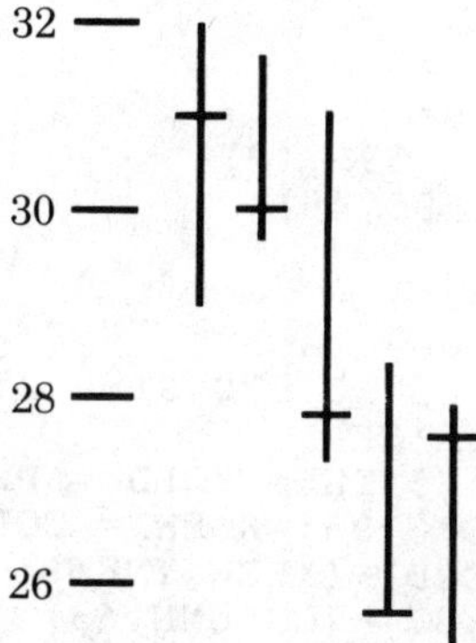

A graph of this type is drawn by the program of Listing 8–7. This program modifies Listing 8–6 to allow drawing the simple line graph of Fig. 8–11(b) or the more complex graph of Fig. 8–11(c).

LISTING 8–7. Line Graphs with Options

```
100 REM * set screen *
110 SCREEN 2: KEY OFF: CLS
120 WINDOW(0,0)-(639,199)
199 '
200 REM * options *
210 GOSUB 6010
220 IF SELECT <>1 AND SELECT <>2 THEN 210 ELSE IF SELECT =1 THEN 310
230 CLS: RESTORE
240 GOSUB 2010: GOSUB 3010: GOSUB 5010: GOTO 340
299 '
300 REM * go to line graph *
310 RESTORE: GOSUB 2010
320 GOSUB 3010
330 GOSUB 4010
340 START$ = INKEY$
```

```
350 IF START$ = "" THEN 340 ELSE CLS: GOTO 210
399 '
1000 REM * graph data - hi lo,close *
1010 DATA 27.8,25.8,27.5,27.3,26.1,26.1
1020 DATA 26.6,24.6,24.6,24.6,22.4,22.4
1030 DATA 23.9,22.4,23.8,23.9,23.5,23.8
1040 DATA 23.9,22.6,22.6,22.6,21.8,22
1050 DATA 24.6,22.1,24.4,23.8,23.3,23.5
1060 DATA 24.5,23.6,24,23.9,23.1,23.1
1070 DATA 23.5,23.4,23.4,23.5,23,23
1080 DATA 22.5,23.1,23,23.9,22.8,23.8
1090 DATA 24,23.4,23.4,23.8,23.1,23.1
1100 DATA 23.3,21.1,22.1,22,21,22
1110 DATA 22,21.4,21.4,22,21.4,21.7
1999 '
2000 REM * draw title and scale *
2010 CLS: LOCATE 2,2: PRINT"DATA-STREAM, INC."
2020 LOCATE 3,5: PRINT"Daily Prices"
2030 PRICE = 32
2040 FOR ROW = 5 TO 19 STEP 2
2050   LOCATE ROW,75: PRINT "-";PRICE;
2060   PRICE = PRICE-2
2070 NEXT ROW
2080 RETURN
2999 '
3000 REM * draw axes *
3010 LINE(595,170)-(595,40)
3020 LINE(25,40)-(595,40)
3030 RETURN
3999 ,
4000 REM * plot line graph *
4010 FOR COLUMN = 25 TO 570 STEP 25
4020   READ HI,LO,PRICE
4030   IF COLUMN = 25 THEN YOLD = PRICE*8-95: XOLD = COLUMN
4040   YNEW = PRICE*8-95: XNEW = COLUMN
4050   LINE(XOLD,YOLD)-(XNEW,YNEW)
4060   LINE(COLUMN,37)-(COLUMN,43)
4070   YOLD = YNEW: XOLD = XNEW
4080 NEXT COLUMN
4090 RETURN
4999 '
5000 REM * plot hi, low, close graph *
5005 VIEW(0,0)-(639,150)
5010 FOR COLUMN = 25 TO 570 STEP 25
5020   READ HI,LO,FINAL
5030   YHI = HI*8-95: YLO = LO*8-95: YCLOSE = FINAL*8-95
5040   LINE(COLUMN,YHI)-(COLUMN,YLO)
5050   LINE(COLUMN-3,YCLOSE)-(COLUMN+3,YCLOSE)
5060   LINE(COLUMN,37)-(COLUMN,43)
5070 NEXT COLUMN
5080 RETURN
5999 '
6000 REM * option menu *
6010 CLS
6020 LOCATE 2,35: PRINT"GRAPH OPTIONS"
6030 LOCATE 5,30: PRINT"1. Simple Line Graph"
6040 LOCATE 7,30: PRINT"2. High, Low, and Close Graph"
6050 LOCATE 23,5: PRINT"Press 1 or 2 to view selected graph."
6060 SELECT$ = INKEY$
```

```
6070 IF SELECT$ = "" THEN 6060
6080 SELECT = VAL(SELECT$)
6090 RETURN
```

The options for the selection are provided by adding lines 200 through 240 to Listing 8–6.

```
200 REM * options *
210 GOSUB 6010                    ←——————— to print the option menu
220 IF SELECT<>1 OR SELECT<>2 THEN 210
        ELSE IF SELECT=1 THEN 310
230 CLS: RESTORE
240 GOSUB 2010: GOSUB 3010: GOSUB 5010: GOTO 340
```

Since this portion of this program may be repeated, the data that is read might be needed again. In order to move the data pointer back to the beginning of the data list, the RESTORE statement is used in lines 230 and 310. Without the RESTORE statement, the program would run out of data when the data pointer reached the end of the data list.

The menu selection of the subroutine starting at line 6000 is shown in Fig. 8–11(a).

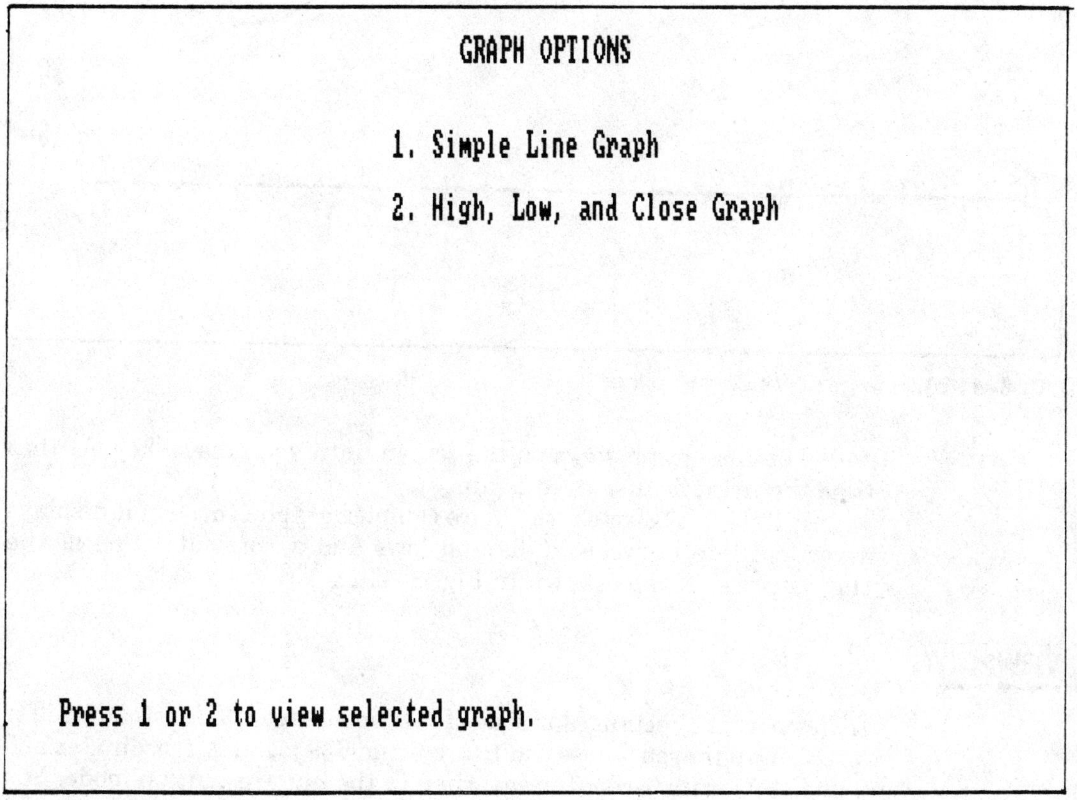

FIG. 8–11(a). Menu options

If item 1 is selected, a simple line graph, as shown in Fig. 8–11(b) is displayed. This graph is drawn by the subroutine beginning at line 4000 of Listing 8–7. The data used is obtained from the expanded list in lines 1010 through 1110. Only the stock closing prices are plotted, even though high, low, and closing prices are all read by the statement at line 4020.

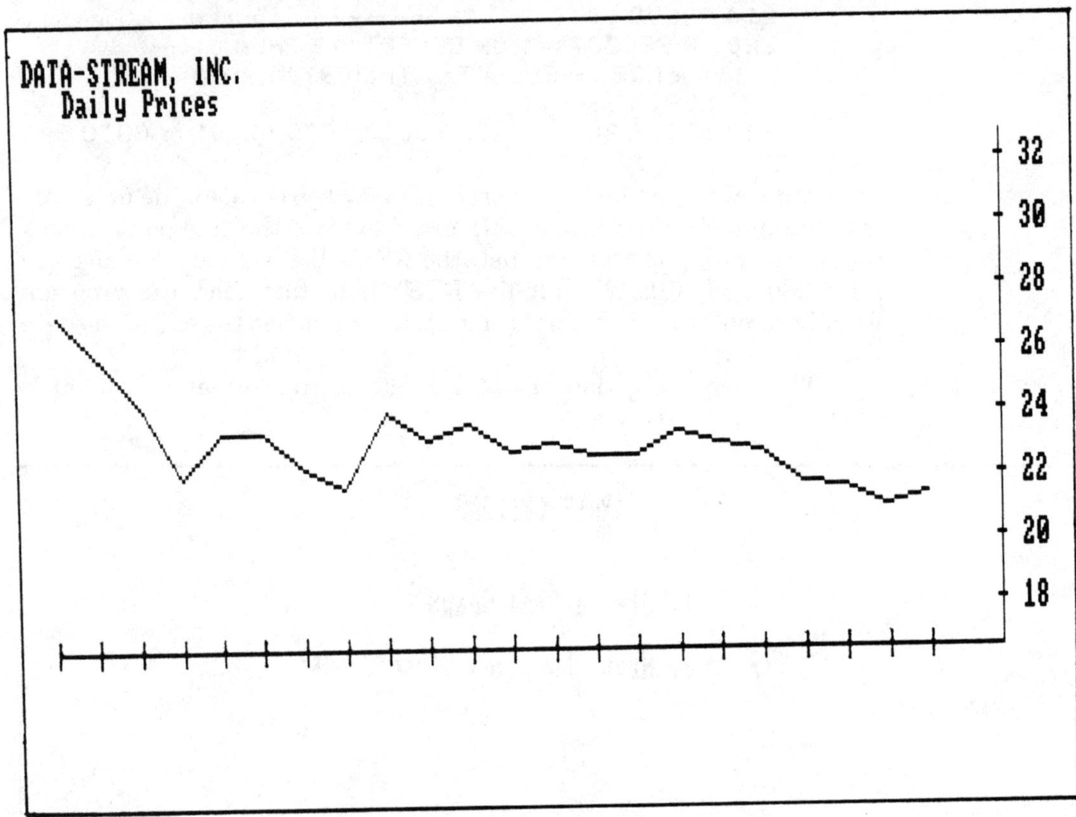

FIG. 8–11(b). Line graph of closing prices

The line graph stays on the screen until you press a key. At that time the menu is displayed again.

If item 2 is selected, the more complex graph is drawn; it displays a vertical line between highs and lows and a horizontal line at the closing price. This is shown in Fig. 8–11(c).

VIEWPORT

A viewport is a rectangular area of the video screen. The screen itself is a rectangular area whose limits are 0 and 639 for its X-coordinates and 0 and 199 for its Y-coordinates when in the high-resolution mode. You saw in Chapter 6 that the WINDOW statement can be used to enlarge a figure (drawn from screen coordinates) so that only a part of the figure

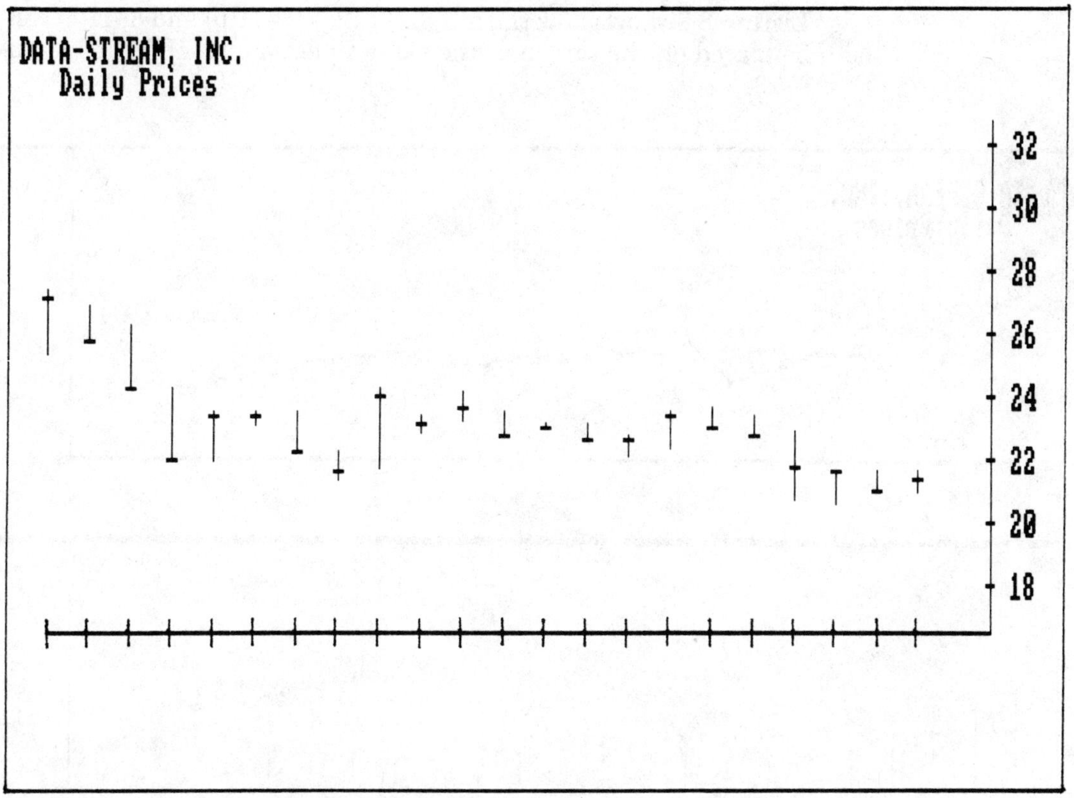

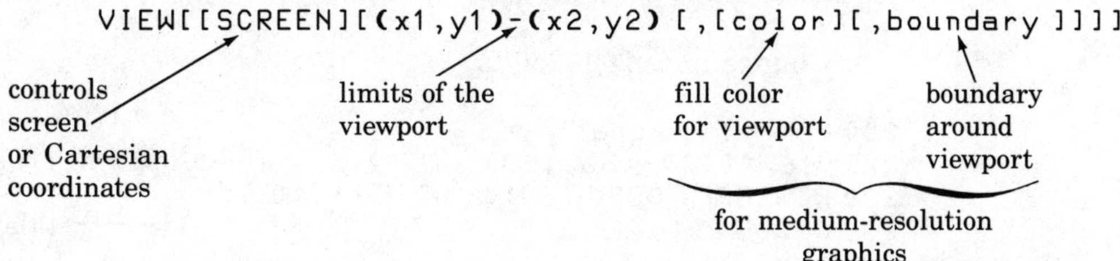

FIG. 8–11(c). Mixed graph of stock prices

filled the screen. The VIEW statement is used to control the placement of viewports on the screen. In fact, as shown in Fig. 8–12, more than one viewport can be placed on the screen at the same time.

The VIEW statement has the format

```
VIEW[[SCREEN][(x1,y1)-(x2,y2) [,[color][,boundary ]]]]
```

controls screen or Cartesian coordinates

limits of the viewport

fill color for viewport

boundary around viewport

for medium-resolution graphics

The SCREEN option serves the same function for VIEW as it does for WINDOW, providing screen coordinates rather than Cartesian coordinates. The limits of the viewport are the opposite corners of the rectangular area where the viewport is to be displayed. The color option will fill the inside of the viewport with color using the codes specified previously. The boundary color is the color used to draw around the viewport.

Listing 8.8 shows how the graphs of Figs. 8–11(b) and 8–11(c) can both be placed on the screen at the same time. The result is shown in Fig. 8–12.

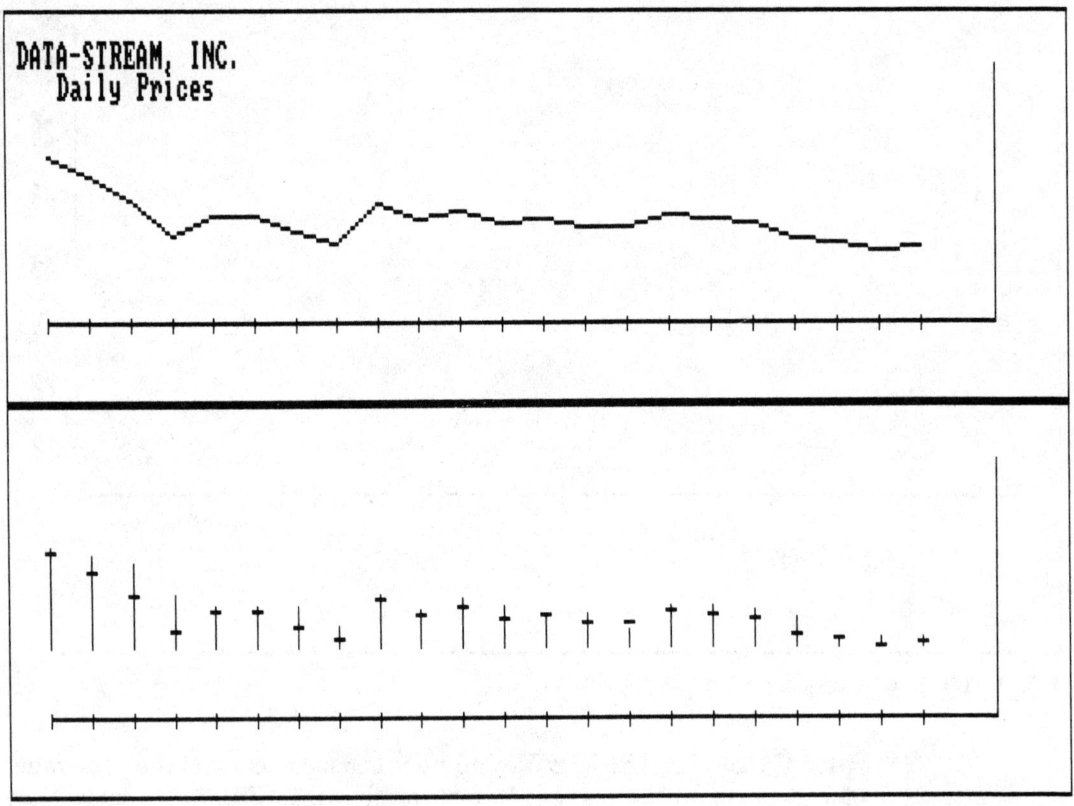

FIG. 8–12. Two views—high-resolution

Listing 8–8 is obtained by the following modifications to Listing 8–7:

Change lines 200–230 to

```
200 REM * line graph *
210 VIEW(0,0)-(639,99)          ←— upper half of screen
220 RESTORE: GOSUB 3010: GOSUB 4010
230 GOSUB 2010                  ←— title
```

Delete line 240.
Change lines 300–320 to

```
300 REM * mixed graph *
310 VIEW(0,100)-(639,199)       ←— lower half of screen
320 RESTORE: GOSUB 3010: GOSUB 5010
```

Delete line 330.
Delete lines 2030, 2040, 2050, 2060, and 2070.

LISTING 8–8. Viewport—High-Resolution

```
100 REM * set screen *
110 SCREEN 2: KEY OFF: CLS
120 WINDOW(0,0)-(639,199)
199 '
200 REM * line graph *
210 VIEW(0,0)-(639,99)
220 RESTORE: GOSUB 3010: GOSUB 4010
230 GOSUB 2010
299 '
300 REM * mixed graph *
310 VIEW(0,100)-(639,199)
320 RESTORE: GOSUB 3010: GOSUB 5010
340 START$ = INKEY$
350 IF START$ = "" THEN 340 ELSE CLS: GOTO 210
399 '
1000 REM * graph data - hi lo,close *
1010 DATA 27.8,25.8,27.5,27.3,26.1,26.1
1020 DATA 26.6,24.6,24.6,24.6,22.4,22.4
1030 DATA 23.9,22.4,23.8,23.9,23.5,23.8
1040 DATA 23.9,22.6,22.6,22.6,21.8,22
1050 DATA 24.6,22.1,24.4,23.8,23.3,23.5
1060 DATA 24.5,23.6,24,23.9,23.1,23.1
1070 DATA 23.5,23.4,23.4,23.5,23,23
1080 DATA 22.5,23.1,23,23.9,22.8,23.8
1090 DATA 24,23.4,23.4,23.8,23.1,23.1
1100 DATA 23.3,21.1,22.1,22,21,22
1110 DATA 22,21.4,21.4,22,21.4,21.7
1999 '
2000 REM * draw title and scale *
2010 LOCATE 2,2: PRINT"DATA-STREAM, INC.";
2020 LOCATE 3,5: PRINT"Daily Prices";
2080 RETURN
2999 '
3000 REM * draw axes *
3010 LINE(595,170)-(595,40)
3020 LINE(25,40)-(595,40)
3025 LINE(0,0)-(639,199),,B
3030 RETURN
3999 ,
4000 REM * plot line graph *
4010 FOR COLUMN = 25 TO 570 STEP 25
4020   READ HI,LO,PRICE
4030   IF COLUMN = 25 THEN YOLD = PRICE*8-95: XOLD = COLUMN
4040   YNEW = PRICE*8-95: XNEW = COLUMN
4050   LINE(XOLD,YOLD)-(XNEW,YNEW)
4060   LINE(COLUMN,37)-(COLUMN,43)
4070   YOLD = YNEW: XOLD = XNEW
4080 NEXT COLUMN
4090 RETURN
4999 '
5000 REM * plot hi, low, close graph *
5010 FOR COLUMN = 25 TO 570 STEP 25
```

```
5020   READ HI,LO,FINAL
5030   YHI = HI*8-95: YLO = LO*8-95: YCLOSE = FINAL*8-95
5040   LINE(COLUMN,YHI)-(COLUMN,YLO)
5050   LINE(COLUMN-3,YCLOSE)-(COLUMN+3,YCLOSE)
5060   LINE(COLUMN,37)-(COLUMN,43)
5070 NEXT COLUMN
5080 RETURN
```

Notice that the title subroutine, beginning at line 2010, is called only once (at line 230). It appears in the upper-left corner of the line graph in Fig. 8–12, as it did in Figs. 8–11(b) and 8–11(c). The height of each graph is half that of Figs. 8–11(b) and 8–11(c) because of the viewports specified. Their widths remain the same.

VIEW can also be used in the medium-resolution mode where the FILL-COLOR and BOUNDARY-COLOR options may be used. The program of Listing 8–9 draws the graphs using these options in the medium-resolution mode. The results are displayed as shown in Fig. 8–13. The top viewport is filled with cyan, and the bottom viewport is filled with magenta. The boundaries of both viewports are drawn in white.

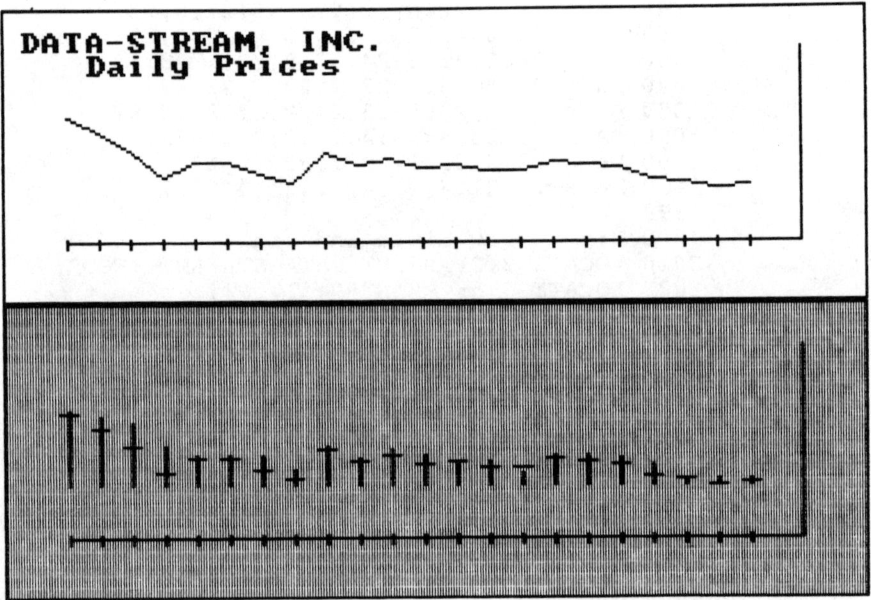

FIG. 8–13. Two views—medium-resolution

LISTING 8–9. Viewport—Medium-Resolution

```
100 REM * set screen *
110 SCREEN 1,1: KEY OFF: CLS
120 WINDOW(0,0)-(319,199)
199 '
```

```
200 REM * line graph *
210 VIEW(0,0)-(319,99),1,3
220 RESTORE: GOSUB 3010: GOSUB 4010
230 GOSUB 2010
299 '
300 REM * mixed graph *
310 VIEW(0,100)-(319,199),2,3
320 RESTORE: GOSUB 3010: GOSUB 5010
340 START$ = INKEY$
350 IF START$ = "" THEN 340 ELSE CLS: GOTO 210
399 '
1000 REM * graph data - hi lo,close *
1010 DATA 27.8,25.8,27.5,27.3,26.1,26.1
1020 DATA 26.6,24.6,24.6,24.6,22.4,22.4
1030 DATA 23.9,22.4,23.8,23.9,23.5,23.8
1040 DATA 23.9,22.6,22.6,22.6,21.8,22
1050 DATA 24.6,22.1,24.4,23.8,23.3,23.5
1060 DATA 24.5,23.6,24,23.9,23.1,23.1
1070 DATA 23.5,23.4,23.4,23.5,23,23
1080 DATA 22.5,23.1,23,23.9,22.8,23.8
1090 DATA 24,23.4,23.4,23.8,23.1,23.1
1100 DATA 23.3,21.1,22.1,22,21,22
1110 DATA 22,21.4,21.4,22,21.4,21.7
1999 '
2000 REM * draw title and scale *
2010 LOCATE 2,2: PRINT"DATA-STREAM, INC.";
2020 LOCATE 3,5: PRINT"Daily Prices";
2080 RETURN
2999 '
3000 REM * draw axes *
3010 LINE(295,170)-(295,40)
3020 LINE(24,40)-(295,40)
3025 LINE(0,0)-(319,199),,B
3030 RETURN
3999 ,
4000 REM * plot line graph *
4010 FOR COLUMN = 24 TO 284 STEP 12
4020   READ HI,LO,PRICE
4030   IF COLUMN = 24 THEN YOLD = PRICE*8-95: XOLD = COLUMN
4040   YNEW = PRICE*8-95: XNEW = COLUMN
4050   LINE(XOLD,YOLD)-(XNEW,YNEW)
4060   LINE(COLUMN,37)-(COLUMN,43)
4070   YOLD = YNEW: XOLD = XNEW
4080 NEXT COLUMN
4090 RETURN
4999 '
5000 REM * plot hi, low, close graph *
5010 FOR COLUMN = 24 TO 284 STEP 12
5020   READ HI,LO,FINAL
5030   YHI = HI*8-95: YLO = LO*8-95: YCLOSE = FINAL*8-95
5040   LINE(COLUMN,YHI)-(COLUMN,YLO)
5050   LINE(COLUMN-3,YCLOSE)-(COLUMN+3,YCLOSE)
5060   LINE(COLUMN,37)-(COLUMN,43)
5070 NEXT COLUMN
5080 RETURN
```

We have explored various ways to display information in graphical form in this chapter. Bar graphs, circle graphs, line graphs, and a mix of bar and line graphs were drawn. We also investigated the capabilities of the high-resolution graphics mode. Menus were used to provide selections from several options. Viewports were used to place multiple displays on the screen at the same time. Several new terms and statements were introduced.

- The modulo operation was used to select color codes.

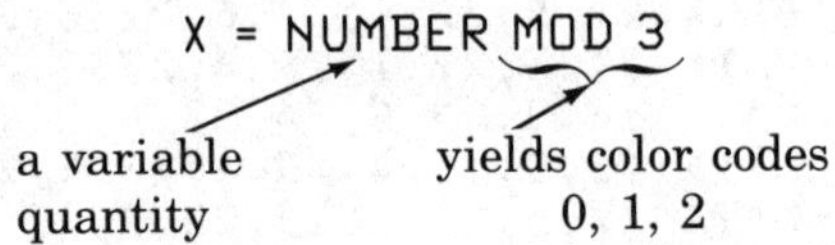

- High-resolution graphics is selected by the SCREEN statement.

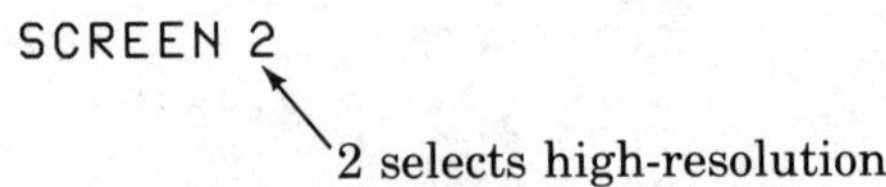

- Viewports can be designated to display rectangular areas on the screen.

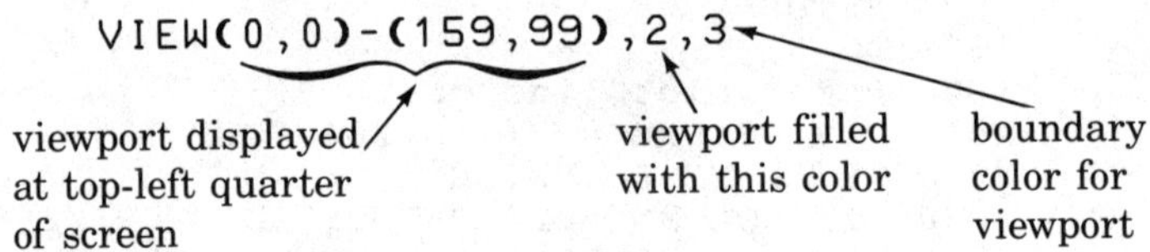

9
GRAPHICS MEMORY USE

Graphics Statements, Functions,
and Terms Introduced

DEF SEG
POKE
OUT
screen memory

The objective of this chapter is to teach you how to place text and graphics directly on the screen by storing data into the memory area dedicated to the screen display.

BASIC statements and terms that we assume you are familiar with are all those used in previous chapters, plus OUT.

BASIC statements and terms that are explained in this chapter are DEF SEG, POKE, OUT, and screen memory.

We have previously used BASICA statements to draw figures, plot points, and print data. We will now create pictures on the screen using BASICA's POKE statement. The POKE statement writes a byte (range of 0–255) into a specified memory location. The format is

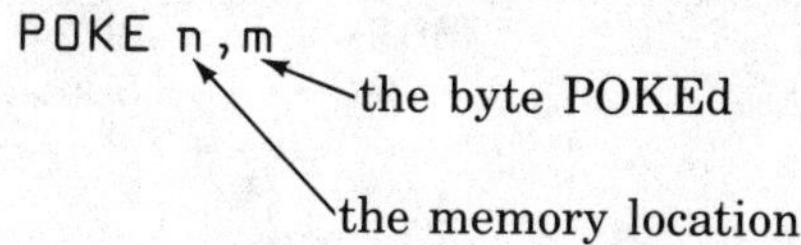

The memory address (n) must be in the range of 0 to 65535. It is an offset from the current segment as defined by the DEF SEG statement discussed in this chapter.

We will be storing codes that represent text and color information directly into the screen memory of the IBM. While it is generally harder to create pictures this way, it is useful in that you can learn how graphics data is represented in the machine.

MEMORY ORGANIZATION

The computer's memory is divided into segments. Each segment can address 65535 bytes (64K). When using BASICA, a predefined segment is used to store all the variable contents and other data. Any PEEK or POKE statements executed would retrieve or store information in this area. To create graphics on the screen, we must POKE data into the screen memory. This memory is stored in a different segment than the one used for BASICA's data. The screen memory segment is B800 (hex). To tell BASICA to use this new segment for storage, we must use the DEF SEG statement. The statement

```
DEF SEG = &HB800
```

tells BASICA to set the current segment to B800 (hex). The '&H' that precedes the B800 specifies a hexadecimal argument. This statement will be used in all our programs in this chapter.

PEEK and POKE statements can only access memory addresses from 0 through 65535 (0 through FFFF hex). DEF SEG is used to define the address where a 64K segment begins. A memory address on the IBM PC is 20 bits long. Therefore, a total of 1,048,576 bytes (2 raised to the 20th power, or 1024K bytes) can be addressed. The actual memory address is calculated by combining the 16-bit segment value (set with the DEF SEG statement in BASICA) and the 16-bit address value given in a PEEK or POKE statement. The segment value is shifted 4 bits to the left, and the address value is added to it. This creates a 20-bit memory address from two 16-bit values.

EXAMPLE

All values listed below are in hexadecimal.

```
      B800      16-bit segment value
     B8000      shifted 4 bits to the left
      1A23      16-bit address value

     B8000
   +  1A23      add
     B9A23      resulting 20-bit memory address
```

Therefore, using a segment value of B800, we can address memory locations B8000 through C7FFF by using PEEK or POKE addresses 0 through FFFF (B8000 + FFFF = C7FFF).

Depending on which text or graphics mode you are using, different amounts of screen memory are used and the data stored in that memory is interpreted differently.

USING TEXT MODE

When using either 40-column or 80-column text mode, each character requires 2 bytes of screen memory. The first byte contains the ASCII character code, and the second byte contains an attribute code. The attribute code controls the foreground and background colors of the character as well as specifying whether it should blink.

In 40-column mode, the screen uses 2000 bytes of memory (40 characters × 25 lines × 2 bytes per character). In 80-column mode, the screen uses 4000 bytes (80 × 25 × 2). This memory begins at the start of our screen memory segment, B800 (hex). This means that the first address of the actual screen memory is B8000 (hex). The value stored in this location is the ASCII code for the character that appears at the upper-left corner of the screen. The value stored in the next location (B8001 hex) is the attribute code for that upper-left character.

The next 2 bytes of screen memory contain the ASCII and attribute codes describing the next character to the right, and so on until the end of that line on the screen. The first character of the next line is stored in the next 2 memory locations. The memory locations used are contiguous for the whole screen in the text mode. The illustration in Fig. 9–1 shows the representation of 40-column text in the screen memory.

The screen memory-address pair can be calculated easily for any location on the screen. The following formula gives the "offset" value for any location on the screen:

```
ASCII value offset = 80 × (ROW -1) + 2 × (COL - 1)
Attribute value offset = ASCII value offset + 1
```

ROW is the screen row number (1 through 25). Row 1 is the top row of the screen and 25 is the bottom row. COL is the column number (1 through 40).

The offset value is the address that we will use in our POKE statement to place data on the screen. It is combined internally with the screen segment value to generate the true 20-bit address for the screen.

EXAMPLE

We compute the offsets necessary to address the character at the upper-right corner of the screen (ROW = 1, COL = 40).

```
ASCII offset = 80 × 0 + 2 × 39 = 78 = 4E hex
Attribute offset = 78 + 1 = 79 = 4F hex
```

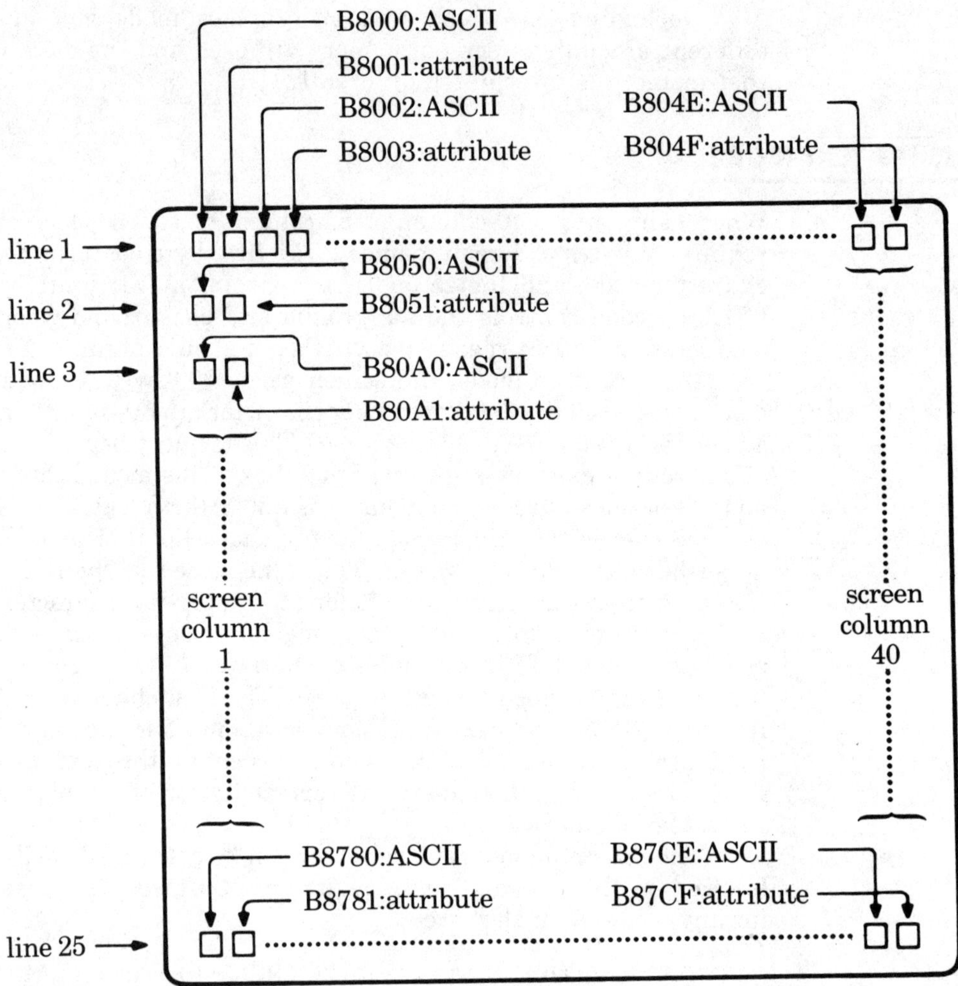

FIG. 9–1. 40-column text mode memory organization

POKEing data into address 78 or 79 (decimal) actually results in the data being put into address B804E or B804F hex.

To compute the offsets for the character at the lower-left corner of the screen (ROW = 25, COL = 1):

$$\text{ASCII offset} = 80 \times 24 + 2 \times 0 = 1920 = 780 \text{ hex}$$

$$\text{Attribute offset} = 1920 + 1 = 1921 = 781 \text{ hex}$$

POKEing data into address 1920 or 1921 decimal actually results in the data being put into address B8780 or B8781 hex.

Looking at our screen map of Fig. 9–1, we see that these are the actual addresses of these points on the screen.

The 80-column text screen is organized identically to the 40-column except that there are now twice as many characters on each line. This means that the screen map will look a bit different, since twice as many addresses must be used. The screen map for the 80-column text mode is shown in Fig. 9–2.

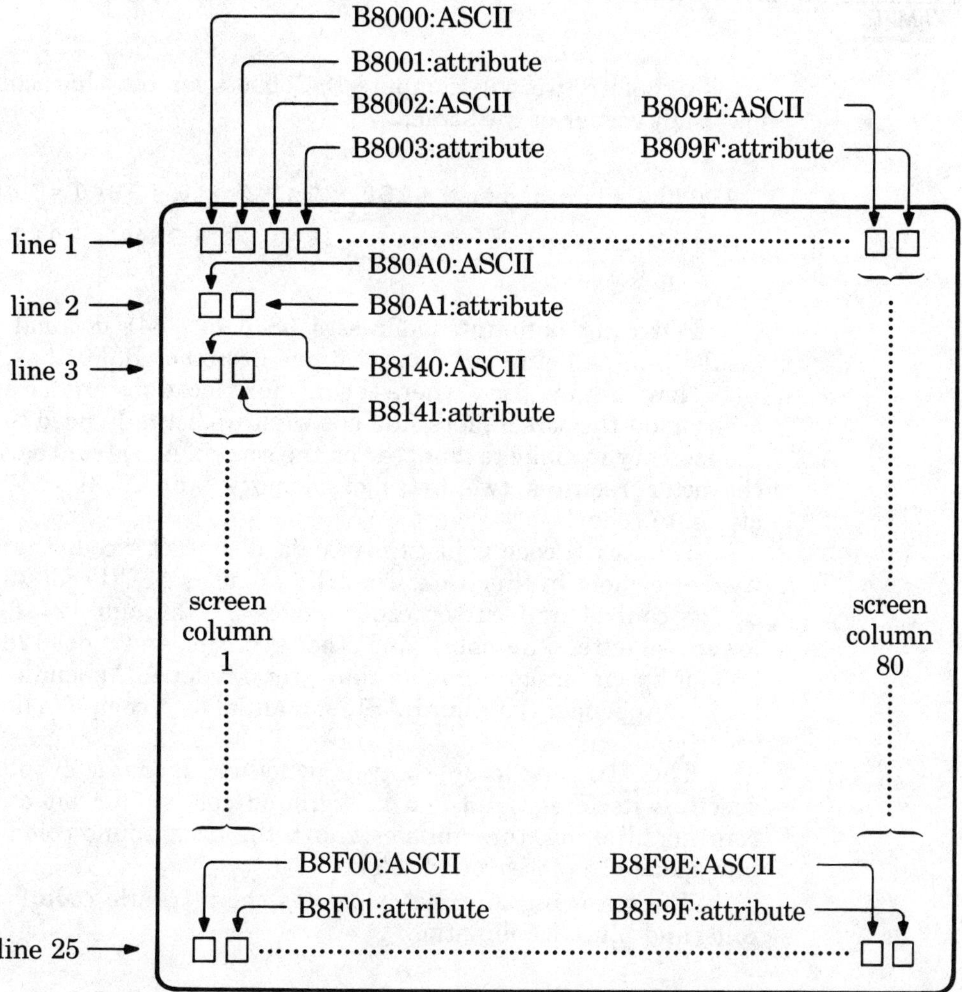

FIG. 9–2. 80-column text mode memory organization

As before, there is a convenient formula that can be used to calculate the offsets for any location on the screen.

```
ASCII value offset = 160 × (ROW -1) + 2 × (COL -1)

Attribute value offset = ASCII value offset + 1
```

Notice that the only difference between this formula and the 40-column version is that the value of 80 in the 40-column version has been changed to 160 in the 80-column version. This reflects the fact that there are now twice as many characters (and thus twice as many bytes) per line than before.

As before, we will compute the offsets for the character at the lower-left corner of the screen.

```
ASCII value offset = 160 × 24 + 2 × 0 = 3840 = F00 hex

Attribute value offset = 3840 + 1 = 3841 = F01 hex
```

POKEing data into addresses 3840 or 3841 decimal actually results in data being put into locations B8F00 or B8F01 hex.

Now that we know where the memory locations are for any given position on the screen, let's find out what we actually need to put into the memory to make text appear on the screen. As we said earlier, each character requires two bytes of memory: an ASCII code and an attribute code.

The ASCII code is just the standard character code that we have used elsewhere in this book. The IBM PC uses ASCII codes 0 through 31 for control and cursor codes, codes 32 through 127 for upper/lowercase letters, numbers, and other symbols, and codes 128 through 255 for special programmable characters. Refer to Appendix A of this book or Appendix G of your BASICA manual for a complete list of these codes.

The attribute code controls whether a character blinks and specifies its foreground and background colors. One bit of the code controls blinking, three bits establish the background color, and four bits specify the foreground color.

The following formula calculates the attribute code for a given color and blink combination:

```
Attribute code = 128 × BLINK + 16 × BACKGROUND + FOREGROUND
```

1—blinking   colors 0–7   colors 0–15
0—not blinking

The program in Listing 9–1 puts several characters on the screen using 40-column text mode. Figure 9–3 shows the result. Lines 310 through 340 generate a red *H* on a black background, a blinking blue *i* on a white background, a blinking bright white + on a brown background, and a yellow *Q* on a blue background.

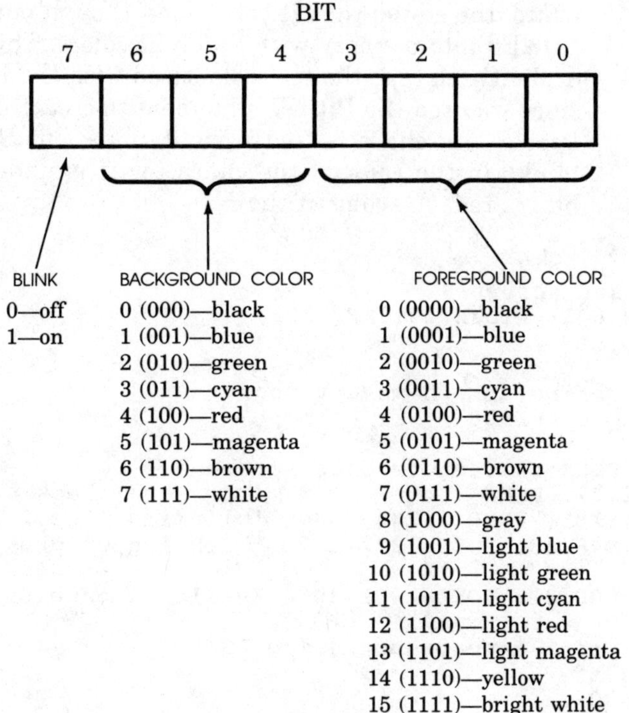

EXAMPLE

Red H on black background:
  Blink = 0 (no)
  Background color = 0 (black)
  Foreground color = 4 (red)
Attribute code = 128 × blink + 16 × background + foreground
  = 128 × 0 + 16 × 0 + 4 = 4
Blinking blue i on a white background:
  Blink = 1 (yes)
  Background color = 7 (white)
  Foreground color = 1 (blue)
Attribute code = 128 × 1 + 16 × 7 + 1 = 241

Notice that the PRINT statement in line 410 causes the z to appear in the upper-left corner of the screen, even though the last character we put on the screen (Q) was positioned in the middle of the screen. This is because we did not explicitly change the cursor location, which is used for all PRINT statements, even though we POKEd characters all over the screen. Notice also that the z was printed in white, the standard text color, even though our other characters were POKEd into memory with different colors. This is because we did not explicitly change the text color used with the PRINT statement. Also, since we used the PRINT statement to create the *z*, the PRINT cursor appears one character to the right, under our *H*. Notice that the cursor blinks in the color of the character it is underneath. In our case, it blinks red, the color of the *H*.

LISTING 9–1. 40-Column Text

```
100 REM * set screen *
110 SCREEN 0,1: WIDTH 40: KEY OFF
120 CLS
199 '
200 REM * define screen memory segment *
210 DEF SEG = &HB800
299 '
300 REM * POKE characters onto screen *
310 POKE 2,72: POKE 3,4          'red H on black background
320 POKE 4,105: POKE 5,241       'blinking blue i on white background
330 POKE 1996,43: POKE 1997,239  'blinking bright white + on brown ba
ckground
340 POKE 1000,81: POKE 1001,30   'yellow Q on blue background
399 '
400 REM * print a character using PRINT *
410 PRINT "z"
420 GOTO 420
```

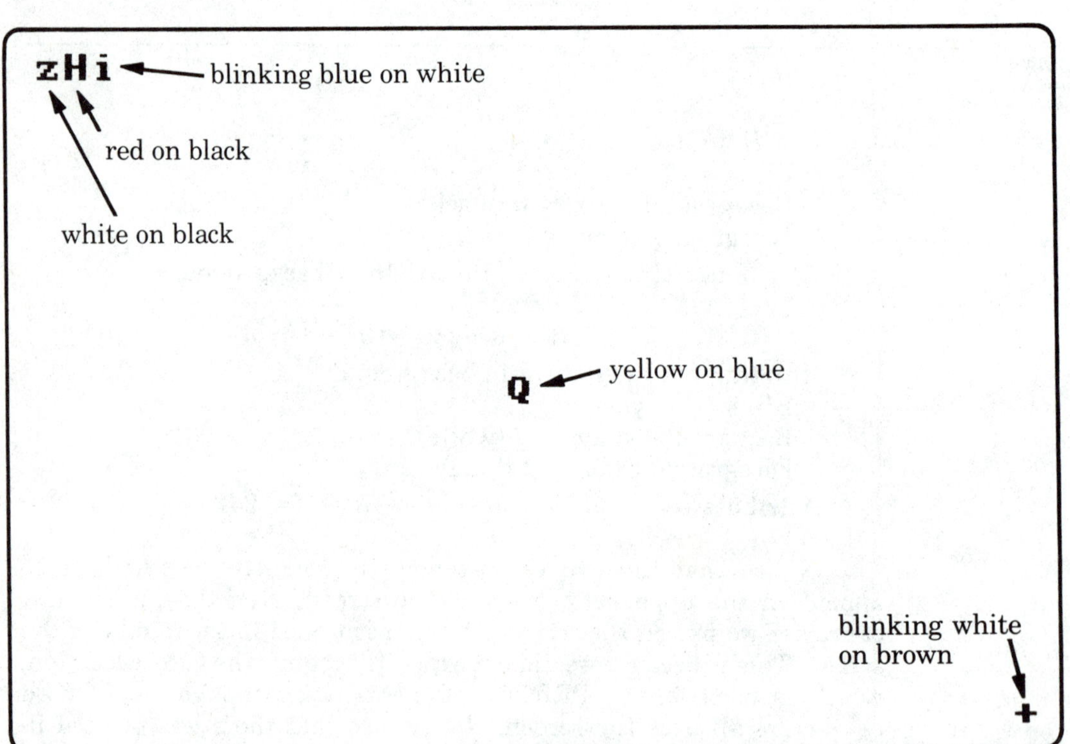

FIG. 9–3. 40-column text

Now let's change the program so that it puts text on the screen in 80-column mode while still using the same addresses as the 40-column version. All we have to do is change the WIDTH in line 110 from 40 to 80.

```
110 SCREEN 0,1: WIDTH 40: KEY OFF
```

becomes

```
110 SCREEN 0,1: WIDTH 80: KEY OFF
```

Upon running this new version, we get the result shown in Fig. 9–4. All the characters are the same, but it looks like they have all moved toward the upper-left corner of the screen by a factor of two. Indeed they have, since the 80-column mode has twice as many characters per line as the 40-column mode. This means that using the same addresses as in the 40-column mode will cause our picture to appear to be reduced in size by half and moved toward the upper-left corner of the screen while the symbols displayed still appear in the same positions relative to each other.

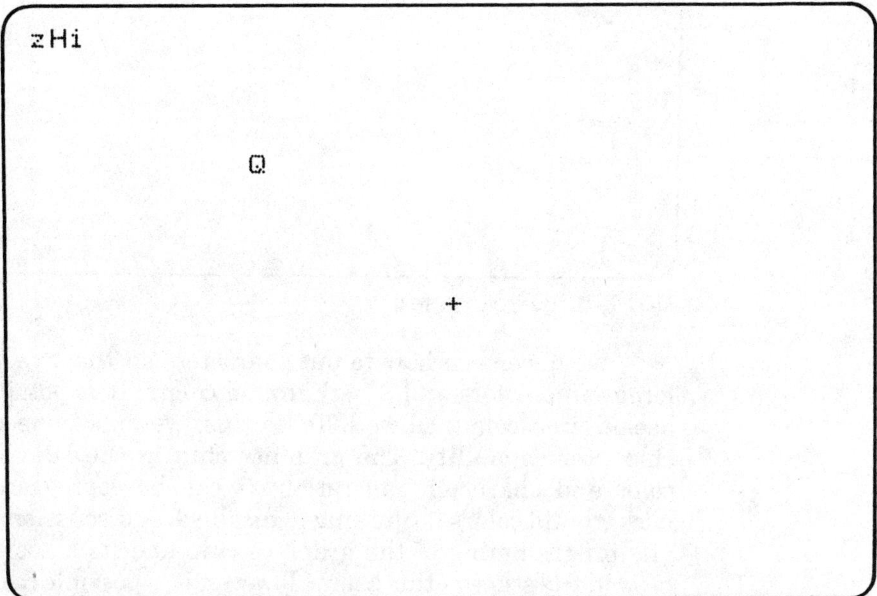

FIG. 9–4. Reduced 80-column text

Now let's change the program once more. We will continue to use the 80-column mode, but this time we will put the *Q* back in the center of the screen and the + back in the lower-right portion of the screen (as they were in the original 40-column version). To do this, we must change lines 330 and 340:

330 POKE 1996,43: POKE 1997,239

becomes

330 POKE 3996,43: POKE 3997,239

340 POKE 1000,81: POKE 1001,30

becomes

340 POKE 2000,81: POKE 2001,30

The resulting screen is shown in Fig. 9–5.

FIG. 9–5. 80-column text

We have seen how to put characters on the screen in any 1 of 16 foreground colors and 8 background colors. It is possible to use all 16 background colors as well. To do this, we must give up the blinking character capability. The graphics chip in the IBM PC controls the color and character generation. It can be reprogrammed to use 16 background colors if blinking is disabled. A discussion of the operation and programming of the graphics chip and its associated circuitry is beyond the scope of this book. However, it is possible to do what we want without understanding all the details. The graphics chip is programmed via several output ports. We can send data to these ports using BASICA's OUT statement.

The OUT statement sends a byte of data (0–255) to a machine output port using the form

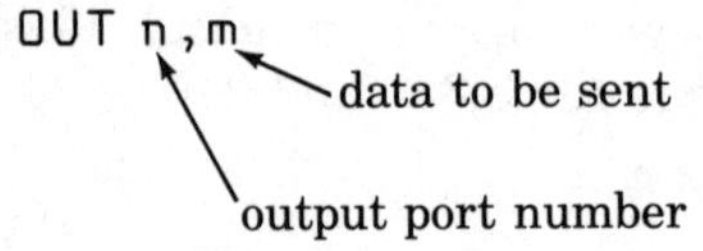

To use 16 background colors in the 40-column mode, we must send the value 8 to output port 3D8 (hex). In the 80-column mode, we must send the value 9 to the same output port. Thereafter, whenever we POKE an attribute code into the screen memory, the high-order bit, which used to control blinking, now completes the 4-bit code for background color.

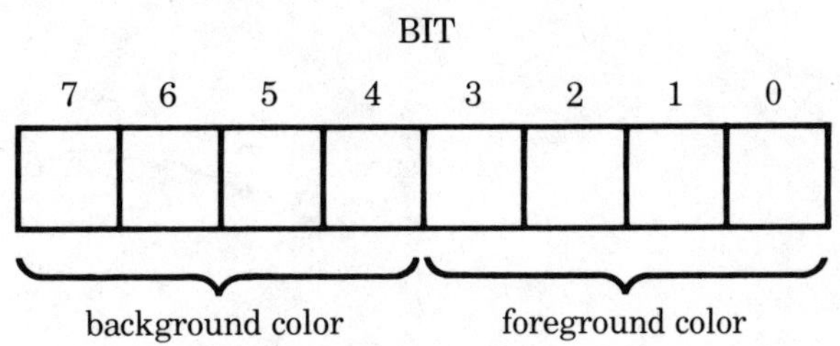

The background color now ranges from 0 through 15 (0000 through 1111 binary), just like the foreground color. The background color codes are the same as the foreground color codes listed earlier.

We will now add this ability to our program. The new version is shown in Listing 9–2. Upon running the program, notice that all the characters that were blinking before are no longer blinking, but do appear in different colors. The result is shown in Fig. 9–6. The *i* that was blinking before now appears as blue on bright white. The blink bit (1) combined with the background bits for normal white (111) became the new background color 1111, or bright white. Likewise, the + that was blinking before now appears as bright white on a yellow background, since the blink bit (1) combined with the background color bits for brown (110) became 1110, or yellow.

LISTING 9–2. 40-Column Text with 16 Background Colors

```
100 REM * set screen *
110 SCREEN 0,1: WIDTH 40: KEY OFF
120 CLS
199 '
200 REM * define screen memory segment *
210 DEF SEG = &HB800
299 '
300 REM * set up blink bit as background bit *
310 OUT &H3D8,8
399 '
400 REM * POKE characters onto screen *
410 POKE 2,72: POKE 3,4          'red H on black background
420 POKE 4,105: POKE 5,241       'blue i on bright white background
430 POKE 1996,43: POKE 1997,239  'bright white + on yellow background
440 POKE 1000,81: POKE 1001,30   'yellow Q on blue background
499 '
500 REM * print a character using PRINT *
510 PRINT "z";
520 GOTO 520
```

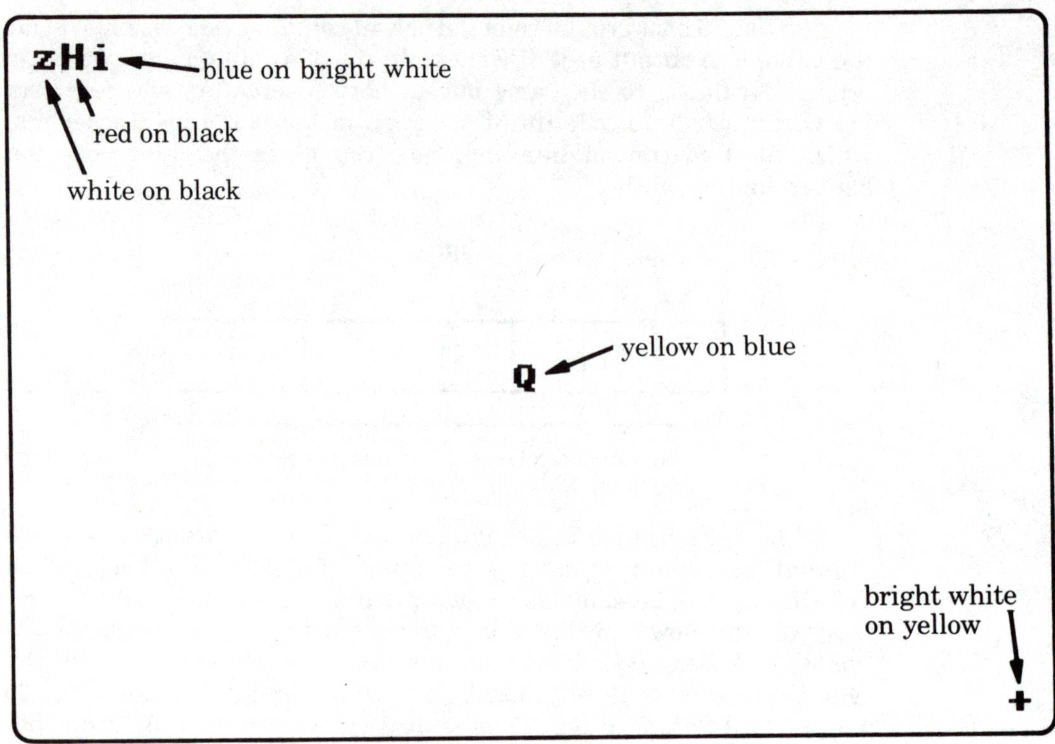

FIG. 9—6. 40-column text with 16 background colors

USING THE MEDIUM-RESOLUTION GRAPHICS MODE

The medium-resolution graphics mode is a bit more complicated to use. The screen memory used in this mode is not quite contiguous: two separate areas of memory are used and alternating lines on the screen are created from alternating areas of memory. Instead of two bytes per character location, the medium-resolution mode uses two bits (underline) per pixel. Thus, one byte of screen memory represents four pixels on the screen. Two bits are required to select the color for the pixel: 0 through 3 (00 through 11 binary), as in BASICA.

EXAMPLE

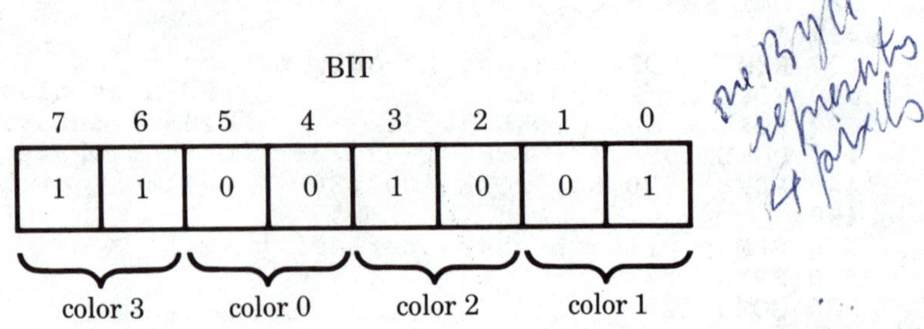

produces a pixel in color 3, followed by a pixel in color 0, followed by a pixel in color 2, followed by a pixel in color 1. The actual color generated depends on the palette selected with the COLOR statement.

The screen memory layout is illustrated in Fig. 9–7. As with the text mode, the screen memory starts at segment B800 (hex). There are 320 pixels across a line in the medium-resolution graphics mode. Since we can store four pixels in one byte of screen memory, we need 80 bytes for each line. The top line of the screen is controlled by addresses B8000 through B804F (4F hex = 79 decimal). Notice that the next line of the screen is controlled by addresses BA000 through BA04F. The third line of the screen is controlled by addresses B8050 through B809F. The set of addresses for each line alternates between memory that started at B8000 and memory that started at BA000. Looking at the last byte of the two bottom rows of the screen, notice that the first set of addresses does not extend right up to the beginning of the second

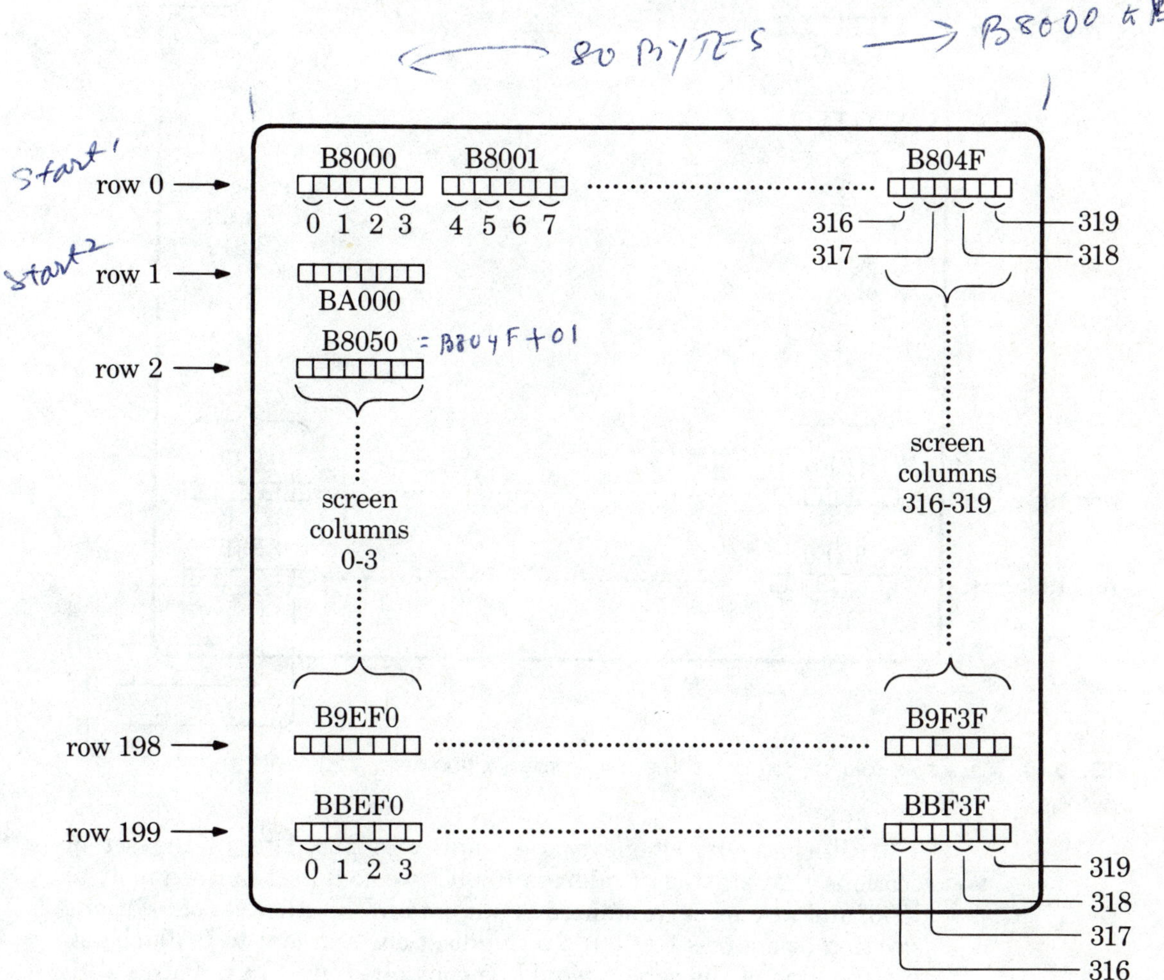

FIG. 9–7. Medium-resolution graphics memory organization

set: the second from the bottom row ends with address B9F3F, rather than B9FFF. Likewise, the bottom row ends at BBF3F, rather than BBFFF.

There are two ways to access these memory locations from BASICA. We could define our segment to be B800. Then POKEing data into locations 0 through 4F would affect the pixels on the first line of the screen, and POKEing data into locations 2000 through 204F (B8000 + 2000 = BA000) would affect the pixels on the second line of the screen, and so on. The resulting screen addresses are shown in Fig. 9–8.

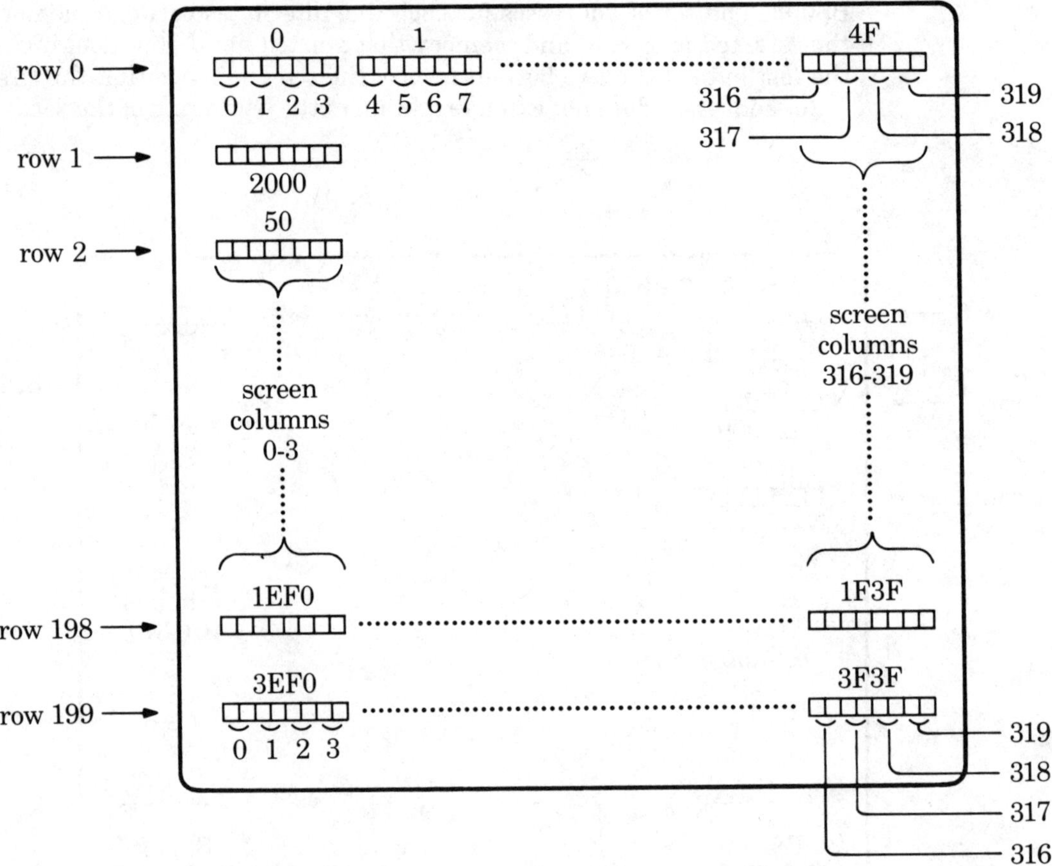

FIG. 9–8. Medium-resolution graphics memory organization with segment offsets

Alternatively, whenever we wanted to put data in the set of locations that started at address B8000, we could set our segment to B800, and whenever we wanted to put data in the other set of locations (starting at address BA000), we could set our segment to BA00. Then the first line of the screen would be controlled by POKE addresses 0 through 4F in the first segment, and the second line of the screen would be controlled by POKE addresses 0 through 4F in the second segment. This method requires much work because we have to constantly switch the segment using the DEF SEG statement.

It would be possible to do all the POKEing for segment B800, then switch the segment once and do all the POKEing for segment BA00, but a person watching the screen would see the first half of the picture drawn from top to botttom, followed by the second half drawn from top to bottom to complete the picture, rather than seeing the entire picture drawn at once from top to bottom.

The program in Listing 9–3 draws a box on the screen in the medium-resolution mode. The box has green sides and a brown top and bottom. The sides are drawn first, using POKEs that alternate between memory areas so that the dots will be drawn continuously from the top to the bottom of the screen. We use only one DEF SEG statement, set to B800, the start of the screen memory.

The POKE statements in line 120 put a single dot at both ends of the current screen line (controlled by the FOR loop).

The POKE statements in line 130 do the same thing but for the other memory area by adding 2000 hex (B8000 + 2000 = BA000) to the FOR loop variable. Lines 210 through 230 generate the brown top and bottom lines of the box by POKEing data into locations 0 through 4F (for the top line) and 3EF0 through 3F3F (for the bottom line). The finished box is shown in Fig. 9–9.

LISTING 9–3. Box Using Both Segments at Once

```
100 REM * set screen *
110 SCREEN 1,0: KEY OFF
120 COLOR 0,0: CLS
130 DEF SEG = &HB800                    'set up graphics segment
199 '
200 REM * make green sides *
210 FOR X = 0 TO &H1EF0 STEP &H50
220   POKE X,&H40: POKE X+&H4F,1        'make line A
230   POKE X+&H2000,&H40: POKE X+&H204F,1   'make line A+1
240 NEXT X
299 '
300 REM * make top and bottom lines brown *
310 FOR X = 0 TO &H4F
320   POKE X,&HFF: POKE X+&H3EF0,&HFF
330 NEXT X
340 GOTO 340
```

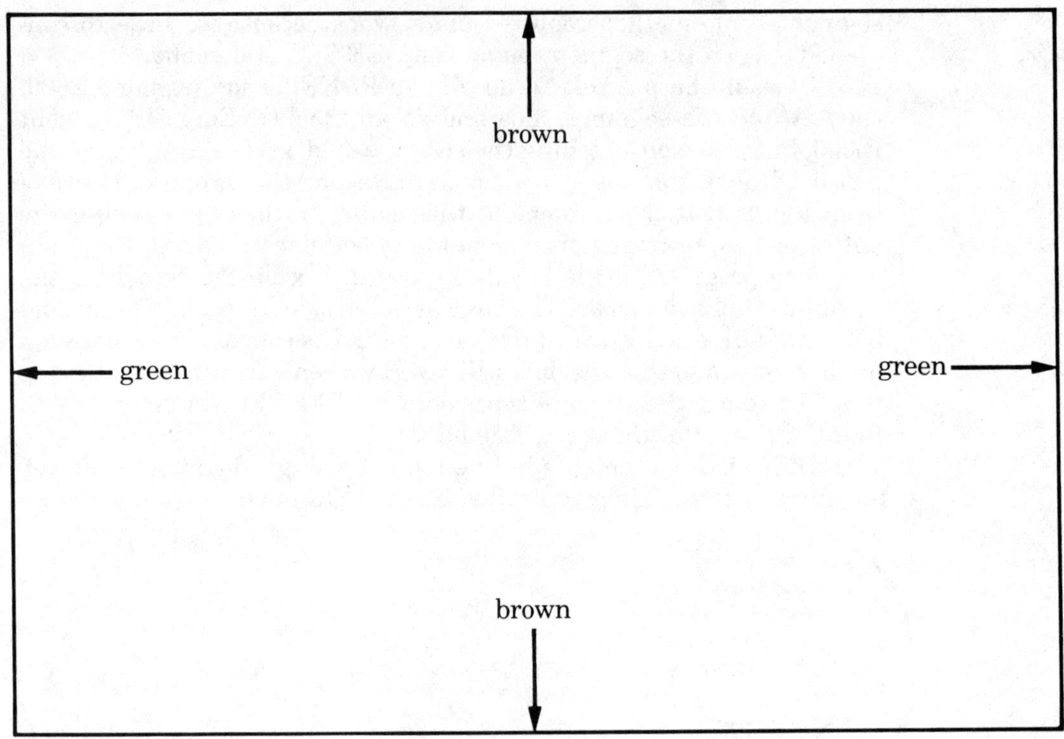

FIG. 9—9. Box

LISTING 9—4. Box Using One Segment at a Time

```
100 REM * set screen *
110 SCREEN 1,0: KEY OFF
120 COLOR 0,0: CLS
199 '
200 REM * make green sides *
210 DEF SEG = &HB800                'use first segment
220 GOSUB 1010                      'POKE data for sides (first half)
230 DEF SEG = &HBA00                'use second segment
240 GOSUB 1010                      'POKE data for sides (second half)
299 '
300 REM * make top and bottom lines brown *
310 FOR X = &H1EF0 TO &H1F3F        'make bottom line using second
320   POKE X,&HFF                   'segment
330 NEXT X
340 DEF SEG = &HB800
350 FOR X = 0 TO &H4F               'make top line using second segment
360   POKE X,&HFF
370 NEXT X
380 GOTO 380
399 '
1000 REM * subroutine for sides *
1010 FOR X = 0 TO &H1EF0 STEP &H50
1020   POKE X,&H40: POKE X+&H4F,1
1030 NEXT X
1040 RETURN
```

The program in Listing 9–4 does the same thing, using two different DEF SEGs. The green sides of the box are drawn using a subroutine (lines 300 through 350), which POKEs data into locations 0 through 1EF0. When the program is run, the first segment, B800, is selected with the DEF SEG in line 110. The subroutine is called, drawing two lines down the sides of the screen. Notice that in these lines, only every other dot is turned on. Next, the segment is set to BA00 and the subroutine is called again. This "fills in" the missing dots in the lines by POKEing to the same addresses in the second segment, thus putting dots on every other line on the second "half" of the screen. Lines 210 and 220 create the bottom line of the screen, POKEing to locations 1EF0 through 1F3F (the segment is still set to BA00). Lines 230 through 250 set the segment back to B800 and POKE in the top line of the screen in locations 0 through 4F.

The program in Listing 9–5 draws the same box on the screen, except that the sides are composed of alternating red and green dots. Run this program and examine the output carefully. The effect of different colored pixels right next to each other sometimes causes those colors to blend together. On our monitor, looking up close, you can see the red and green dots. From further away, it looks like there are yellow dots on every other line with occasional red specks between them. This effect will vary from monitor to monitor.

The program uses only one DEF SEG statement (similar to Listing 9–3) but it draws all the red dots first, then draws all the green dots, and finally draws the brown top and bottom lines. This allows you to see what happens when the green pixels are introduced in such close proximity to the red ones. The output is shown in Fig. 9–10.

LISTING 9–5. Box with Alternating Colors

```
100 REM * set up screen *
110 SCREEN 1,0: KEY OFF
120 COLOR 0,0: CLS
130 DEF SEG = &HB800                     'set up graphics segment
199 '
200 REM * make first half of sides red *
210 FOR X = 0 TO &H1EF0 STEP &H50
220   POKE X,&H80: POKE X+&H4F,2
230 NEXT X
299 '
300 REM * make second half of sides green *
310 FOR X = &H2000 TO &H3EF0 STEP &H50
320   POKE X,&H40: POKE X+&H4F,1
330 NEXT X
399 '
400 REM * make top and bottom lines brown *
410 FOR X = 0 TO &H4F
420   POKE X,&HFF: POKE X+&H3EF0,&HFF
430 NEXT X
440 GOTO 440
```

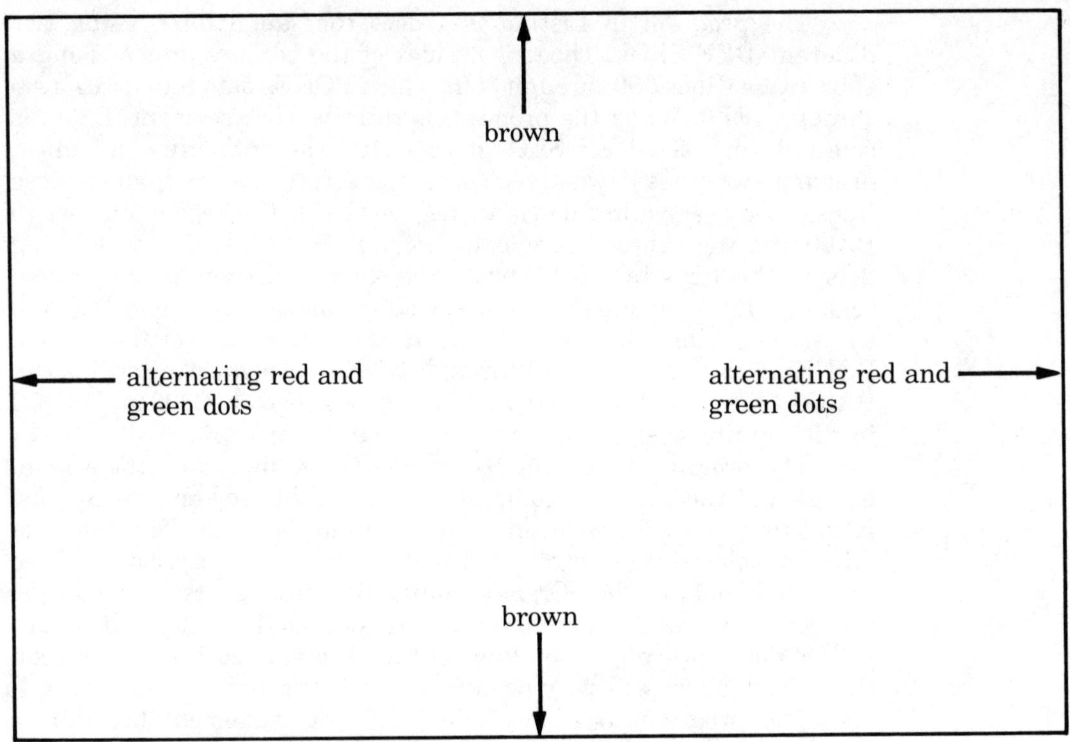

FIG. 9–10. Box with alternating colors

MIXING GRAPHICS AND TEXT

It is possible to put 40-column text onto the screen in the medium-resolution graphics mode. There are two ways to do this. The easiest way is to simply use the PRINT and LOCATE statements as you would normally. The other way is to copy into screen memory the stored pixel patterns for the character you want to print from a special table. This method is very cumbersome and has no advantages when used as part of a BASIC program. It could be done quickly using an assembly-language subroutine; however, programming in IBM assembly language is beyond the scope of this book. For our purposes, we will use LOCATE and PRINT.

Normally when using the PRINT statement in the medium-resolution graphics mode, the text appears in the foreground color (color 3) of whichever palette was selected with the COLOR statement. It is possible to change this color with a POKE to address 4E (hex) in BASICA's data segment. To do this, we will need to add the following line to our program:

```
DEF SEG: POKE &H4E, color
```

The DEF SEG with no agrument sets the current segment to the segment that BASICA uses to store its internal data. The "color" parameter is the new color that you want the text PRINTed to appear in. This may be set to either 1, 2, or 3 (not 0). After this statement is executed, all text PRINTed will appear in this color. We will change our program of Listing 9–5 so that it will print some text in the middle of the screen in different colors as well as drawing a box. The new version of the program is shown in Listing 9–6. The output is shown in Fig. 9–11.

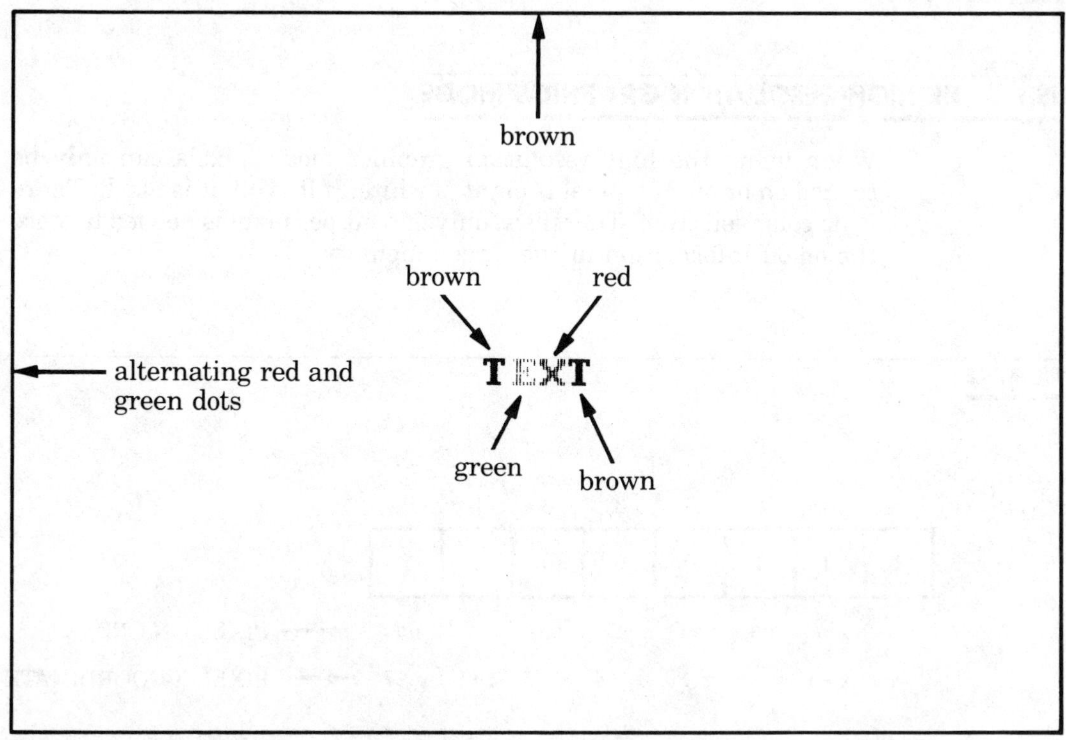

FIG. 9–11. Multicolored 40-column text

LISTING 9–6. Multicolored 40-Column Text

```
100 REM * set up screen *
110 SCREEN 1,0: KEY OFF
120 COLOR 0,0: CLS
130 DEF SEG = &HB800                        'set up graphics segment
199 '
200 REM * make first half of sides red *
210 FOR X = 0 TO &H1EF0 STEP &H50
220   POKE X,&H80: POKE X+&H4F,2
230 NEXT X
299 '
300 REM * make second half of sides green *
310 FOR X = &H2000 TO &H3EF0 STEP &H50
320   POKE X,&H40: POKE X+&H4F,1
330 NEXT X
399 '
400 REM * make top and bottom lines brown *
410 FOR X = 0 TO &H4F
```

```
420   POKE X,&HFF: POKE X+&H3EF0,&HFF
430 NEXT X
499 '
500 REM * put multi-color text on screen *
510 DEF SEG                              'change segment
520 LOCATE 12,18: PRINT "T";             'brown T
530 POKE &H4E,1: PRINT "E";              'green E
540 POKE &H4E,2: PRINT "X";              'red X
550 POKE &H4E,3: PRINT "T";              'brown T
560 GOTO 560
```

USING THE HIGH-RESOLUTION GRAPHICS MODE

When using the high-resolution graphics mode, pixels can only be turned on or off. If a pixel is on, it is white. If it is off, it is black. There is no color selection. Therefore, only one bit per pixel is needed to store the on/off information in the screen memory.

EXAMPLE

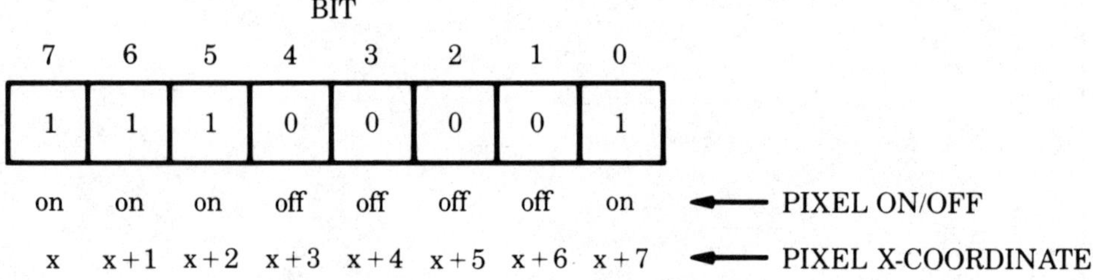

A screen line in high-resolution mode is 640 pixels wide. Therefore, since each byte contains information about 8 pixels, 80 bytes are required for each screen line. This is the same number as for the medium-resolution mode. Each line is generated from alternating screen memory areas, the same as in medium-resolution mode. Therefore, as we can see in Fig. 9–12, the screen memory organization is exactly the same as for medium-resolution mode.

The program in Listing 9–7 generates our familiar box around the edge of the screen. The addresses used to POKE screen data are identical to our earlier programs. The only differences are the actual values POKEd and the initialization to SCREEN 2 for high-resolution mode. We now use 80 rather than 40 (hex) to turn on the leftmost pixel in the first byte of each screen line. The output is identical to that of the program of Listing 9–4 except that all sides of the box are now white instead of green or brown.

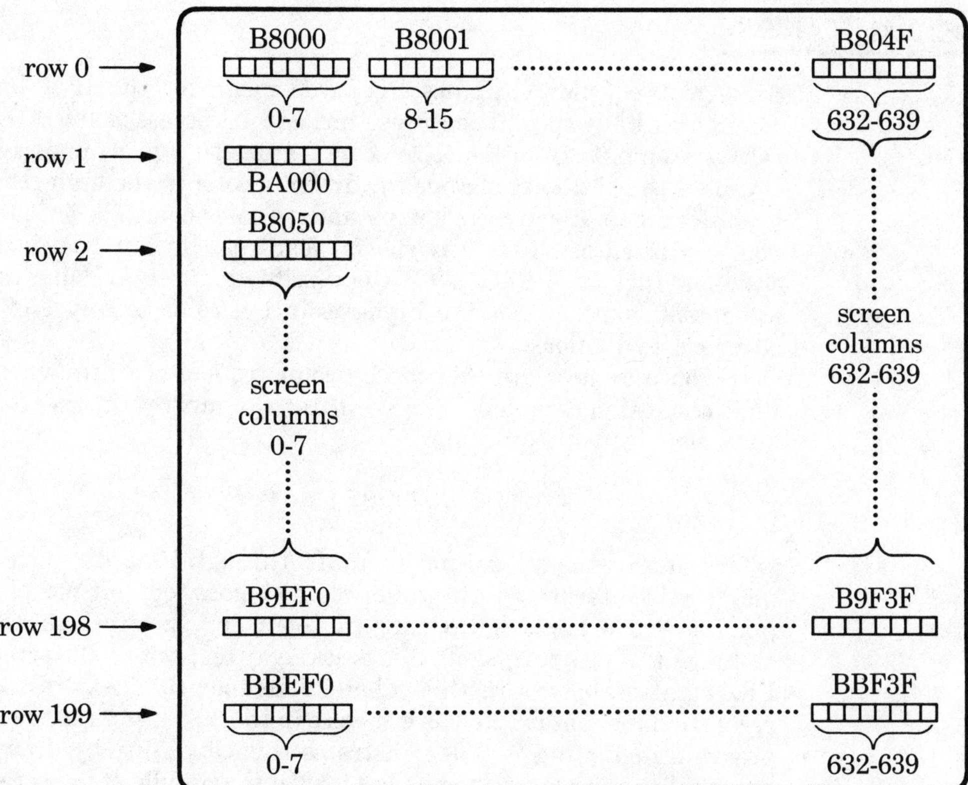

FIG. 9–12. High-resolution graphics memory organization

LISTING 9–7. High-Resolution Box

```
100 REM * set up screen *
110 SCREEN 2: KEY OFF: CLS
120 DEF SEG = &HB800                    'set up graphics segment
199 '
200 REM * make first half of sides *
210 FOR X = 0 TO &H1EF0 STEP &H50
220  POKE X,&H80: POKE X+&H4F,1
230 NEXT X
299 '
300 REM * make second half of sides *
310 FOR X = &H2000 TO &H3EF0 STEP &H50
320  POKE X,&H40: POKE X+&H4F,1
330 NEXT X
399 '
400 REM * make top and bottom lines brown *
410 FOR X = 0 TO &H4F
420  POKE X,&HFF: POKE X+&H3EF0,&HFF
430 NEXT X
440 GOTO 440
```

Some of the Color Graphics PC cards made for the IBM by other companies have special features that can be accessed by POKE and OUT statements from BASICA. One feature that is common to many boards is the ability to change the drawing color in the high-resolution graphics mode. If you have a nonstandard color board, be sure to check your documentation for any special features. On our board, the MA Systems, Inc., PC PEACOCK, it is possible to do this. Using the OUT statement, you can set the high-resolution color to any 1 of the 16 standard text colors.

You may now use this chosen color instead of white when doing high-resolution graphics. To do this, we must put the following statement into our program:

```
OUT 985, color
```

where color is the color number from 0 through 15. Data in the screen memory is interpreted the same way as before, one bit per pixel. If a pixel is turned on, it appears in the color specified in the OUT statement. If it is turned off, it is black. Any text put on the screen with PRINT also appears in this color. Remember that text in the high-resolution mode is printed as if it were in the 80-column text mode. The program in Listing 9–8 demonstrates this capability by drawing our box in blue and placing some blue text in the middle of the screen. The result is shown in Fig. 9–13.

LISTING 9–8. High-Resolution Box in Blue with Text

```
100 REM * set up screen *
110 SCREEN 2: KEY OFF: CLS
120 DEF SEG = &HB800                        'set up graphics segment
130 OUT 985,1                               'set special color to blue
199 '
200 REM * make first half of sides *
210 FOR X = 0 TO &H1EF0 STEP &H50
220   POKE X,&H80: POKE X+&H4F,1
230 NEXT X
299 '
300 REM * make second half of sides *
310 FOR X = &H2000 TO &H3EF0 STEP &H50
320   POKE X,&H40: POKE X+&H4F,1
330 NEXT X
399 '
400 REM * make top and bottom lines brown *
410 FOR X = 0 TO &H4F
420   POKE X,&HFF: POKE X+&H3EF0,&HFF
430 NEXT X
499 '
500 REM * put blue text on screen *
510 LOCATE 12,35: PRINT "Blue Text";
520 GOTO 520
```

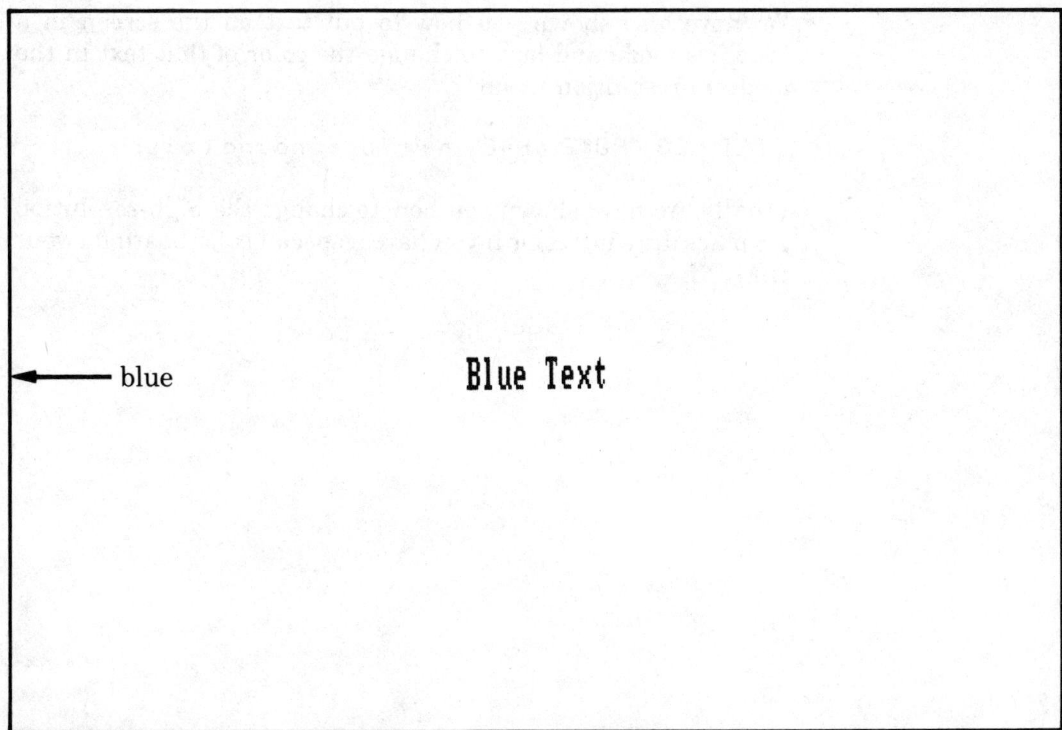

FIG. 9—13. High-resolution box in blue with text

SUMMARY

In this chapter, we have shown you how the screen memory is organized and used in the test, medium-resolution graphics mode, and high-resolution graphics mode.

- We have shown you how to use the DEF SEG statement to change BASICA's memory segment.

```
DEF SEG = segment address
```

- We have shown you how to use the character and attribute codes to put text on the screen.

```
POKE address, ASCII code
POKE address + 1, attribute code
```

- We have shown you how to use 16 background colors in text mode.

```
OUT &H3D8,8      in 40-column mode
OUT &H3D8,9      in 80-column mode
```

- We have also shown you how to put text on the screen in a graphics mode and how to change the color of that text in the medium-resolution mode.

```
DEF SEG: POKE &H4E, new foreground color
```

- Finally, we have shown you how to change the high-resolution graphics drawing color if you have a special color board for your IBM PC.

```
OUT 985, drawing color
```

10
SOUND AND PLAY MUSIC

Graphics Statements, Functions,
and Terms Introduced

SOUND
PLAY
tune definition language

Your objective in this chapter is to learn how to add sound effects to programs containing animation in order to obtain a more realistic simulation.

BASIC statements and terms that are explained in this chapter are PLAY, SOUND, and tune definition language.

Sound can be created from a speaker in the IBM PC through the use of two statements, SOUND and PLAY. The statements can be used to create music; however, in this book, we will explore the nonmusical sounds (noise) that can enhance your graphics programs. The SOUND statement is the simpler of the two and will be discussed first.

Table 10–1 gives frequencies that will produce four octaves for notes about Middle C, which has a frequency of 523.25.

TABLE 10–1

FOUR-OCTAVE SCALE

NOTE	FREQUENCY	NOTE	FREQUENCY	NOTE	FREQUENCY	NOTE	FREQUENCY
C	130.81	C	261.63	C*	523.25	C	1056.50
D	146.83	D	293.66	D	587.33	D	1174.70
E	164.81	E	329.63	E	659.26	E	1318.50
F	174.61	F	349.23	F	698.46	F	1396.90
G	196.00	G	392.00	G	783.99	G	1568.00
A	220.00	A	440.00	A	880.00	A	1760.00
B	246.94	B	493.88	B	987.77	B	1975.50

*Middle C

SOUND STATEMENT

The SOUND statement uses two parameters—frequency and duration—to control the output of the speaker.

The desired frequency is measured in Hertz (cycles per second) and is specified as a numeric expression in the range of 37 through 32767. The computer will not accept a number outside this range. When trying to execute a SOUND statement with a frequency greater than 32767, the computer will print "Overflow in xxx" where xxx is the line number of the offending SOUND statement. When trying to execute a SOUND statement with a frequency less than 37, the computer will print "Illegal function call in line xxx".

The duration is measured in clock ticks. A clock tick occurs 18.2 times per second.

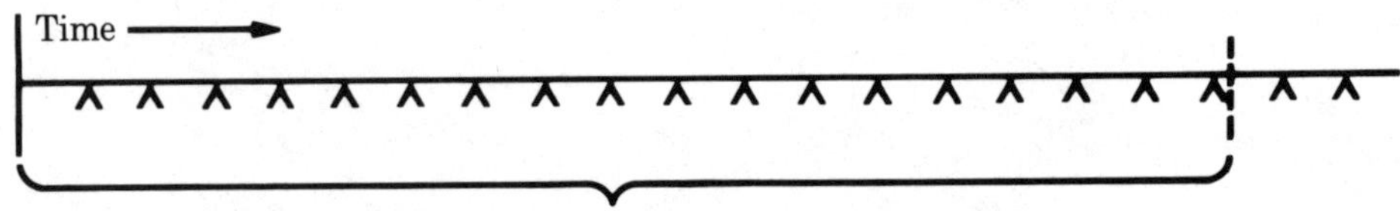

The specified duration must be a numeric expression in the range of 0 through 65535. If a number larger than 65535 is used, the computer will print "Illegal function call in line xxx".

When a SOUND statement is executed, the program normally continues (while the sound is being produced) until another SOUND statement is reached.

EXAMPLE

```
110 SCREEN 1,0:CLS
120 SOUND 440,50
130 CIRCLE(160,100),90
990 END
```

The statement in line 120 will turn on a sound. The circle will then be drawn. The sound will continue for the entire 50 clock ticks even though the program has ended.

After you have tried the previous example, add the following line and run the revised program:

```
150 SOUND 880,60
```

The computer will play the sound in line 120 and draw the circle. The computer does not play the second sound until the first one has finished. The program ends, and the "Ok" appears on the screen before the second sound starts. The sound at line 150 will continue for its complete 60 clock ticks even though the program has long ended.

SOUND WITH ANIMATION

Listing 6–5 of Chapter 6 produced an animated clock face. Sound can be added to that program to give "ticks" as the minute hand moves and "chimes" when each hour has passed. The program of Listing 10–1 includes these sounds utilizing the following modifications to Listing 6–5.

```
add        345 IF BETA = 360 THEN GOSUB 1210   ← hour chime

change     350 SOUND 37,.2                      ← tick

delete     380                                  ← was delay

add        420 KOLOR$ = "2"; GOSUB 1110 ⎫
                                        ⎬ ← 12 o'clock
add        430 GOSUB 1210               ⎭
```

Also, add the following subroutine:

```
1200 REM * hour chime *
1210 IF NUMBER = 1 THEN RETURN   ← no chime
1220 FOR STRIKE = 1 TO NUMBER-1
1230   SOUND 220,4               ← chime
1240   SOUND 32767,1             ← silence
1250 NEXT STRIKE
1260 RETURN
```

The complete revised clock with sound is given in Listing 10–1.

LISTING 10–1. Clock with Sound

```
100 REM * set screen & PI *
110 SCREEN 1,0: KEY OFF
120 COLOR 0,0: CLS
130 PI = 3.141593
199 '
200 REM * clock face *
210 CIRCLE(160,100),90,,,,1
220 CIRCLE(160,15),3,3: CIRCLE(160,185),3,3
230 CIRCLE(75,100),3,3: CIRCLE(245,100),3,3
299 '
300 REM * move hands *
310 ALPH=360.25
320 FOR NUMBER = 1 TO 12
330   FOR BETA=360 TO 3 STEP -3
340     KOLOR$="2": GOSUB 1100
345     IF BETA = 360 THEN GOSUB 1210
```

```
350    SOUND 37,.2
360     KOLOR$="0": GOSUB 1010
370     ALPH=ALPH-.25: KOLOR$="2": GOSUB 1010
390     KOLOR$="0": GOSUB 1100
400   NEXT BETA
410 NEXT NUMBER
420 KOLOR$ = "2": GOSUB 1110
430 GOSUB 1210
499 '
500 END
599 '
1000 REM * clock subroutine *
1010 DRAW"c"+KOLOR$+"bm 160,100;ta=alph;u4014e4f414"
1020 RETURN
1100 '
1110 DRAW"c"+KOLOR$+";bm 160,100;ta=beta;u6014e4f414"
1120 RETURN
1200 REM * hour chime *
1210 IF NUMBER = 1 THEN RETURN
1220 FOR STRIKE = 1 TO NUMBER-1
1230   SOUND 220,4
1240   SOUND 32767,1
1250 NEXT STRIKE
1260 RETURN
```

SOUND OFF

Sounds can be turned off by inserting a SOUND statement that has a
zero duration. Suppose you want to stop the first sound in the first
example of this chapter immediately after the circle has been drawn.
Add the following statement:

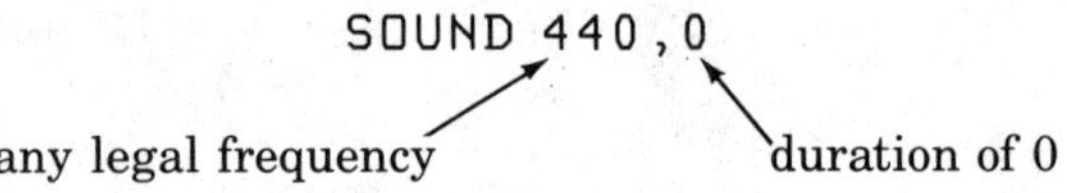

Try the following example to hear the effect of SOUND with zero
duration.

EXAMPLE

```
110 SCREEN 1,0; COLOR 0,0; CLS
120 SOUND 440,50
130 CIRCLE(160,100),90
140 SOUND 440,0          ◄——— turns off sound
150 SOUND 880,60         ◄——— turns on new sound
990 END
```

> Note: A zero duration SOUND statement will turn off any current
> sound statement being executed. If a nonzero duration
> SOUND statement is reached, the computer will complete the
> current sound before starting the new sound.

Periods of silence can also be created by specifying the highest legal value for the frequency parameter.

Therefore, you have two methods of creating silence:

1. Turning off the sound
2. Creating a period of silence

The use of the two forms of silencing SOUND are demonstrated in the program of Listing 10–2. The program produces a series of rising notes followed by a series of falling notes.

You have control of three variables:

1. The size of the step between frequencies
2. The duration of the note sound
3. The duration of the silence between notes

A wide variety of sounds can be made by varying these three variables.

The silence between notes is controlled in lines 230 and 240 by the statement

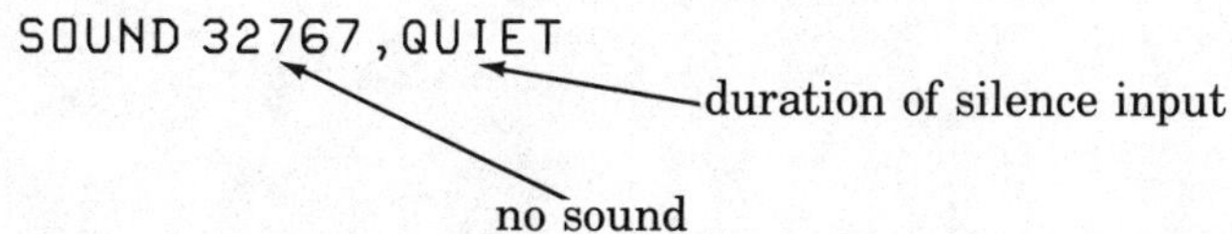

An experiment with the three variables can be ended by pressing a key. The key press is recognized at the end of the current series of falling notes at lines 410 and 420 by the statements

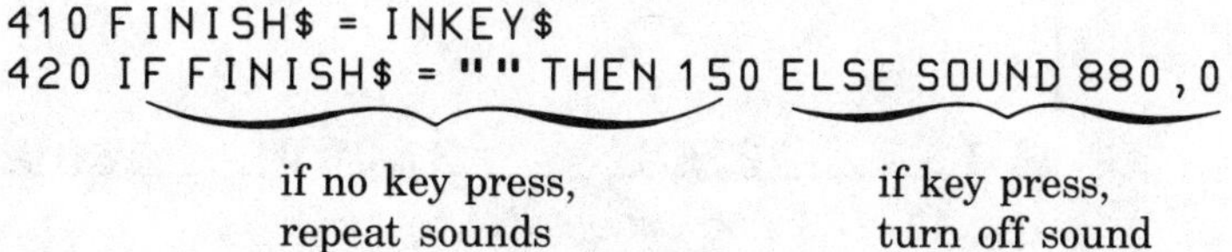

When the sound is turned off, the screen is cleared, and new variables can be entered for a new experiment.

You should spend considerable time running the Sound Experiment program with different values to discover the variety of sounds that can be produced. Sample inputs are shown in Fig. 10–1.

LISTING 10–2. Sound Experiment

```
100 REM * playing with sound *
110 CLS
120 INPUT "step (0-120)";INC
130 INPUT "sound duration (0-65535)";LONG
140 INPUT "silent duration (0-65535)";QUIET
199 '
200 REM * sound up *
210 FOR I=1000 TO 880 STEP -INC
220  SOUND I,LONG
230  SOUND 32767,QUIET
240 NEXT
299 '
300 REM * sound down *
310 FOR I=1000 TO 880 STEP -INC
320  SOUND I,LONG
330  SOUND 32767,QUIET
340 NEXT
399 '
400 REM * repeat or stop ? *
410 FINISH$=INKEY$
420 IF FINISH$="" THEN 210 ELSE SOUND 880,0
430 GOTO 110
```

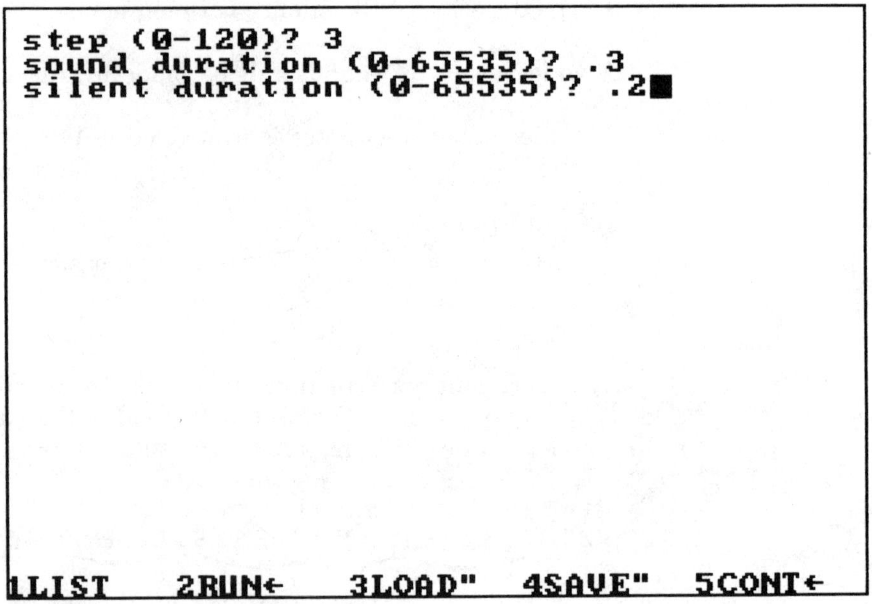

FIG. 10–1. Sound experiment inputs

MODIFIED HURDLER

It is often very simple to modify an existing program so that sound effects can be added. Sounds can often be added in places where time delays exist. Sometimes the insertion of a few simple lines is sufficient.

Visualize the display of the hurdler program of Listing 7–8 in Chapter 7. The hurdler runs toward the hurdle, leaps over it, and continues running toward the next hurdle. Enter and run the following example while keeping the picture of the hurdler in your mind.

EXAMPLE 1

```
110 FOR N = 1 TO 10
120   SOUND 37,.25
130   SOUND 32767,5
140 NEXT N
150 SOUND 32767,15
160 GOTO 110
990 END
```

The FOR-NEXT loop produces the sound of the hurdler's footsteps. Line 150 produces a period of silence as the hurdler glides over the hurdle. Line 160 causes the series of sounds to repeat.

This sequence of lines seems to produce a fairly realistic sound of the hurdler running. However, you should also consider the sound of a hurdle being knocked down. Enter and run Example 2, which incorporates some changes and additions to Example 1.

EXAMPLE 2

```
100 FOR H = 1 TO 10
110   FOR N = 1 TO 10
120     SOUND 37,.25
130     SOUND 32767,5
140   NEXT N
150   IF H/2<>INT(H/2) THEN SOUND 32767,15 ELSE GOSUB 1010
160 NEXT H
990 END
999 '
1010 SOUND 32767,5
1020 SOUND 2000,.1
1030 SOUND 32767,.2
1040 SOUND 2000,.1
1050 SOUND 32767,10
1060 RETURN
```

Next, imagine the hurdle clearing the odd-numbered hurdles (1, 3, 5, etc.) and knocking down the even-numbered hurdles (2, 4, 6, etc.).

The sound of footsteps between hurdles is made by lines 110 through 140, as in Example 1. However, line 150 provides for a choice of clearing the hurdle or knocking it down. The equality or inequality of

H/2 and the integer value of H/2 determines the sound made. H/2 will equal INT(H/2) for all even-numbered hurdles. H/2 will not equal INT(H/2) for the odd-numbered hurdles. The choice as it occurs at line 150 is shown in Fig. 10–2.

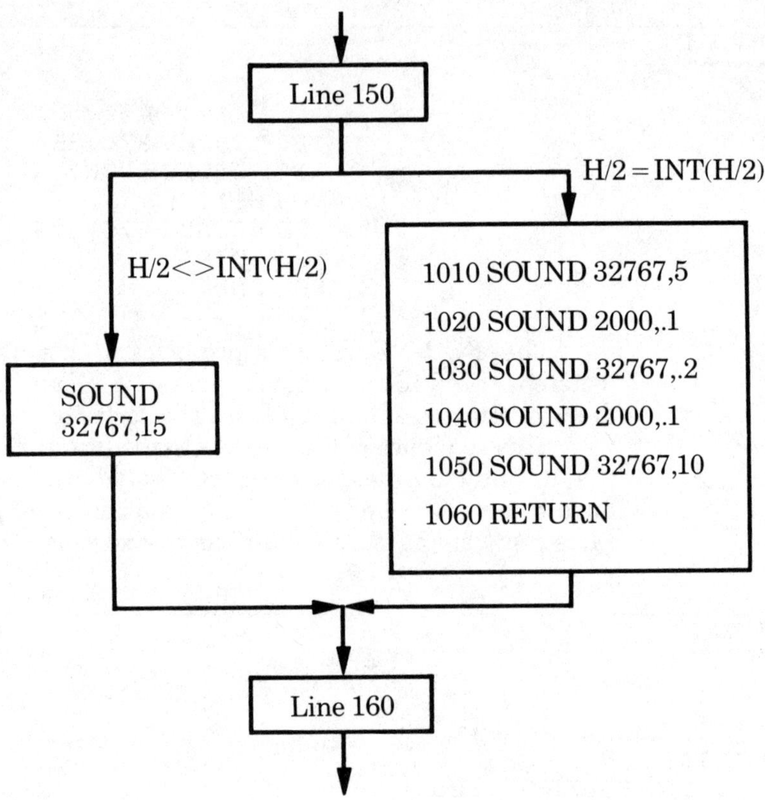

FIG. 10–2. Choice of sounds

The sound for clearing the hurdle is SOUND 32767,15 in line 150. The sound for knocking down the hurdle is provided in the subroutine at line 1010.

```
1010 SOUND 32767,5      ←— short silence
1020 SOUND 2000,.1      ←— hurdler hits hurdle
1030 SOUND 32767,.2            then
1040 SOUND 2000,.1      ←— hurdle hits ground
1050 SOUND 32767,10     ←— short silence before
                           hurdler recovers and
                           runs for next hurdle
```

Programming the sounds in Examples 1 and 2 is actually more complicated than adding the sounds to an existing program. The complete Hurdler with Sound program is given in Listing 10–3. If you compare it with Listing 7–8, you will notice the following changes.

SOUND 37,.25 is inserted at lines 835 and 925.

Line 2010 has been changed to provide a subroutine after
THEN.

```
2010 IF POINT(X+1,112)=1 OR POINT(X+2,112)=1 OR
     POINT(X+3,112)=1 OR POINT(X+10,110)=1
     THEN GOSUB 4010
```

SOUND 2000,.1: SOUND 32767,.2: SOUND 2000,.1 is contained
in the subroutine at line 4040.

```
4000 REM * hurdle down *
4010 PUT(X-2,100),F%,PSET
4020 PUT(X-2,115),E%,PSET
4030 X = X-18: Q=1
4040 SOUND 2000,.1: SOUND 32767,.2: SOUND 2000,.1
4050 RETURN
```

LISTING 10–3. Hurdler with Sound

```
100 REM * dimension arrays & set screen *
110 SCREEN 1: KEY OFF: CLS
120 DIM A%(36),B%(36),C%(36),D%(36),E%(12),F%(36)
199 '
200 REM * draw figure 1 *
210 LINE(11,189)-(11,188): LINE-(12,188): LINE-(12,185)
220 LINE-(14,183): LINE-(14,179): LINE-(11,182): LINE-(10,181): LINE-
(13,178)
230 LINE-(15,178): LINE-(15,177): LINE-(14,176): LINE-(14,174): LINE-
(17,174)
240 LINE-(17,176): LINE-(16,177): LINE-(16,178): LINE-(17,178): LINE-
(20,175)
250 LINE-(21,176): LINE-(17,180): LINE-(17,185): LINE-(19,183): LINE-
(21,185)
260 LINE-(20,186): LINE-(19,185): LINE-(17,187): LINE-(15,185): LINE-
(13,186)
270 LINE-(13,189): LINE-(11,189)
299 '
300 REM * draw figure 2 *
310 LINE(26,189)-(26,188): LINE-(27,188): LINE-(27,185)
320 LINE-(29,183): LINE-(29,179): LINE-(26,182): LINE-(25,181): LINE-
(28,178)
330 LINE-(30,178): LINE-(30,177): LINE-(29,176): LINE-(29,174): LINE-
(32,174)
340 LINE-(32,176): LINE-(31,177): LINE-(31,178): LINE-(33,178): LINE-
(36,181)
350 LINE-(35,182): LINE-(32,179): LINE-(32,189): LINE-(30,189): LINE-
(30,188)
360 LINE-(31,188): LINE-(31,185): LINE-(29,185): LINE-(28,186): LINE-
(28,189)
370 LINE-(26,189)
399 '
400 REM * draw figure 3 *
410 LINE(45,189)-(45,188): LINE-(46,188): LINE-(46,185): LINE-(45,185
): LINE-(45,183)
420 LINE(46,185)-(45,186): LINE-(44,186): LINE-(44,180): LINE-(40,176
): LINE-(41,175)
```

```
430 LINE-(44,178): LINE-(45,178): LINE-(45,177): LINE-(44,176): LINE-
(44,174)
440 LINE-(47,174): LINE-(47,176): LINE-(46,177): LINE-(46,178): LINE-
(48,178)
450 LINE-(51,181): LINE-(50,182): LINE-(47,179): LINE-(47,184): LINE-
(48,183)
460 LINE-(49,184): LINE-(50,183): LINE-(48,181): LINE-(47,182): LINE-
(47,189): LINE-(45,189)
499 '
500 REM * draw hurdler position & downed hurdle *
510 DRAW"bm63,185;ul14ulbr3l7u2r2d1r5ulbd1bl1u3"
520 LINE(61,178)-(57,180): LINE-(56,179): LINE-(60,178)
530 DRAW"hlllhle2fld1flr1"
540 LINE(62,177)-(64,176): LINE-(65,177): LINE-(62,178)
550 DRAW"buld6r2d2l1"
560 LINE(71,190)-(70,189),2: LINE-(73,188),2: LINE-(73,187),2: LINE-(
74,187),2
570 LINE-(74,190),2: LINE-(73,190),2: LINE-(73,189),2: LINE-(71,190),
2
599 '
600 REM * store figures *
610 GET(10,174)-(24,190),A%
620 GET(25,174)-(39,190),B%
630 GET(40,174)-(54,190),C%
640 GET(55,168)-(69,184),D%
650 GET(70,185)-(74,190),E%
660 GET(85,168)-(99,184),F%
670 CLS
699 '
700 REM * draw hurdles *
710 DRAW"bm83,115;c2r3ulllu3lld3lldl"
720 DRAW"bm155,115;r3ulllu3lld3lldl"
730 DRAW"bm233,115;r3ulllu3lld3lldl"
750 LINE(0,0)-(319,199),,B
799 '
800 REM * put figures for animation *
810 FOR DELAY=1 TO 50: NEXT DELAY
820 FOR X = 302 TO 16 STEP -6
830   PUT(X,100),A%,XOR
835   SOUND 37,.25
840   GOSUB 2010: IF Q=1 THEN GOTO 980
850   IF INKEY$="j" THEN GOSUB 3010
860   GOSUB 2010: IF Q=1 THEN GOTO 980
870   FOR DELAY = 1 TO 50: NEXT DELAY
880   PUT(X,100),A%,XOR
890   PUT(X,100),B%,XOR
900   FOR DELAY = 1 TO 50: NEXT DELAY
905   GOSUB 2010: IF Q=1 THEN GOTO 980
910   PUT(X,100),B%,XOR
920   PUT(X-3,100),C%,XOR
925   SOUND 37,.25
930   FOR DELAY = 1 TO 50: NEXT DELAY
935   GOSUB 2010: IF Q=1 THEN GOTO 980
940   PUT(X-3,100),C%,XOR
950   PUT(X-3,100),B%,XOR
960   FOR DELAY = 1 TO 50: NEXT DELAY
965   GOSUB 2010: IF Q=1 THEN GOTO 980
970   PUT(X-3,100),B%,XOR: GOTO 980
980   Q=0
```

```
990 NEXT X
1000 END
1999 '
2000 REM * test points *
2010 IF POINT(X+1,112)=1 OR POINT(X+2,112)=1 OR POINT(X+3,112)=1
     OR POINT(X+10,112)=1 THEN GOSUB 4010
2020 RETURN
2999 '
3000 REM * hurdle subroutine *
3010 PUT(X,100),F%,AND
3020 FOR N = 0 TO 21 STEP 3
3030   PUT(X-N,94),D%,XOR
3040   FOR DELAY = 1 TO 50: NEXT DELAY
3050   PUT(X-N,94),D%,XOR
3060 NEXT N
3070 X = X-24
3080 PUT(X,100),A%,XOR
3090 RETURN
3999 '
4000 REM * hurdle down *
4010 PUT(X-2,100),F%,PSET
4020 PUT(X-2,115),E%,PSET
4030 X = X-18: Q = 1
4040 SOUND 2000,.1: SOUND 32767,.2: SOUND 2000,.1
4050 RETURN
```

PLAY STATEMENT

The PLAY statement is a more versatile method for making sounds. It provides a way to pack many notes into a single statement with a wide variety of choices for defining notes and pauses. PLAY has the following format:

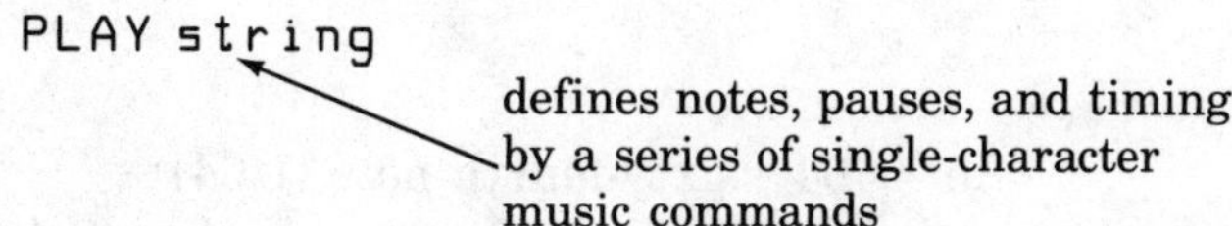

The concept of the PLAY statement is similar to that of the DRAW statement described in Chapter 5. The DRAW statement imbeds a "graphics definition language" in its string; the PLAY statement inbeds a "tune definition language" in its string.

A note to be played can be specified in two different ways by single-character commands.

1. You may combine a specified octave and note name.
    a. O n The letter *O* (octave) is followed by a number (n). The number *n* may range from 0 to 6. Zero (0) is the lowest, and six (6) is the highest.
    b. A through G with optional #, +, or −. The # or + signs indicate a sharp; the − sign indicates a flat. A through G are the standard notations used in music symbolism.

2. N n The letter N (note) is followed by a number (n). The number n may be in the range of 0 through 84. This covers the range of 7 octaves described in method 1. A zero used for n gives a rest (no sound). Thus, the N command provides a way to produce any note that can be produced by the combined octave (0) and note name (A–G).

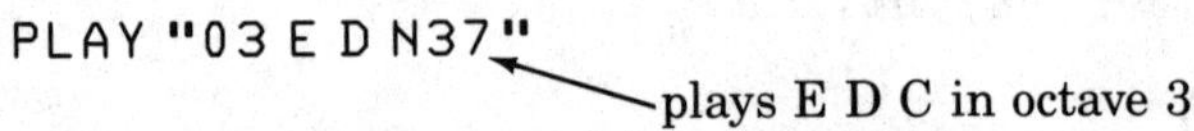

The length of a note is controlled by the L command. The note length is calculated as 1/n where n is the value following the L command.

n = 1 whole note (1/1)
n = 2 half note (1/2)

.

n = 4 quarter note (1/4)

.
.

n = 8 eighth note (1/8)

.
.

n = 64 sixty-fourth note (1/64)

If you want to change the length of a single note, the value for the length may follow the note symbol (N) with the letter L omitted.

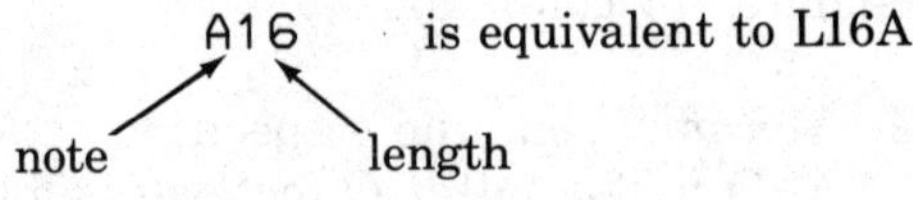

PLAY "CDEF16GA"   plays notes CDEGA
with length 32 and
note F with length 16

In the normal mode, each note plays 7/8 of the time specified by the value following the letter *L*. However, this time can be controlled by the following three PLAY commands:

MN music normal   (Each note plays for 7/8 of the time specified by L.)

ML music legato   (Each note plays for the full time specified by L.)

MS music staccato   (Each note plays for 3/4 of the time specified by L.)

The tempo of a series of notes is set with the T command.

```
T n
```

n may range from 32 through 255;
32 is slowest, 255 is fastest


```
PLAY "T40 CDE"
```

plays slower than PLAY "T240 CDE"

Rests between notes are set with the P (pause) command.

```
P n
```

n may range from 1 through 64;
the length of the pause is 1/n,
as in the L (length) command


```
PLAY "T40 CD P2 EF"
```

rest of 1/2 between D and E

Music is normally played in the foreground. That is, each sound will not start until the previous sound is finished. A certain amount of sound can be played in the background. If the MB command is used in a PLAY statement, each note or sound is placed in a buffer. This allows your BASIC program to continue executing other statements while music plays in the background. The buffer will hold up to 32 notes or rests for background play.

MF ← music foreground, the default state

MB ← music background (up to 32 notes or rests)

Finally, a substring labeled X may be executed within the PLAY string. Songs often repeat a series of notes one or more times. The X substring is useful at those times.


```
510 A$ = "DEFGA"
520 PLAY "CCC;XA$;DD;XA$;CC"
```

The n argument in all the PLAY commands can be a constant, such as 15. It can also be a variable, providing an equal sign (=) precedes the variable name.


```
650 FOR Z = 1 TO 9
660   PLAY "C D E N=Z;"  ←—plays 4 notes:
670 NEXT Z                        C D E 1
                                  C D E 2
                                  C D E 3
                                     .
                                     .
                                  C D E 9
```

A semicolon (;) is required when you use the variable format and when you use the X command. Otherwise, a semicolon between commands is optional, with the following exceptions: a semicolon cannot follow MF, MB, MN, ML, or MS.

NOISY ENGINE

Graphics for moving pistons of a four-cylinder engine were contained in the program of Listing 2–6 in Chapter 2. The pistons moved silently up and down with a red area representing the firing of each piston in turn. The movement was accomplished by flipping pages to display different positions of the pistons. This was done in lines 700 through 750 of the program.

```
700 REM * flip pages *
710 FOR PAGE = 0 TO 5
720   SCREEN 0,1,PAGE,PAGE
730   FOR DELAY = 1 TO 80: NEXT DELAY
740 NEXT PAGE
750 GOTO 710
```

Notice the time delay at line 730. We mentioned earlier in this chapter that time delays are places where sound can be added to existing programs. This seems like an ideal place to add the sound of the engine.

Pages 0, 1, 2, and 3 display the pistons in position for firing. The sounds should be made only when each of these pages is displayed. After some experimentation, we decided to replace the time delay with the following statement:

```
730 IF PAGE<4 THEN PLAY "T255 N20 L64 P16"
```

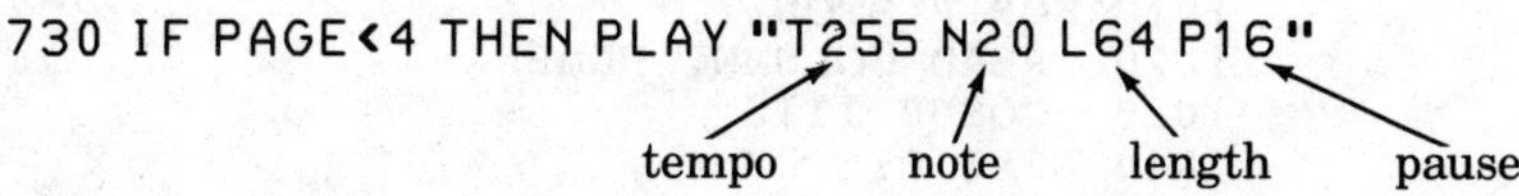

The frequency of the sound is controlled by the note value. Tempo, length, and pause work together to define the note and rest lengths. The complete modified program is shown in Listing 10–4.

LISTING 10–4. Noisy Engine

```
100 REM * set screen *
110 KEY OFF
120 WIDTH 40
130 SCREEN 0,1
140 CLS
199 '
200 REM * define A$ *
210 A$ = CHR$(32)+CHR$(32)
220 FOR NUMBER = 1 TO 12
230   A$ = A$+CHR$(220)
240 NEXT NUMBER
299 '
300 REM * define B$ *
310 B$ = ""
320 FOR NUMBER = 1 TO 5
330   B$ = B$+CHR$(32)+CHR$(219)+CHR$(219)
340 NEXT NUMBER
399 '
400 REM *define C$ *
410 C$ = CHR$(32)
420 FOR NUMBER = 1 TO 14
430   C$ = C$+CHR$(219)
440 NEXT NUMBER
499 '
500 REM * draw engine on 6 pages *
510 FOR AP = 0 TO 5
520   SCREEN 0,1,AP,0
525   COLOR 9
530   LOCATE 7,13
540   PRINT A$;
550   FOR ROW = 9 TO 14
560     LOCATE ROW,13
570     PRINT B$;
580   NEXT ROW
590   LOCATE 15,13
600   PRINT C$;
605 COLOR 7
610 GOSUB 1010
620 NEXT AP
699 '
```

```
700 REM * flip pages *
710 FOR PAGE = 0 TO 5
720   SCREEN 0,1,PAGE,PAGE
730   IF PAGE<4 THEN PLAY "MF T255 N20 L64 P16"
740 NEXT PAGE
750 GOTO 710
799 '
1000 REM * subroutine for piston data *
1010 FOR PISTON = 1 TO 4
1020   READ COLUMN, NUMBER
1030   GOSUB 1110
1040 NEXT PISTON
1050 RETURN
1099 '
1100 REM * subroutine to draw pistons *
1110 FOR ROW = 8 TO NUMBER
1120   LOCATE ROW,COLUMN
1130   PRINT CHR$(179);
1140 NEXT ROW
1150 LOCATE ROW,COLUMN
1160 PRINT CHR$(219);
1170 IF NUMBER = 12 THEN LOCATE ROW+1,COLUMN: COLOR 12,0,0:
                  PRINT CHR$(177);: COLOR 7,0,0
1180 RETURN
1199 '
1200 REM * data for pistons *
1210 DATA 16,9,19,10,22,11,25,12
1220 DATA 16,10,19,11,22,12,25,11
1230 DATA 16,11,19,12,22,11,25,10
1240 DATA 16,12,19,11,22,10,25,9
1250 DATA 16,11,19,10,22,9,25,10
1260 DATA 16,10,19,9,22,10,25,11
```

After entering and running the program, try changing any of the four PLAY commands to alter the sound. Save the program on disk, as it will be modified again in the next section.

CHANGING ENGINE NOISE

A noisy engine often needs tuning. Therefore, the next program allows you to input values for PLAY commands to change the engine's sound. The following inputs are provided:

1. Tempo (32 through 255)
2. Note (1 through 84)
3. Length (1 through 64)
4. Pause (1 through 64)

The program, Engine Tune-up, contains the following changes to Listing 10–4 to allow for the inputs and to execute the sounds:

```
100 REM * set screen and input *
110 SCREEN 0,1: WIDTH 40: KEY OFF: CLS
```

```
120 LOCATE 2,2: INPUT"Tempo (32-255)";SPEED
130 LOCATE 3,2: INPUT"Note (1-84)";TONE
140 LOCATE 4,2: INPUT"Length (1-64)";LONG
150 LOCATE 5,2: INPUT"Pause (1-64)";REST

730 IF PAGE<4 THEN PLAY "MF T=SPEED;N=TONE;L=LONG;P=REST;"
```

Make these changes to Listing 10–4. Then experiment with all four variables. Figure 10–3 shows values used to duplicate the sounds of Listing 10–4. See how well you can tune the engine with your own values. A possible variation of the program would allow sounds of the engine starting slowly and building up speed to its optimum operating sound. Another option would be to provide for instant control of engine speed through the use of joysticks or keyboard input.

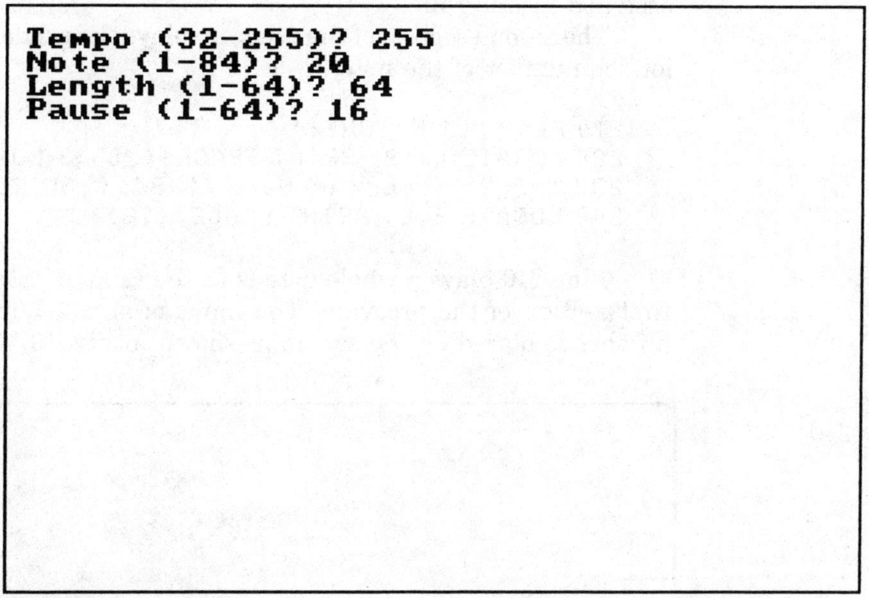

FIG. 10–3. Noise inputs

A SOUND GAME

You have probably played the computer game Guess My Number, which has been programmed under many names. It picks a random number and then requests you to guess what it is. Clues such as "Guess Higher" and "Guess Lower" are usually provided to help you find the number. A similar game can be written using musical notes and the numbers associated with the notes.

The PLAY statement allows you to choose from 0 through 84 values for the N (note) command. Since the zero value is a rest (no sound), we will confine our Note Guessing game values to the range of 1 through 84.

In the first section of the program, the screen is initialized. The random-number generator is then seeded, variables are initialized, and the random note is selected.

```
100 REM * set screen and initialize *
110 SCREEN 0,1: WIDTH 40: KEY OFF: CLS
120 RANDOMIZE
130 COLOR 5,0,5
140 TRY = 1: SUCCESS = 0
150 TONE = INT(RND*(84+1))
```

The TRY variable is used to tabulate the number of guesses made. SUCCESS is used to select a choice of two branches taken in the third section of the program. If SUCCESS = 0, one branch is taken. If SUCCESS = 1, a second branch is taken. The random note (TONE) is assigned in line 150.

The second section of the program plays the random note and asks for the number of the note.

```
210 PLAY "L1 N=TONE;"
220 LOCATE 10,2: PRINT SPACE$(20);: LOCATE 10,2
230 INPUT "Number of Note (1-84)";GUESS
240 LOCATE 2,2: PRINT SPACE$(16);
```

Line 210 plays a whole note with the random value chosen in the first section of the program. The input prompt requesting the note's number is placed on the screen as shown in Fig. 10-4.

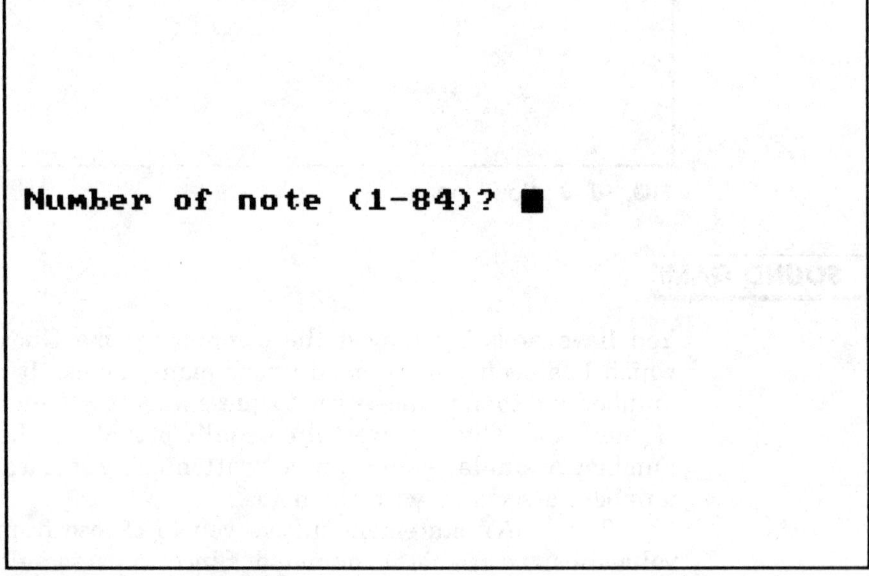

FIG. 10—4. Input prompt

The third section compares the guess with the random number. If the numbers are not equal, a branch to a subroutine is made. The subroutine contains clues for a new guess. If the numbers are equal, the SUCCESS variable is set to 1. Line 320 causes the computer to return to the second section if the guess is unsuccessful. If success has been achieved, the computer moves on to section 4.

```
310 IF TONE<>GUESS THEN GOSUB 1010 ELSE SUCCESS = 1
320 IF SUCCESS = 0 THEN 220
```

The logic of section 3 is shown in Fig. 10–5.

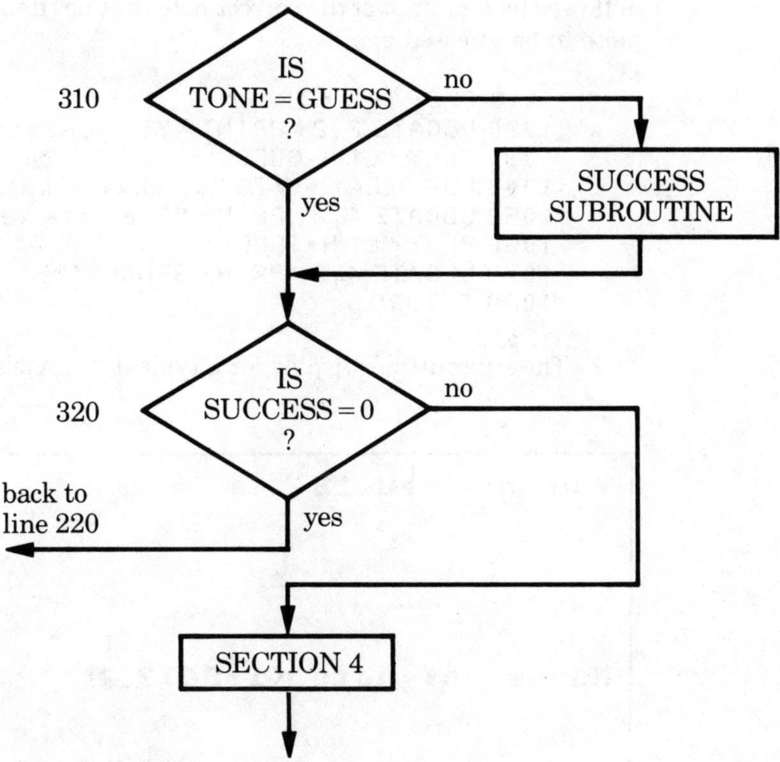

FIG. 10–5. Success logic

The fourth section is reached only when the numbers match. A FOR-NEXT loop is used to flash the screen with different border colors while a note of different value is played for each border.

```
410 CLS
420 FOR NUMBER = 1 TO 15
430   COLOR 1,0,NUMBER
440   PLAY "MF L16 N=NUMBER;"
450   FOR DELAY = 1 TO 50: NEXT DELAY
460 NEXT NUMBER
```

Section 5 displays the number of guesses made before achieving success and asks whether a new game is desired.

```
510 LOCATE 10,2: PRINT "You guessed it in";TRY; "tries";:
    INPUT "Play again";ANSWER$
520 IF LEFT$(ANSWER$,1)="Y" OR LEFT$(ANSWER$,1)="y" THEN CLS:
    GOTO 130
530 END
```

The subroutine played when the guess and random number values do not match tabulates the number of tries at line 1010. It then prints a prompt of your guess and plays the note for that value. This is followed by a prompt of the correct note (but not its value) and plays the note to be guessed again.

```
1010 CLS: TRY = TRY+1
1020 LOCATE 2,2: PRINT "You guessed":GUESS
1030 PLAY "L1 N=GUESS;"
1040 FOR DELAY = 1 TO 50: NEXT DELAY
1050 LOCATE 4,2: PRINT "The note was"
1060 PLAY "L1 N=TONE;"
1070 LOCATE 4,2: PRINT SPACE$(16)
1080 RETURN
```

The subroutine's display for a typical guess is shown in Fig. 10–6.

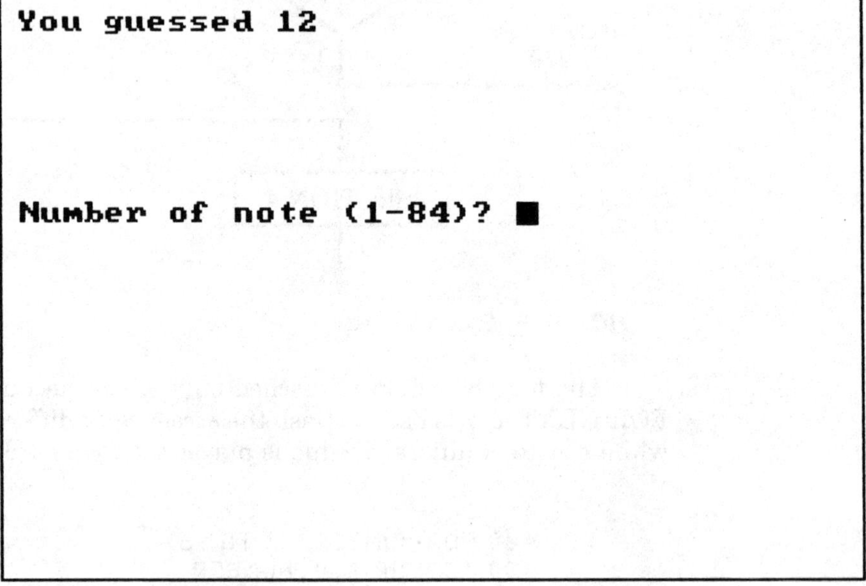

FIG. 10–6. Clue display

The complete program is shown in Listing 10–5.

LISTING 10–5. Note Guessing

```
100 REM * set screen and initialize *
110 SCREEN 0,1:WIDTH 40: KEY OFF: CLS
120 RANDOMIZE: CLS
130 COLOR 5,0,5
140 TRY = 1: SUCCESS = 0
150 TONE = INT(RND*(84+1))
199 '
200 REM * play note and get guess *
210 PLAY"L1 N=TONE;"
220 LOCATE 10,2: PRINT SPACE$(20);: LOCATE 10,2
230 INPUT "Number of Note (1-84)";GUESS
240 LOCATE 2,2: PRINT SPACE$(16);
299 '
300 REM * compare tones *
310 IF TONE<>GUESS THEN GOSUB 1010 ELSE SUCCESS=1
320 IF SUCCESS=0 THEN 220
399 '
400 REM * success *
410 CLS
420 FOR NUMBER = 1 TO 15
430   COLOR 1,0,NUMBER
440   PLAY "MF L16 N=NUMBER;"
450   FOR DELAY = 1 TO 50: NEXT DELAY
460 NEXT NUMBER
499 '
500 REM * play again? *
510 LOCATE 10,2: PRINT"You guessed it in";TRY;"tries ";:
    INPUT "Play again";ANSWER$
520 IF LEFT$(ANSWER$,1)="Y" OR LEFT$(ANSWER$,1)="y" THEN CLS:
    GOTO 130
530 END
599 '
1000 REM * wrong note *
1010 CLS:TRY=TRY+1
1020 LOCATE 2,2: PRINT "You guessed";GUESS
1030 PLAY "L1 N=GUESS;"
1040 FOR DELAY = 1 TO 50: NEXT DELAY
1050 LOCATE 4,2: PRINT "The note was"
1060 PLAY "L1 N=TONE;"
1070 LOCATE 4,2: PRINT SPACE$(16)
1080 RETURN
```

SUMMARY

This chapter presented an introduction to the use of the SOUND and PLAY statements. The creation of music was omitted so that we could focus on the sound capabilities for accompanying graphics animation.

- The SOUND statement has two parameters—frequency and duration—which control the output of a speaker.

SOUND frequency, duration

a number in the   duration in the range of
range of   0 through 65535
37 through 32767   (measured in clock ticks
                               occurring 18.2/second)

SOUND 500,0   turns off sound

any legal   0 duration
frequency

SOUND 32767,20   gives a period of silence

silence   any legal duration

- The PLAY statement contains a string of single-character commands.

PLAY string   defines notes, pauses, and timing

String characters consist of

O n   Octave
          range 0 through 6
A–G   Letter names for notes
N n   Note
          range 0 through 84; 0 is a rest
L n   Length of note (calculated as 1/n)
          range 1 through 64
MN   Music normal (note plays 7/8 of time specified by L)
ML   Music legato (note plays full time specified by L)
MS   Music staccato (note plays 3/4 of time specified by L)
T n   Tempo
          range 32 through 255 (32 slowest; 255 fastest)
P n   Pause
          range 1 through 64 (pause length 1/n, as in the L command)
MF   Music foreground
MB   Music background

This table lists all the ASCII codes (in decimal format) and the characters associated with each code. The characters can be displayed using the statement PRINT CHR$(n), where n is the ASCII code. The standard interpretations of ASCII codes 0 through 31 (usually used for control functions or communications) are listed in a separate column titled "Control Character."

Each of the characters may also be entered from the keyboard. Hold the Alt key down while pressing the digits of the ASCII code on the numeric keypad. Some of the codes have a special meaning to the BASIC program editor. Since the BASIC program editor uses its own interpretation of the codes, a character other than the one shown in the table may be displayed.

ASCII value	Character	Control character	ASCII value	Character	Control character
000	(null)	NUL	016	►	DLE
001	☺	SOH	017	◄	DC1
002	☻	STX	018	↕	DC2
003	♥	ETX	019	!!	DC3
004	♦	EOT	020	¶	DC4
005	♣	ENQ	021	§	NAK
006	♠	ACK	022	▬	SYN
007	(beep)	BEL	023	↨	ETB
008	◘	BS	024	↑	CAN
009	(tab)	HT	025	↓	EM
010	(line feed)	LF	026	→	SUB
011	(home)	VT	027	←	ESC
012	(form feed)	FF	028	(cursor right)	FS
013	(carriage return)	CR	029	(cursor left)	GS
014	♫	SO	030	(cursor up)	RS
015	☼	SI	031	(cursor down)	US

ASCII value	Character	ASCII value	Character
032	(space)	064	@
033	!	065	A
034	''	066	B
035	#	067	C
036	$	068	D
037	%	069	E
038	&	070	F
039	'	071	G
040	(	072	H
041	)	073	I
042	*	074	J
043	+	075	K
044	,	076	L
045	-	077	M
046	.	078	N
047	/	079	O
048	0	080	P
049	1	081	Q
050	2	082	R
051	3	083	S
052	4	084	T
053	5	085	U
054	6	086	V
055	7	087	W
056	8	088	X
057	9	089	Y
058	:	090	Z
059	;	091	[
060	<	092	\
061	=	093	]
062	>	094	∧
063	?	095	—

ASCII value	Character	ASCII value	Character
096	`	128	Ç
097	a	129	ü
098	b	130	é
099	c	131	â
100	d	132	ä
101	e	133	à
102	f	134	å
103	g	135	ç
104	h	136	ê
105	i	137	ë
106	j	138	è
107	k	139	ï
108	l	140	î
109	m	141	ì
110	n	142	Ä
111	o	143	Å
112	p	144	É
113	q	145	æ
114	r	146	Æ
115	s	147	ô
116	t	148	ö
117	u	149	ò
118	v	150	û
119	w	151	ù
120	x	152	ÿ
121	y	153	Ö
122	z	154	Ü
123	{	155	¢
124	¦	156	£
125	}	157	¥
126	~	158	Pt
127	⌂	159	ƒ

<table>
<tr><td colspan="2">ASCII</td><td colspan="2">ASCII</td></tr>
<tr><td>value</td><td>Character</td><td>value</td><td>Character</td></tr>
<tr><td>160</td><td>á</td><td>192</td><td>└</td></tr>
<tr><td>161</td><td>í</td><td>193</td><td>┴</td></tr>
<tr><td>162</td><td>ó</td><td>194</td><td>┬</td></tr>
<tr><td>163</td><td>ú</td><td>195</td><td>├</td></tr>
<tr><td>164</td><td>ñ</td><td>196</td><td>─</td></tr>
<tr><td>165</td><td>Ñ</td><td>197</td><td>┼</td></tr>
<tr><td>166</td><td>ª</td><td>198</td><td>╞</td></tr>
<tr><td>167</td><td>º</td><td>199</td><td>╟</td></tr>
<tr><td>168</td><td>¿</td><td>200</td><td>╚</td></tr>
<tr><td>169</td><td>⌐</td><td>201</td><td>╔</td></tr>
<tr><td>170</td><td>¬</td><td>202</td><td>╩</td></tr>
<tr><td>171</td><td>½</td><td>203</td><td>╦</td></tr>
<tr><td>172</td><td>¼</td><td>204</td><td>╠</td></tr>
<tr><td>173</td><td>¡</td><td>205</td><td>═</td></tr>
<tr><td>174</td><td>«</td><td>206</td><td>╬</td></tr>
<tr><td>175</td><td>»</td><td>207</td><td>╧</td></tr>
<tr><td>176</td><td>░</td><td>208</td><td>╨</td></tr>
<tr><td>177</td><td>▒</td><td>209</td><td>╤</td></tr>
<tr><td>178</td><td>▓</td><td>210</td><td>╥</td></tr>
<tr><td>179</td><td>│</td><td>211</td><td>╙</td></tr>
<tr><td>180</td><td>┤</td><td>212</td><td>╘</td></tr>
<tr><td>181</td><td>╡</td><td>213</td><td>╒</td></tr>
<tr><td>182</td><td>╢</td><td>214</td><td>╓</td></tr>
<tr><td>183</td><td>╖</td><td>215</td><td>╫</td></tr>
<tr><td>184</td><td>╕</td><td>216</td><td>╪</td></tr>
<tr><td>185</td><td>╣</td><td>217</td><td>┘</td></tr>
<tr><td>186</td><td>║</td><td>218</td><td>┌</td></tr>
<tr><td>187</td><td>╗</td><td>219</td><td>█</td></tr>
<tr><td>188</td><td>╝</td><td>220</td><td>▄</td></tr>
<tr><td>189</td><td>╜</td><td>221</td><td>▌</td></tr>
<tr><td>190</td><td>╛</td><td>222</td><td>▐</td></tr>
<tr><td>191</td><td>┐</td><td>223</td><td>▀</td></tr>
</table>

ASCII value	Character		ASCII value	Character
224	α		240	$\equiv$
225	β		241	$\pm$
226	Γ		242	$\geq$
227	π		243	$\leq$
228	Σ		244	$\lceil$
229	σ		245	$\rfloor$
230	μ		246	$\div$
231	τ		247	$\approx$
232	Φ		248	$\circ$
233	θ		249	$\bullet$
234	Ω		250	$\cdot$
235	δ		251	$\sqrt{}$
236	∞		252	^{n}
237	$\emptyset$		253	^{2}
238	ϵ		254	■
239	$\cap$		255	(blank 'FF')

USEFUL TABLES

OPERATING MODES OF THE COLOR/GRAPHICS ADAPTER

MODE	HORIZONTAL RESOLUTION	VERTICAL RESOLUTION	NUMBER OF PIXELS	COLORS AVAILABLE
Text	40	25	1,000	16 foreground
	80	25	2,000	8 background
				16 border
Medium-Resolution Graphics	320	200	64,000	3 foreground
				16 background
High-Resolution Graphics	640	200	128,000	black and white only

COLOR CODES FOR TEXT MODE

CODE	COLOR	USE
0	black	foreground, border, background
1	blue	foreground, border, background
2	green	foreground, border, background
3	cyan	foreground, border, background
4	red	foreground, border, background
5	magenta	foreground, border, background
6	brown	foreground, border, background
7	white	foreground, border, background
8	gray	foreground, border
9	light blue	foreground, border
10	light green	foreground, border
11	light cyan	foreground, border
12	light red	foreground, border
13	light magenta	foreground, border
14	yellow	foreground, border
15	bright white	foreground, border
16	* black	foreground
17	* blue	foreground
18	* green	foreground
19	* cyan	foreground
20	* red	foreground
21	* magenta	foreground
22	* brown	foreground
23	* white	foreground
24	* gray	foreground
25	* light blue	foreground
26	* light green	foreground
27	* light cyan	foreground
28	* light red	foreground
29	* light magenta	foreground
30	* yellow	foreground
31	* bright white	foreground

* signifies blinking color

NUMBER CODE	COLOR
0	black
1	blue
2	green
3	cyan
4	red
5	magenta
6	brown
7	white
8	gray
9	light blue
10	light green
11	light cyan
12	light red
13	light magenta
14	yellow
15	bright white

PALETTE COLORS FOR MEDIUM-RESOLUTION GRAPHICS

NUMBER CODE	PALETTE 0	PALETTE 1
0	background	background
1	green	cyan
2	red	magenta
3	brown	white

BINARY/HEXADECIMAL/DECIMAL EQUIVALENT VALUES

BINARY	HEXADECIMAL	DECIMAL
0000	0	0
0001	1	1
0010	2	2
0011	3	3
0100	4	4
0101	5	5
0110	6	6
0111	7	7
1000	8	8
1001	9	9
1010	A	10
1011	B	11
1100	C	12
1101	D	13
1110	E	14
1111	F	15

EFFECT OF PUT ACTION

		XOR			OR			AND		
		ARRAY COLOR			ARRAY COLOR			ARRAY COLOR		
		0 1 2 3			0 1 2 3			0 1 2 3		
	0	0 1 2 3			0 1 2 3			0 0 0 0		
Screen	1	1 0 3 2			1 1 3 3			0 1 0 1		
Color	2	2 3 0 1			2 3 2 3			0 0 2 2		
	3	3 2 1 0			3 3 3 3			0 1 2 3		

FOUR-OCTAVE SCALE FOR SOUND

NOTE	FREQUENCY	NOTE	FREQUENCY
C	130.81	C*	523.25
D	146.83	D	587.33
E	164.81	E	659.26
F	174.61	F	698.46
G	196.00	G	783.99
A	220.00	A	880.00
B	246.94	B	987.77
C	261.63	C	1046.50
D	293.66	D	1174.70
E	329.63	E	1318.50
F	349.23	F	1396.90
G	392.00	G	1568.00
A	440.00	A	1760.00
B	493.88	B	1975.50

*Middle C

AND A logical operator that returns a value of true when two conditions are compared and both are true; otherwise, it returns a value of false.

Apage The active page for the screen when in the text mode.

Catenation The operation that joins two strings together into a single string.

CHR\$ A function that returns the one-character string whose ASCII code is n in the form

```
CHR$(n)
```

CIRCLE A statement used to draw a circle or ellipse (or a part of one or the other) with center (x,y) and radius r. Its format is

```
CIRCLE(x,y),r[,color[,start,end[,aspect]]]
```

CLS A statement that clears the screen. (Changing the screen mode or width also clears the screen. The screen may also be cleared by pressing Ctrl-Home on the keyboard.)

COLOR A statement that sets colors on the screen. In the text mode the foreground, background, and border colors can be set with

```
COLOR[foreground][,[background][,border]]
```

In the medium-resolution graphics mode, COLOR can set the background color and one of two palettes to be used for the foreground color.

```
COLOR[background][,[palette]]
```

Concatenation See Catenation.

COS A function that returns the trigonometric cosine value for an angle specified in radians.

```
COS(angle)
```

DATA A statement used to store numeric and/or string constants that are accessed by a READ statement.

DEF SEG A statement that defines the current "segment" of memory storage. Subsequent address-oriented statements will define the actual physical memory address as an offset to this segment.

DIM A statement that specifies the maximum value for array variable subscripts. It also allocates memory space accordingly.

DRAW A statement that draws an object that is specified by commands contained in a string following the word *DRAW*. A graphics definition language is used to form the string.

ELSE Used in an IF-THEN statement to provide an alternate path for program flow in case the if condition is false.

END A statement that terminates program execution, closes all files, and returns to the command level.

FOR-NEXT Statements that form the beginning and ending of a series of instructions performed in a loop a given number of times.

GET A graphics statement that reads points from a rectangular area of the screen into an array. The area is specified by the coordinates of two opposite corners of the rectangle. (This statement should not be confused with the GET statement used for files, which was not used in this book.)

GOSUB A statement that causes a branch to a subroutine. A RETURN statement returns control to the main program to the statement that follows the most recent GOSUB statement.

GOTO A statement that causes an unconditional branch out of the normal program sequence to a specified line number.

HEX$ A function that returns a string representing the hexadecimal value of the specified decimal number.

IF-THEN-ELSE A statement used to make a decision regarding program flow based on whether a specified condition is true or false. If ELSE is omitted, a false condition would cause the program to continue at the next line number (next greatest in magnitude).

INKEY$ A string variable used to read a single character from the keyboard.

INPUT A statement that reads an input from the keyboard during program execution. The program pauses and a question mark is displayed. A prompt string may be used. It will appear before the question mark. Execution of the program resumes when data has been entered and the enter key pressed.

INT A function that returns the largest integer that is less than or equal to a specified value.

KEY A statement that sets or displays the soft (function) keys. KEY LIST returns a list of the functions currently assigned to the soft keys. KEY OFF turns off the display of the key functions. KEY ON turns on the display of the key functions, which are displayed at the bottom of the screen.

LEFT$ A function that returns the leftmost n characters of a specified string, as

```
A$ = LEFT$(X$,n)
```

LEN A function that returns the number of characters in a specified string, as

```
N = LEN(X$)
```

LINE A statement that draws either a line or a box on the screen. Two coordinate pairs are used to specify the end points of a line or the opposite corners of a box.

LOCATE A statement that positions the cursor on the active screen by row and column. Optional parameters turn the blinking cursor off or on and define its size.

LPRINT A statement that causes the computer to output data to a printer.

**MID$** A function that returns a specified part of a specified string. In the form shown, it returns a string of length m characters from A$ beginning with the nth character.

```
MID$(A$,n,m)
```

MOD An arithmetic operator used in modulo arithmetic. It gives the integer value that is the remainder of an integer division. Thus, 6 MOD 4 = 2, since the remainder of 6 divided by 4 is 2.

NEXT Used to end a FOR-NEXT loop. See FOR-NEXT.

ON...GOSUB Branches to one of several specified subroutine line numbers, depending on the value of an expression placed between the words ON and GOSUB.

OR A logic operator that returns a value of true when two conditions are compared and either one, or both, of the conditions are true. It returns a value of false when the two compared conditions are both false.

OUT A statement that sends a byte to a machine output port. In the following statement, n represents the output port number (in the range of 0–65535), and m represents the data to be sent (in the range of 0–255) to that port:

```
OUT n,m
```

PAINT A statement used to fill a closed area on the screen with the specified color. It is used in the graphics modes only. In the following statement, (x,y) is a point within the area to be painted, paint is the color used for painting, and boundary is the color of the boundary of the area:

```
PAINT(x,y), paint, boundary
```

PEEK A function that returns a byte of data read from the indicated memory location.

```
V = PEEK(n)
```

PLAY A statement used to play music or make complicated sounds. The string following the word *PLAY*, in the example, is made up of commands from a "tune definition language."

```
PLAY string
```

POINT A function that returns the color of the specified point on the screen. It is used in the graphics modes only. Its format is

```
POINT(x,y)
```

POKE A statement that writes a byte of data into a memory location. In the form shown, n (range of 0–65535) is the memory location where the byte is to be written. It is an offset from the current segment as defined by the DEF SEG statement. The data to be written (m) must be in the range of 0–255.

```
POKE n,m
```

PRESET and PSET Statements that draw a point at the specified position on the screen. The color of the point may also be set as shown.

```
PSET(x,y),color
PRESET(x,y),color
```

PRESET and PSET are almost identical. The only difference is when no color is given to PRESET, the background color is selected. Both are used in graphics mode only.

PRINT A statement that displays data on the screen. The question mark (?) may be used as a short way of entering PRINT when you are using the BASIC program editor.

PSET A statement used to draw a point at the specified position on the screen. See PRESET and PSET.

PUT A statement used in graphics to write colors onto a specified area of the screen. The location is specified by the X,Y coordinates of the upper-left corner of the area. The colors have been placed in an array by a previous GET statement. The interaction with what is already on the screen is determined by the action parameter (selected from PSET, PRESET, XOR, OR, and AND).

```
PUT(x,y), array[,action]
```

RANDOMIZE A statement that reseeds the random-number generator. If the random-number generator is not reseeded, the RND function will return the same sequence of random numbers each time a program containing it is run.

READ A statement that reads values from a DATA statement and assigns them to variables. See DATA.

REM A statement that inserts explanatory remarks in a program. These remarks are not executed, but are output as entered when the program is listed.

RESTORE A statement that allows DATA statements to be reread from a specified line.

```
RESTORE[line]
```

If line is not specified, the DATA statement is reread from the first DATA statement in the program.

RETURN A statement that brings you back from a subroutine. The return is made to the statement immediately following the GOSUB statement that transferred the program to the subroutine.

**RIGHT$** A function that returns the rightmost n characters of a string A$.

```
RIGHT$(A$,n)
```

RND A function that returns a random number between 0 and 1. A numeric expression may follow the word RND. In the form shown, three possibilities exist.

```
RND(x)
```

1. If x is positive or not included, RND(x) generates the next random number in the current sequence.
2. RND(0) repeats the last number generated.
3. If x is negative, RND(x) generates the particular sequence for the given x, effectively reseeding the random-number generator with the value of x.

SCREEN A function that returns the ASCII code for the character on the active screen at the specified row and column.

```
SCREEN(row,column)
```

SCREEN A statement that sets the screen attributes by subsequent statements.

```
SCREEN[mode][,[burst][,[apage][,vpage]]]
```

Mode is an integer value (0, 1, or 2). Burst enables or disables the color. Apage and vpage are valid in the text mode only. They determine the active and visual pages. If omitted, vpage defaults to apage.

SCREEN An option that can be used with VIEW or WINDOW to determine the direction and origin of the Y coordinate for the display screen.

SIN A function that calculates the trigonometric sine function of an angle that is specified in radians.

```
SIN(angle)
```

SOUND A statement that generates sound through the speaker in the desired frequency (37–32767 Hertz) and duration (0 to 65535 clock ticks). The clock ticks 18.2 times per second. If the duration is zero (0), the current SOUND statement that is running is turned off.

SPACE$ A function that returns a string consisting of the specified number (n) of spaces.

```
SPACE$(n)
```

SPC A function that skips a specified number (n) of spaces in a PRINT statement.

```
PRINT SPC(n)
```

STEP A parameter used in a FOR-NEXT loop to specify the increment (n) of the control variable.

```
FOR X = 1 to 10 STEP n
```

STR$ A function that returns a string representation of the value of a specified numeric expression (x).

```
STR$(x)
```

STRING$ A function that returns a string of length n whose characters all have a specified ASCII code (m) in the form

```
STRING$(n,m)
```

It returns the first character of another string (A$) a specified number of times (n) when in the form

```
STRING$(n,A$)
```

THEN A decision branch point in an IF-THEN statement. If the condition of the IF-THEN statement is true, the statement following THEN is executed. Otherwise, the statement following THEN is ignored.

VAL A function that returns the numeric value of a specified string, as

```
V = VAL(A$)
```

VARPTR$ A function that returns a character form of the address of a specified variable in memory.

```
V$ = VARPTR$(A)
```

VIEW A statement used to control placement of viewports on the screen. The SCREEN option provides control of the positive Y direction of the viewport. The specified limits determine where the opposite corners of the viewport are to be displayed.

Vpage Selects which page is to be displayed on the screen. The visual page may be different from the active page. Vpage is used only in the text mode.

WIDTH A statement that sets the number of characters in an output line. After outputting the specified number of characters, BASIC adds a carriage return. When in medium-resolution, WIDTH 80 forces the screen into high-resolution. When in high-resolution, WIDTH 40 forces the screen into medium-resolution. Changing the screen width causes the screen to be cleared and sets the border screen color to black.

WINDOW A statement that controls the minimum and maximum X,Y coordinates that can be displayed, thus clipping off areas that would normally be displayed. The SCREEN option can be used to control the positive Y-coordinate direction.

XOR A logic operator that returns a value of true when two conditions are compared and one, but not both, of the conditions are true. Otherwise, it returns a value of false.

INDEX